THE COMPLETE POLYGRAPH HANDBOOK

THE COMPLETE POLYGRAPH HANDBOOK

Stan Abrams

Lexington Books

D.C. Heath and Company

Lexington, Massachusetts/Toronto

Library of Congress Cataloging-in-Publication Data

Abrams, Stanley.
  The complete polygraph handbook / Stan Abrams.
    p.   cm.
  Includes bibliographies and index.
  ISBN 0-669-15345-1 (alk. paper)
  1. Lie detectors and detection—United States. I. Title.
HV8078.A227 1989
363.2'54—dc19   86-46308
                                        CIP

Published simultaneously in Canada
Printed in the United States of America
International Standard Book Number: 0-669-15345-1
Library of Congress Catalog Card Number 86-46308

The paper used in this publication meets the minimum requirements of
American National Standard for Information Sciences—Permanence of
Paper for Printed Library Materials, ANSI Z39.48–1984. ∞™

88 89 90 91 92 8 7 6 5 4 3 2 1

THIS BOOK IS DEDICATED TO MY CHILDREN, JARED AND
KENDRA, WHO HAVE BROUGHT LIGHT AND HAPPINESS TO
MY LIFE AND HAVE MOTIVATED ME TO REACH JUST A LITTLE
BIT FURTHER.

CONTENTS

FIGURES

TABLES

If and when convincing evidence is produced that reasonably scientific methods of exposing falsehood either in or out of the courtroom are available, these methods should be properly utilized by the legal profession. Lawyers, judges, and law professors know that there is today in our courtroom entirely too much individual perjury and that it is usually difficult, and often impossible, for even an experienced trial lawyer to expose on cross-examination many of the lies of false-swearing witnesses. The legal profession can no longer assume a complacent attitude concerning our present methods of exposing mendacity.

—William Wicker

PREFACE

There has never been any doubt that life contains deception. Deception is characterized as a moral wrong, but it is part of almost everyone's existence. It is very much a part of childhood but continues throughout the adult years as well. Deception is found in the lowest reaches of human life up to the highest levels of politics, business, and even religion. Certainly, there is no reason to assume that it is different in other societies or professions.

It has long been recognized that swearing to God that one will tell the whole truth does not preclude the commission of perjury in court. As far back as 1906, Freud indicated that "There is a growing recognition of the untrustworthiness of statements made by witnesses."[1] Moreover, these lies often cannot be exposed by even an experienced trial lawyer, and juries tend to accept lies as factual. Mendacious behavior is not always displayed in the demeanor of the witness; in fact, the most effective liars appear sincere and candid. Throughout the years attempts have been made to find an approach that can successfully differentiate between truth and deception. Word association tests, hypnosis, truth serums, and more recently voice analysis have all been tried but with few positive results. Only polygraphy has stood the test of time. After ninety years of research and use in the criminal realm, it remains the most effective means of determining truthtelling and lying. But like a pendulum, in some years it is well accepted and flourishes, but in other years it clearly loses ground.

The courts have demanded infallibility, but when the findings for validity were reported to be high, a concern arose that testimony of this nature would influence the jury to the point of usurping its role. This Catch 22 has resulted in little progress being made in the last ten years in having polygraph evidence admitted into testimony. The accuracy of the approach is still the major reason for rejecting polygraph testimony. Undoubtedly, validity is difficult to determine because of the complexity of the procedure. Different examiners employing varying techniques on various kinds of cases complicate the evaluation of the procedure. More than this, however, as will be discussed in chapter 13, confusion is caused by inconsistent findings when reviews of the literature are made. The findings of the report of the Office of Technical Assessment were negative, indicating that polygraph accuracy is only slightly better than chance,[9] but that office did not study polygraph validity at all; its findings were based on blind chart interpretation. The weakness of the report's conclusions was demonstrated by Patrick and Iacono, who obtained complete accuracy for the guilty and 90 percent correct judgments for the innocent,[3] but 98 percent accuracy for the guilty and only 50 percent for the innocent when blind scoring was carried out. Obviously, it is the validity of the original testing that is meaningful, not the blind evaluations of these original charts.

A second area that most decidedly has been a major complicating factor in the perception of polygraphy in general is that of commercial testing. This is the realm that deals with preemployment examinations, employee screening tests, and periodic testing. At the protests of labor unions, many states have enacted antipolygraph legislation. Charges of inadequate test procedures, examiner incompetency, insufficient research, low validity, and a breach of civil rights have influenced society's view of noncommercial or specific testing. The courts have become aware of these issues, and it is unlikely that they differentiate between the two types of testing.

Despite these negative factors, much use is being made of polygraphy by law enforcement agencies in every state. Testing results have been admitted into evidence on a stipulated basis in thirty eight states and admitted over objection in eighteen. At the federal level, polygraphy has been accepted into evidence in ten of the eleven circuits.[4] It is still frequently used by law enforcement to eliminate suspects, and prosecution will often agree to drop the charges if a suspect can demonstrate his or her truthfulness on a polygraph test. Defense attorneys need to know the facts and use this procedure to determine how best to serve their clients. Wide use of polygraphy occurs in the government, where it is employed by the Customs Bureau, Treasury Department, Postal Service, Defense Department, FBI, CIA, CID, and armed services.

A new use for this procedure involves the periodic testing of those on probation and parole to determine if they have reoffended and to serve as a deterrent. Initial findings indicate that this kind of testing is effective in protecting society, reducing recidivism, and lessening overcrowded prison conditions. This approach probably soon will be used throughout the country, particularly in the realm of child abuse.

Over half of the states have polygraph licensing laws, but it is also true that twenty seven states have antipolygraph legislation. At the present time a strong move has been made at the federal level that will almost completely eliminate employee testing programs at the nongovernmental level. Because of this, the polygraph field will experience significant changes. Many examiners rely on this type of testing for their livelihoods and probably will be forced out of business by these laws. If large numbers of polygraphists terminate their memberships in the local and national societies, these organizations will lose some of their current power. Attendance at the presently thirty accredited polygraph schools likely will be reduced, and a number of these schools will discontinue their operation.

What happens in the United States will influence other countries as well. About twenty countries use polygraph, including Canada, Japan, Israel, South Africa, Mexico, India, Poland, and Australia, but are involved in specific testing in criminal rather than commercial situations.

My previous book, published in 1977, predicted the increased use of the polygraph in courts and a definite decrease in usage in the commercial realm. Only the latter prediction proved accurate. In the next ten years the use of polygraphy in the employment sector outside of the government may disappear. Research probably will increase, and more college-educated people will tend to enter the field. These occurrences may induce a greater acceptance of polygraph testimony by the courts. This should most certainly be the case, for if psychiatric and psychological testimony is ruled admissible, then so too should this psychological procedure. The polygraph approach continues to be the most accurate and reliable psychological test that exists, but it is not and never will be infallible.

THE HISTORY OF POLYGRAPHY

1

It is in knowing the past that we are able to predict the future. And in knowing how an individual reacted before, we can best estimate his later responses.

—Stan Abrams

People lie. They lie for many reasons. Sometimes lying avoids hurting others, but most of the time deception is for self-serving purposes. People deceive to gain something or to stay out of trouble. Untruthfulness occurs regardless of religious background, nationality, race, age, or sex, and as has become evident in recent years, high economic or social status does not preclude this behavior. In the 1980s the lies of those holding some of the country's highest political and religious positions have been exposed.

Although it is clear that everyone responds in a deceptive manner at times, there is great variation in the frequency and even in the manner in which this is accomplished. Ekman, author of *Telling Lies*, reported many leg and foot movements associated with deceiving others.[1] Those deceiving will look away from listeners, fidget with their clothing, and stammer. Both John Reid and Richard Arther would agree that there are definite and interpretable expressive movements associated with responding in an untruthful manner. However, some sophisticated liars are quite capable of presenting an innocent demeanor. They remain perfectly still and look directly at their accuser without demonstrating anger or guilt. They do it well, as they should, for they have been doing it all their lives. When they were caught in a lie, they did not learn to tell the truth but instead learned to deceive more effectively and more believably. Although these people may not expose their lies in external behavior, they are unable to control what is occurring inside of them. The changes in their heart rate, blood pressure, even digestive processes proclaim to all who can read these messages that they are lying. At some level, this internal response was recognized by primitive societies that developed magical means of deciphering hidden messages to learn who told the truth and who lied.

The scientific approach to detecting deception began in the work of Cesare Lombroso in 1895, over a hundred years ago. Employing a measure of pulse rate in actual criminal cases, he was able to determine which suspects lied.[2] Larson reported that Lombroso used only heart rate, but Trovillo noted that he used a measure of blood pressure as well.[3] The procedure that he used included showing the subject a picture of an object from the crime scene or simply mentioning something about the criminal act itself and then ascertaining what physiologic changes took place in the subject.

Following the successes attained by Lombroso, in 1914 Benussi studied the value of measuring respiratory changes associated with deception.[4] By comparing inspirations (I) and expirations (E) he found that the duration of inspiration increased following lying and the opposite occurred with truthfulness. Those who observed the subjects' behavioral reactions during deceptive behavior achieved only 50 percent of the accuracy of Benussi's I/E ratio, which obtained complete accuracy for an evaluation of breathing changes. Although Burtt was able to partially corroborate these findings, he achieved greater success with a measure of blood pressure (91 percent) in comparison to Benussi's I/E ratio (73 percent).[5] In 1917 Marston used a discontinuous measure of systolic blood pressure over the left brachial artery, reporting that this approach resulted in "a practically infallible test of the consciousness of an attitude of deception."[6] His procedure was to interview the subject by combining both neutral material and data associated with the crime in question. When the pressure of the blood pressure cuff became too uncomfortable, it was released and the interview was stopped. Shortly after that, the cuff pressure was again increased and the questions continued. At the request of the Psychological Committee of the National Research Council, he attempted to determine the effectiveness of this approach for use during World War I. His findings in a study of a criminal population were indicative of complete accuracy. In 1923, he reported that he had achieved an average accuracy of over 95 percent.[7]

In that same year, Marston attempted to have the findings of the discontinuous measure of blood pressure test of deception admitted into evidence in *United States v. Frye*.[8] The results of this landmark decision have affected not only polygraphy but science in general and have set the national standard for the admission of almost all new scientific evidence. Over the years, however, the facts of *Frye* have become so twisted that the exact details of what transpired in the matter probably will never be known. According to the original version of the facts, James Alphonso Frye confessed to the murder of Dr. Brown but later recanted. To ascertain his truthfulness in his denial of having committed the homicide, Dr. Marston, who was both a psychologist and an attorney, examined him with a lie detector. This was not a polygraph for it measured only one area of physiologic functioning. Marston's approach was a primitive precursor to the polygraph technique as it is known at this time, but he found Frye to be truthful and attempted to have these findings presented into evidence. The court, however, ruled that this testimony was not admissible because it was not accepted by the scientific community. The jury found Frye guilty of second-degree murder. The verdict was appealed, and a higher court affirmed the decision to reject the testimony of the lie detection findings.

Three years after Frye's sentencing, according to unreliable sources, another individual confessed and Frye was released from prison.[9] This information may have grown out of statements made in Marston's book, *The Lie Detector Test*.[10] It has been assumed for years that Marston's test had, in fact, been accurate and the jury was in error in finding Frye guilty. According to Starrs' recent investigation into the case, however, no one else confessed to Brown's murder and Frye most definitely was not released from prison after serving only three years.[11] In fact, he remained there for almost eighteen years. From this data it might appear that Frye was guilty, Marston's findings were incorrect, and that the accuracy of his blood pressure measure was not as great as he believed.

John Larson did not support allowing Marston's lie detection test to be admitted into evidence. Larson believed that the test lacked sufficient experimentation and standardization. In 1921 he developed his own approach combining some of the features of Benussi's respiratory studies and Marston's work in blood pressure.[12] He used the ink polygraph developed by Dr. James MacKenzie in 1908, which was composed of sensors that measured blood pressure, pulse, and respiration.[13] Larson's instrument differed considerably from Marston's in that it provided a continuous measure of physiologic changes that occurred. Respiration was employed not to determine deception but rather to ascertain the effect of respiratory changes on heart activity. He replaced the blood pressure technique used by Marston with an occlusion plethysmograph that measured relative blood pressure and blood volume. This is much closer to what is presently employed to evaluate cardiovascular changes in contemporary polygraph instrumentation. Instead of an interview approach, he used word association technique by inserting a word associated with the criminal act at every third word. Later, he reported that better results were obtained when direct questions were asked and the subject responded with either yes or no.[14] Larson also evaluated the effectiveness of the galvanometer, but he determined that it would only duplicate the findings of the sphygmograph and that it would be too sensitive, and therefore invalid, when highly emotional questions were asked. Even twenty-five years ago Larson demonstrated that high accuracy could be attained with blind scoring of charts. He also indicated that a definite weakness existed in generalizing from laboratory studies to real life situations because the laboratory subject cannot experience the same degree of emotional arousal as a subject in a criminal investigation.[15]

When Larson was experimenting with the polygraph technique at Berkeley, he was assisted by Leonarde Keeler, who was then a high school student. Keeler went on to study psychology, and Larson continued into medicine and then psychiatry. In 1926 Keeler modified Larson's instrumentation so that it was compact enough to be portable. He became involved in manufacturing polygraph instruments and founded the first polygraph school. In 1931 he added the galvanometer to the instrument, making it a significant part of the lie detection process.[16] He improved on the techniques developing stimulation and guilty knowledge tests.[17] In the case of the former, this was a method for enhancing the fear of the guilty suspect by demonstrating how readily his deception could be determined through the polygraph tracing. The guilty knowledge or peak of tension test (POT) allowed for a comparison of responses that included a number of nonsignificant items and a question that related to the crime. For example, various calibers of guns would be listed, and if only the guilty individual knew which gun was used in a shooting, only he and not the innocent should react to that question.

In 1917 Marston was asked to evaluate his approach for use in the war. In 1941, Wolfle, a psychologist at the University of Washington, received a request from the American Psychological Association to determine the validity of the procedure for the government's use in World War II. Basing his findings on a review of the literature, observations of the technique, and interactions with individuals who had considerable experience in polygraphy in both law enforcement and research, Wolfle reported that it would be valuable.[18] He indicated that the methods were adequately developed, the instruments served their purposes, but only a small number of adequately trained examiners were available at that time. Dr. Wolfle stated that it could be highly useful when well-trained polygraphists were available. Shortly after this, in May 1944, a resolution was passed by the Forensic Society of the American Psychiatric Association on the use of polygraphy. Eliasberg studied the technique and presented a number of recommendations that the society accepted.[19] It was determined that this approach could provide reliable results, but only when employed by trained physicians and psychologists who could evaluate the data by applying other techniques along with it and using other independently obtained information.

Although the original research was conducted by psychologists, physiologists, and physicians, they lost interest in this area of research and the void was then filled by polygraphists. John Reid, in particular, accomplished a great deal to advance polygraphy in an attempt to make it a more scientific and objective procedure. Reid and Imbau wrote the major textbooks for polygraphists, but in addition, Reid developed a measure of muscular movements to detect the use of countermeasures.[20] In 1947 he reported on two procedures that he instituted—the guilt complex test and the control question technique.[21] Prior to Reid's use of the control question, the subject's physiologic response to the crime question was compared with neutral items; A large difference indicated deception, whereas a minor difference or no difference was indicative of truthfulness. The control question, however, was an assumed lie that was developed during the interview stage of the examination. Examinees were asked a number of questions that they responded to with denial but that the polygraphist could be almost certain were lies. These items did not relate to the case under study. Therefore, innocent individuals were responding deceptively on the test only to the control questions, and the guilty lied on both the control and the crime (relevant) questions. Under this procedure the innocent demonstrated greater physiologic responses to the control questions, but the guilty, although lying to both, reacted more to the relevant questions because they presented the greater threat. This approach enhanced the accuracy of the technique.

Backster carried this approach even further. He refined the control question and explained it in terms of the concept of a psychological set.[22] In essence, he stated that the examinee will be oriented toward the greatest threat and this will be demonstrated in physiologic reactivity to those questions. Backster also has been successful in promoting the use of a standardized approach to testing and the development of a numerical scoring system, resulting in a more objective system that has increased the validity (accuracy) and the reliability (consistency) of the field. Polygraphy now has achieved the level of being more a science than an art.

Not only have changes occurred in technique and methodology, but instrumentation has been improved and expanded. New sensors have been developed that are more sensitive and therefore more effective. Many schools require a college degree for entry, and course curriculum has expanded, to include a six-month internship. As is discussed in chapter 13, polygraph validity and reliability are quite high. A poll of a sample of members of the Society for Psychophysiologic Research indicated that 63 percent felt polygraphy to be a valuable diagnostic tool.[23] From this and previous surveys, it would appear that the polygraph approach has met the *Frye* standard and is now accepted by the scientific community. One final stumbling block to admissibility in court is the frequently raised argument that polygraphy testimony will have too great an effect on the jury and that will usurp the jury's role.

There have been other lie detector techniques, but few have stood the test of time. Voice analysis is still being employed, but as is shown in chapter 2, its validity has not been demonstrated by research.

A major area of growth in polygraph usage has been in business, which is where a large percentage of polygraphists make their livelihoods. Preemployment testing can be helpful in eliminating individuals who might not be desirable for a particular position because of a background of drug use, employee theft, or other activities of this nature. Employee screening as used by the government, for example, can reduce security risks, and periodic testing can deter employee theft. Workers who know that they will be polygraphed every six months to determine whether they have stolen anything should refrain from this behavior. Although all three of these approaches have been shown to be effective methods of curtailing problems of this nature, labor unions have come out strongly against these procedures. Claims of inappropriate government use of these approaches resulted in an investigation of polygraph usage in the government. In 1963 John Moss chaired the congressional committee that evaluated the use of polygraphs in government, reviews of literature, and reports of researchers and examiners.[24] The committee also relied on a report by Orlansky, who had evaluated polygraph procedures in 1962[25] and concluded that objective data had not been compiled by the governmental agencies that employed polygraphy despite the great many tests that were administered. He claimed that there were no statistics to demonstrate the effectiveness of this approach as used by the government. Within the Department of Defense he found no set of standards for the regulation of the polygraph techniques, and he strongly felt that research was needed in the areas of validity and reliability.

The Moss committee in April 1963 reported that "There is no 'lie detector,' neither mechanical nor human."[26] Despite the fact that two of the Committee's witnesses, Drs. Orne and Kubis, testified that they attained accuracies as high as 80 to 90 percent, the Moss committee stated that polygraphy had not been proven to be valid in either laboratory or field research. (It is important to recognize that political motivations can strongly bias investigations of this nature.) Although this report resulted in a reduction of polygraph usage in the government, it also spurred research activity in both government and the private sector.

The polygraph approach, however, was too large a target, for as long as it was used with job applicants and employees, some legislators actively fought against its use. Because unions have large voting blocs that cannot be ignored, this battle has to continue. In June 1974 the polygraph approach once again was investigated.[27] A House Committee chaired by Moorehead heard the testimony of polygraphists, scientists, representatives from governmental agencies, and labor unions. After the testimony was heard, the membership of the committee was changed, Bella Abzug became chairperson; and none of those actually present at the hearings were involved in the preparation of the final report. This committee recommended that polygraph usage be completely discontinued by all government agencies for all purposes. These recommendations were not followed.

The transcripts of these sessions provide the real flavor of the meetings. When a union member testifies, he is treated with respect and lauded for the work that he has done. In direct contrast to this, the legislators were very businesslike with any witnesses who favored polygraphy and responded to them tersely. When politicians evaluate a technical or scientific procedure, it can be assumed that under the guise of an objective investigation their own purposes will be served. The news media, whose first purpose is to sell their product, thrive on sensationalism; they distort the facts to the public, which generally accepts that distortion as gospel. If polygraphy were ever eliminated, it would not be because science has demonstrated that it is an invalid technique but rather because of the self-serving motives of those who ignore and distort facts for their own aims.

Like a giant larva that hatches every ten years, another investigation into polygraphy was conducted in the 1980s. When President Reagan requested an increase in polygraph screening tests of government employees because of continued leaks of information, Congress requested an evaluation of polygraphy by the Office of Technology Assessment (OTA). In 1983 that office reported its conclusions, which indicated that polygraphy is a complex procedure that is difficult to assess.[28] The report concluded that there is evidence for the validity of testing of specific incidents associated with criminal investigations but little research available for the validity of polygraph testing in large-scale screening related to an unauthorized disclosure situation or in personal security screening. It indicated that a good deal of research is required to fully determine polygraphy's validity.

One point that will be made again in later chapters bears repeating here. Any scientific group that is requested to evaluate a particular procedure by a legislative body must guard rigidly against biases. Because it is clear that legislators have intended to support unions and eliminate polygraph testing from employee screening, there must be strong safeguards instituted against inadvertent prejudice favoring answering the legislators needs. The OTA selected ten studies believed to be scientifically acceptable investigations of specific control question techniques. Of these, six were based on studies using the blind reevaluation of verified polygraph results. Complete accuracy had been attained by the original examiners. In these cases the OTA did not evaluate polygraph accuracy but rather the validity of the blind interpretation of polygraph charts. Inevitably, this led to a misleading finding and understated the accuracy of this approach. These data have been published and accepted as an objective and scientific evaluation of polygraph validity and have had far-reaching consequences on the polygraph procedure in scientific circles, for the public, and in the courts as well. Inevitably, they will reduce the likelihood of polygraph testimony being admitted into evidence.

House Resolution 1212 was enacted into law in June 1988 and will take effect in January 1989. The law precludes most pre-employment and employee screening tests within the business community. It excludes those employees who provide security services and companies that manufacture or distribute controlled drugs. Employee screening tests will be allowed when an economic loss has occurred, but rigid guidelines determine how they will be conducted. Federal, state, and local governments and private companies that contract with government intelligence agencies will be exempt from these restrictions as well.

The ACLU has indicated an interest in restricting further polygraph testing in law enforcement and government. Certainly the unions would favor the latter. Therefore, it can be expected that the battle will continue in the coming years.

This law will have a great effect on the polygraphy profession. Membership in professional societies will be reduced, fewer schools will continue training examiners, and fewer educational opportunities will be available for individuals who remain active in the field. On the positive side, this conflict has made scientists much more aware of polygraphy and its uses. It can be expected that this will motivate them to do research in polygraphy. In addition, some of those who are already involved in forensic fields might become interested enough to obtain appropriate training as examiners. Both of these factors will increase the likelihood of the admissibility of polygraph testimony into court. It may well be that a new and stronger science of polygraphy will emerge.

THE OTHER LIE DETECTORS

2

For most of us the truth is no longer a part of our minds; it has become a special product for experts.

—Jacob Bronowski

The philosopher Diogenes is said to have carried a lantern around Athens at midday searching for an honest man. He was not alone. The search for truth is eternal, and people continue trying to determine what others think and feel. Because others cannot be trusted to be always honest, special techniques and instruments have been developed to produce results that are more reliable than the words of men and women.

In ancient times primitive societies developed complex procedures for ascertaining the truth. These methods were intermingled with mysticism and magic, and the accused's faith in these devices helped reveal what was true and what was false. Some of these rituals had a foundation based on logical physiological principles learned either by accident or observation. Asians, for example, determined deception by having those suspected of lying chew dry rice and then spit it out. In those who fear being apprehended in deception, the digestive processes, including salivation, slowed down, and spitting out the dry rice became difficult; those who were honest and believed in the power of their gods and in this technique felt little fear and so their salivation was not inhibited. For the same reason, the Arabs achieved some degree of success by applying a hot iron to the tongues of the accused and finding that only the guilty were burned. In India those who were suspected were made to hold fire in their hands, and in Africa the accused had to place their hands in boiling water.[1] Miraculously, it is said that only the innocent escaped from developing the incriminating blisters. Research in hypnosis has demonstrated that if individuals in the hypnotic state are touched with a piece of ice and told that it is a hot iron, a blister will form. Perhaps the same suggestions and beliefs that operate in hypnosis to cause a blister can inhibit this response as well.

Trial by torture was almost guaranteed to obtain a confession if not the truth. During the barbarity of the Spanish Inquisition torture persisted as long as the accused's denial, with no limit to the variety of atrocities that were committed in the name of truth. Inhumanity persists and undoubtedly always will. While in Sri Lanka some years ago, I was informed by the police that they routinely beat prisoners until the truth is obtained. At the same time in India, two men had their eyes burned out in order to obtain a confession but what was more unfortunate, they were later found to be innocent. It was reported that in the Philippines, tiny snakes that flee into any dark openings, in this case the orifices of the body, were placed on the accused and allowed to remain there until an admission was obtained. This manner of behavior is not limited to Third World countries; during World War II both Allied and Axis countries used physical torture and more sophisticated methods to gather information.

Trial by torture was replaced by the third degree, in which relay teams of police question a suspect under bright lights while he or she is deprived of sleep and food.[2] Approaches of this nature have been replaced in some regions with more humane and more sophisticated techniques. Brain washing is an extension of the third degree that is effective in securing all manner of admissions. It grew out of the Chinese Communist program of "Szu-Hsiang Kai-Tsao," which means ideological remodeling, and consists of confession and reeducation.[3] Placed in isolation in small cramped quarters with little or no sleep, the prisoner is condemned for his or her acts and urged to confess. Every admission is rewarded, and each resistance is followed by emotional assaults. In an atmosphere of fear, never knowing whether he or she will live or die, the prisoner begins to feel the need to confess and reform. As this reeducation process progresses, prisoners begin to identify with and become part of the group indoctrinating them. Brainwashed American fliers in Korea confessed to using germ warfare; Cardinal Mindzenty confessed to spying, and Patty Hearst joined the Symbionese Liberation Army. Underlying this transformation are three significant elements—disability, dependency, and dread. The result is described in Orwell's *1984:* "We shall squeeze you empty, and then we shall fill you with ourselves."[4]

The role of the court and the jury is to detect lies—to discriminate between the witness who perjures and the one who tells the truth. The oath—whether swearing on the Bible to tell the truth or kissing the Bible as was done in the past—serves little purpose. The person who heeds the oath does not lie and the person without moral values lies regardless of the oath. Judges and jury members determine truthfulness based on an individual's demeanor, appearance, speech, and attire. Recognizing this, defending attorneys have their clients dress neatly and conservatively. Some attorneys hire specialists in linguistics to teach their clients to respond in a believable and acceptable manner. Although those trained and experienced in dealing with the criminal population are apt to recognize mendacious behavior, naive jury members can be taken in by sophisticated witnesses. Even experienced trial lawyers have difficulty in exposing the lies of those who perjure themselves on the witness stand. There is little doubt that a great deal of lying behavior occurs in the courtroom and is not brought to the awareness of either judge or jury. It has been reported, however, that judges are more successful as finders of fact than a jury, which is one reason that most defendants prefer a jury trial.

Science has developed various techniques that attempt to reach the truth. Some experts still believe that hypnosis can be an effective approach to differentiating truth from deception. Hypnosis has been used in the forensic realm to enhance the recall of witnesses and victims. Hypnosis can accomplish this, but it does so at the cost of increasing inaccurate memories as well. With defendants or others in which the results of hypnosis can be self-serving, the majority opinion by far is that subjects are capable of lying under hypnosis. Moreover, sophisticated individuals can mislead even an experienced hypnotist into thinking that they are hypnotized even though this is not the case. In the Hillside strangler case, for example, the professionals involved were of differing opinions as to whether Bianche actually entered a hypnotic state.

In evaluating various methods for obtaining information from witnesses, Kubis concluded that hypnosis was of limited value when used with individuals who were unwilling to reveal information. Orne, in studying the literature, reported that inducing a hypnotic state in a resistant subject was highly unlikely.[5] This writer, who has worked in forensic hypnosis for many years, has only once obtained information from a defendant that was detrimental to his case. This defendant repeatedly denied any involvement in a homicide under various hypnosis techniques—direct questioning, revivification (regressing back to the time in question and reliving it), and seeing the whole thing as if it were a movie. The subject then was told to hallucinate a blackboard on which the words yes or no would appear in response to questions. When asked if he fired a gun on January 3, he reported that the word yes appeared printed on the board. At this he abruptly opened his eyes and stalked off in anger. It was judged that this indirect admission of guilt was not related to being under the hypnotist's control but rather was due to fatigue and even lack of intelligence in the subject. Partial confessions of this nature probably can be obtained from a long continuous interrogation. This view is consistent with the majority view that people will not do anything in the hypnotic state that they will not do when not hypnotized.

There is a slight possibility that false confessions can be obtained from subjects in hypnotic states because subjects are most suggestible at this time. Kroger described a case where he hypnotized a girl who reportedly was a witness to her girlfriend's murder but who under hypnosis confessed to having done the murder herself.[6] Polygraph testing of four adults who swore that she was in their presence at the time of the killing strongly argued against her having been either a witness or the perpetrator. Because of the risks of a false confession and the ease with which an individual is capable of lying under hypnosis, it is generally accepted that hypnosis is not a valid means of differentiating between truth and deception.

Drugs—specifically the so-called truth serums such as scopolamine, sodium pentothal, and sodium amytal—for a while appeared to be an effective method for determining the truth. It was assumed that individuals in a heavily drugged state did not have the capability of deceiving. Appearance, slurred speech, and difficulty in responding suggested that the drugged subject lacked the defenses to feign a response. This theory, however, was contradicted by the research results. Wolfe was a member of the Emergency Committee of the National Council during World War II and recommended against the use of this approach as a lie detector, saying that the enthusiasm of those favoring the use of this procedure was not well founded.[7] Inbau reported that although success was achieved in experimental situations, it was effective in determining truthfulness in only 50 percent of the cases in actual investigations.[8] Other investigators have concluded that a deceptive person can continue to be deceptive under narcosis but repressed material can be retrieved if the subject has nothing to lose in exposing this information. In the experience of the author, these drugs do not necessarily help investigators obtain the truth but do cloud the subject's thinking and judgment and tend to reduce internal controls so that a more effective interrogation can be conducted. In a drugged state the subject is less capable of defending against a barrage of probing questions and is more apt to slip and reveal information that can be employed as a lever to reach for other details relevant to the case.

Another interesting approach that has never been found to be predictably useful is a word association test combined with a measure of reaction time. A list of neutral words is interspersed with words that relate to the crime in question. The subject then is requested to say the first thing that occurs to him or her in response to the stimulus word. The interpretation of this test not only includes a study of the responses to the critical items but to the neutral words that follow. Although suspects may be able to inhibit their responses to the critical item, guilty knowledge may leak out in response to the neutral words that follow when defenses are somewhat reduced. It has been found that with repetition innocent individuals tend to repeat the words they previously used for both neutral and critical stimuli, but the guilty tend to vary their reactions to the key items. Differences in reaction time to the critical items are also evaluated, and research indicated that the guilty take two to three times as much time to respond to a relevant word as the innocent do. This rather complicated approach has all the disadvantages of the guilty knowledge tests. It requires information that relates to the crime and is known by the perpetrator and investigators but not the innocent suspects. Consequently, this procedure never really has experienced wide usage.

The polygraph literature distinguishes between the school that uses any and all information in reaching a decision and the school that rigidly adheres to evaluations of the polygraph tracings. Backster has espoused the latter view, indicating that it enhances the use of a standardized approach, increases objectivity, and is more readily defended in court. There is no doubt that the more information available to the examiner, the higher the degree of accuracy obtained. This is demonstrated in all of the validity studies in which examiners score verified charts. The original polygraphist was accurate in all instances, but examiners who blindly scored charts without any information other than knowing the relevant and control questions did not achieve an equal degree of accuracy. A study by Holmes found that an average accuracy of 75 percent was attained in a blind analysis of twenty-five charts when only the control and relevant questions were known but that validity increased to 83 percent when additional data such as police reports, description of the subject's demeanor and behavior during examination, and reports of witnesses were included.[9]

The Arther and Reid schools emphasize the advantage of using information other than the tracings, particularly expressive moments. There is no doubt that an individual's position, inflection, gestures, and facial expression provide conscious and unconscious messages that can be interpreted by others. The question is how validly these can be evaluated. Successful evaluation depends in part on the experience and training of the examiner, who must be able to differentiate the generalized anxiety and fears of neurotics from the fears of the guilty. The inability to look an investigator in the eye, a tremor of the hand, and a stammer in the voice may be indicative of deception but also can indicate the presence of an emotional disturbance. If subjects' behavior could be videotaped and analyzed to compare expressive movements during truthful and deceptive responses, a good likelihood exists that accurate estimates of truthfulness could be attained. Although the potential for videotaping exists, it is highly unlikely that a polygraphist could have the equipment, time, and expertise to include it as part of a examination. Even if videotaping were feasible, there is not sufficient research to show that this technique would have adequate validity to be accepted by the courts. The examiner should be aware of and use this information, but results must be shown in the tracings to the extent that other examiners will make the same decisions.

A new instrument that has developed out of the increased number of sex crimes is the penile plethysmograph. Although it has been used to diagnose and evaluate the treatment progress of sexual deviants, it also is being employed to indirectly determine if a person is truthful when he denies having committed a sexual crime.[10] In an accusation of child abuse, a transducer loop similar to the device employed in polygraphy to measure blood flow in the fingers, is wrapped about the penis. The subject is shown sexually stimulating pictures of nude children and women, and with sexual arousal an increased flow of blood to the penis results in varying degrees of erection. If the male does not show a response to the children's pictures but does to the women's, he is assumed not to have been involved in child abuse.

Research findings have demonstrated that some individuals are capable of blunting their aberrant sexual responses by fantasizing of nonsexually stimulating subjects during testing. Moreover, they have been able to create a reaction to normal stimuli to which they would not normally respond. In addition, they have caused false negative results (a guilty person appearing to be innocent) through physically manipulating the transducer or by physically stimulating themselves during the examination. The false pattern obtained through this dissimulation is believed to be undetectable to even a sophisticated examiner. Because of these inadequacies, this approach is not considered valid. The examiner should remember this if a discrepancy occurs between plethsymograph and polygraph findings.

None of the techniques described above is being used to any extent at this time in the general area of lie detection. Voice analysis, however, is being employed to a fair extent and will be discussed in some detail.

In 1970 Charles McQuiston, a co-inventor of the psychological stress evacuator (PSE), founded the Dektor Corporation, which manufactures the PSE and trains examiners. Fred Fuller developed a similar device, the voice stress evaluator (VSE), which operated in a like manner. These systems are reported to be capable of detecting deception without the use of attached body sensors by measuring physiologic changes in the voice associated with stress. The subject is taperecorded in an examination process comparable to a polygraph test in which irrelevant, relevant, control, and even guilt complex questions are asked. The test can be administered telephonically and the tape processed at some later time. An employer can ask an employee a series of prepared questions and send the tape to be evaluated. Although McQuiston has denied that a test can be adequately administered surreptitiously, without using the control question format, some specialists in voice analysis have employed it in this manner. If this could be carried out with a degree of accuracy, it could be an effective tool in wide variety of areas, including in negotiations with other countries.

The tape is processed through the voice analysis instrument, which displays inaudible stress-related voice components. The foundation for this is found in the physiologic tremor (muscle microtremor) that occurs in the muscles that control exhalation during speech. It is reported that only a three-day training period is required to learn to operate these instruments. An additional two weeks is needed for instruction in interviewing and interrogation.

In a survey of the users of the PSE, McQuistion reported than in over 10,000 cases not one error was reported and that there was 99.85 percent agreement with polygraph findings in 5,574 cases.[11] Unfortunately, anecdotal information of this nature is of little value; a determination of the validity of the voice analysis approach must be made through objective controlled studies. During the 1974 congressional hearings on the use of polygraphs and similar devices by federal agencies, various governmental departments described their research results that the PSE was not sufficiently reliable and dismantled the instrumentation for other use. According to the army, valid results were obtained in less than one-third of the tests, indicating a validity at less than chance. In agreement with this, the air force studied two of these instruments and indicated that they were not useful in the detection of deception. The National Security Agency studied one PSE and one VSA, and, finding that they were not sufficiently reliable, declared them surplus and relegated them to other research unrelated to lie detection. At the 1978 congressional hearings, Dr. Brenner of the University of Oregon and Dr. Branscomb of the Massachusetts Institute of Technology reported their research results on the PSE.[13] They indicated that some research has shown this device to be valid as a measure of stress and that the basis for its operation—stress sensitive frequency modulation of the voice—is consistent with earlier evidence. However, they found that it was subject to serious technical limitations resulting in its reliability being questionable. The subjects in their investigation were able to alter their vocal response to the extent that nineteen out of twenty examiners successfully concealed their responses. They found that PSE scores varied according to the quality of the taperecordings and the PSE patterns and varied with the speed of transcribing the material through the instrument. The response words also affected the scores, and scoring in general was found to be subjective.

Horvath made a comparison of voice analysis and the GSR in a simple numbers test using sixty volunteer students.[14] Agreement (reliability) for PSE was .38 as compared to .92 for the GSR. Accuracy for the PSE was at chance level but was greater than chance for the GSR. In a comparison mock crime study of PSE and polygraph, Kubis concluded that high validity existed for the polygraph approach, observations of behavior was second in effectiveness, and voice analysis was the worse. Neither of the two voice analysis instruments was effective in differentiating between the thief, look outs, and innocent suspects in a simulated theft.[15] Suzuki et al. measured voice pitch, intensity, and deviation on seventy-five answers to relevant crime questions in actual criminal cases in which verification had been shown.[16] None of these three methods exceeded chance accuracy, and the authors concluded that these particular voice measures were neither reliable nor useful.

Although voice analysis is being employed as a lie detection device, research findings indicate that this instrumentation is not a valid test at this present time. It is assumed that, like all of the other approaches, it will fall into disuse.

THE PSYCHOPHYSIOLOGIC BASES OF POLYGRAPHY

3

One could not pluck a flower without touching a star.

—Loren Eiseley

Physiology studies the various processes of the body and how they function. Anatomy studies the structure of the organism. The science that investigates the relationship between behavior, physiology, and anatomy is psychophysiology. These three fields cover a massive amount of data, some of which is related to the field of polygraphy. The field requires knowledge of the functions of certain parts of the body but the polygraphist does not need to learn about vision, hearing, or the urinary system. This chapter discusses those parts and functions of the body that directly affect the polygraph process.

THE CELL

The basic structural unit of all living matter is the cell. It is composed of protoplasm, which can be defined as the living substance of all plants and animals.

The cell is surrounded by a semipermeable cell wall, which allows for the passage of substances such as food, waste, and oxygen. Humans, who are multicellular, are made up of trillions of cells that have become structurally differentiated in order that they can perform specific functions. Thus, there are reproductive, muscle, nerve, gland, blood, and connective cells, and in each of them metabolism occurs. Metabolism can be described as the life process of cells and organisms, which involves the building up and destruction of protoplasm. It includes the taking in of food and oxygen and the digestion of the food and its assimilation for energy through oxidation (the use of oxygen to help break down the food). Undigested matter and other waste products are eliminated, and cells are repaired after an injury occurs. The food that is broken down then is used for energy, which permits the body to function and is used to increase the protoplasm (growth).[1]

TISSUES

A tissue consists of many cells that serve the same purpose. The four primary tissues are connective, which includes bone, cartilage, tendons, and ligaments; muscular, in which the cells can contract to allow movement; nervous tissue, which is capable of receiving stimuli (irritability) and conducting nerve impulses from one point to another (conductability); and epithelial tissue, which covers the outer surfaces of the body as well as the majority of the inner organs. When different tissues combine to serve a specialized function, they are considered an organ. A number of organs operating together to serve a particular purpose are an organ system. There is little need to present data on the urinary, reproductive, and digestive systems, but the endocrine, circulatory, respiratory, and nervous systems are relevant to the study of polygraphy.

THE ENDOCRINE SYSTEM

Secretion is a basic function of protoplasm, and in the glands, the chemical activity of these cells has become highly specialized and produces chemicals. There are excretory glands, such as for salivation and sweat, which have ducts that empty onto the surface. Endocrine glands, however, are ductless, and their secretions are emptied into the blood or lymph. The endocrine system is comprised of a number of different glands that produce hormones that serve either an excitatory or inhibitory influence. Along with the nervous system, they play a major role in regulating the activities of the organism. The following glands are significant to polygraphy:

1. **The Pituitary Gland** is composed of an anterior section and a posterior section. In the anterior portion substances are secreted that control skeletal growth and mediate the activities of the thyroid, pancreas, and adrenal cortex. The posterior

part contains the hormone vasopressin, which is produced by the hypothalamus and acts on the smooth muscles of the blood vessels, causing them to constrict and thereby increasing blood pressure. The diameter of the blood vessels is modified through chemical and neural means and controls the amount of blood supplied and to what regions of the body it is moved. In contrast to the skeletal muscles that produce voluntary movements, the smooth muscles deal with involuntary acts. They propel various substances through the body passages, including food through the digestive tract, the expulsion of waste matter, and blood through the blood vessels. These muscles are innervated by nerve fibers from the autonomic nervous system and the visceral motor centers of the brain. They regulate the diameter of the passages of the lungs as well as the blood vessels so that the amount of oxygen taken in can be controlled as well.

2. **The Thyroid Gland** lies in the midportion of the neck. Through its hormones it regulates basal metabolism (cellular oxidation and heat production) as well as mental development, growth, and body temperature.

3. **The Adrenal Glands** are located on the upper surface of each kidney and consist of an external cortical portion (cortex) and an inner part (medulla). Although they serve many important roles, of most significance to polygraphists is the effect of the hormones epinephrine and norepinephrine from the medullary section. They initiate many of the physiologic reactions that are like those caused by the stimulation of the sympathetic nervous system. There is an increase in the secretion of epinephrine during emotional states like anger and fear, and this increase helps the organism cope with the stress that has caused these emotional states. As will be seen shortly, epinephrine mobilizes the body for action. The adrenal gland and its hormones play a significant role in enhancing the organism's likelihood of survival during periods of threat.

4. **The Sweat Glands** are not part of the endocrine system because they do not secrete internally but externally. Because they affect electrodermal activity, however, they are important to the examiner. The sweat glands help regulate temperature and aid in excretion. Their number varies with their position in the body, with about 400 per square centimeter on the palms of the hand and only seventy per square centimeter on the back. Ordinarily about 500 to 1,000 cubic centimeters are excreted daily, but an individual can sweat that much in a single hour of exertion. Sweating is regulated by the sympathetic nervous system, but there is evidence of a sweat center in the hypothalamus of the brain. Special centers are also involved in the so-called emotional sweating areas in the soles of the feet and palms of the hands. These respond to such emotional reactions as fear, anger, and anxiety. Because hydration of the skin assists in locomotion, tactual sensitivity, discrimination, and grasping abilities, it can be assumed that the perspiration that occurs during a threatening situation helps the organism cope with this threat. Not only is the sweating in these areas readily brought about, but it would appear that despite the fact that little absorption takes place

in the skin, the sweat glands are able to reabsorb the perspiration. Therefore, there is an immediate sweating reaction to threat and just as immediate drying when the threat is eliminated that cannot be accounted for by evaporation alone.[2]

The sweat gland activity is not a simple matter of degree of perspiration but rather can be shown to vary from one hand to the other and even among different parts of the hand. This depends on a number of factors, including the stimulus and the task that one has to perform. That is, there is specificity of response based on factors that determine the degree and location of hydration, and these rather independent responses are under the control not only of the autonomic nervous system but the central nervous system as well. This would seem to be particularly true of electrodermal and cardiovascular activity.

The electrodermal response is measured through either conduction or resistance to electrical activity but the former is preferred because a linear measure can be obtained through it. Conductiveness is enhanced or resistance reduced by the hydration that takes place during stress. (It should be recognized that it is only a theoretical assumption that electrodermal activity is a measure of the sweat gland activity and not some other factor.) An immediate electrodermal reaction in response to threat can be observed in the form of a sudden rise in the pen and a drop when the fear is reduced.

THE CIRCULATORY SYSTEM

The circulatory system is composed of structures that transport body fluids throughout the various regions of the body. It is made up of a blood vascular system and a lymphatic system. The former consists of the heart and various blood vessels, whereas the lymphatic system transports lymph from tissues to the point where it enters blood vessels.

The major mode of transportation in the body is blood. It moves nutrients, oxygen, water, and hormones needed for metabolic and secretory activity to various cells. It transports waste products from cells, hormones from glands, antibodies to defend against disease, and excess body heat to the lungs and surface of the body to regulate temperature. Blood, therefore, is involved in nutrition, respiration, excretion, protection and regulation.[3]

The heart is a hollow muscular organ that lies between the lungs. It is surrounded by a double-walled pericardium with four chambers. The upper region consists of a right and left atrium, and the lower area of a right and left ventricle. Veins return deoxygenated blood (blood that has passed through the body so that the oxygen has been used) from the entire body with the exception of the lungs. The superior (upper) vena cava brings deoxygenated blood from the upper portions of the body, and the inferior (lower) vena cava transports deoxygenated blood from the lower parts of the body to the right atrium.

From here blood passes downward through the cuspid valve into the right ventricle. It, in turn, leaves the right ventricle through the semilunar valves and enters the pulmonary artery, which carries the still deoxygenated blood to the lungs. Here it becomes oxygenated and is then transported by four pulmonary veins into the left atrium. Blood then continues through the bicuspid valve into the left ventricle. From here the still oxygenated blood moves through the aortic valve (the semilunar valve) into the aorta. This is the pathway taken by blood, but it tends to be misleading because blood is entering both atria and ventricles simultaneously. When the atria contract, blood is forced through the respective valves into the ventricles. The valves close, preventing a return of blood into the atria. As the ventricles contract, blood leaves the right ventricle entering the pulmonary artery, and blood is forced out of the left ventricle into the aorta. Once again the valves close, preventing a flow of blood back into the ventricles. The purpose of the valves is to maintain the flow of blood in the correct direction. If there is a deformity in the valve, blood will tend to leak past it. This can be heard with a stethoscope; one does not hear the sharp clear heart sounds but, rather, a murmur. Figure 3–1 shows the pathway of the blood through the heart.

When blood leaves the left ventricle through the aortic valve into the aorta, it is ejected into the aorta by the heart's contraction. The force of blood entering the aorta distends it, but when the heart relaxes between contractions, the distended aorta recoils, forcing a majority of the blood forward. Some, however, spurts backward, sealing the aortic valve. As it rebounds off of the valve, a similar situation, but to a lesser degree, is created as when the heart contracted. The blood moves forward in the artery again. From the view of the examiner, as the heart contracts the blood is forced forward in the arteries and through the arm to which the blood pressure cuff is affixed. The resulting thickening of the arm due to an increased supply of blood and increased blood pressure causes pressure to be brought against the inflated cuff and results in air being forced through the tubing and raising the pen. The upward vertical swing of the pen graphically displays the contraction of the heart. As the heart relaxes between contractions, the arm narrows and the pressure against the cuff is reduced. As this occurs, the pen begins to drop, but before the tracing can reach its former base line, the secondary spurt of blood moves forward after rebounding off the aortic valve. Once again, but to a lesser degree, the arm size increases and sends the pen on another but smaller rise. This second rise in the cardiotracings is called the dicrotic notch. When this second surge of blood passes through, the arm returns to its original size, and the pen continues its drop to its original base line. With the next contraction, the cycle starts again. Knowing how many seconds apart each vertical line is on the chart paper, the examiner can readily compute the heart rate. A systole is the contraction phase of the heart activity, and the diastole is when the heart is at rest. An extra systole or

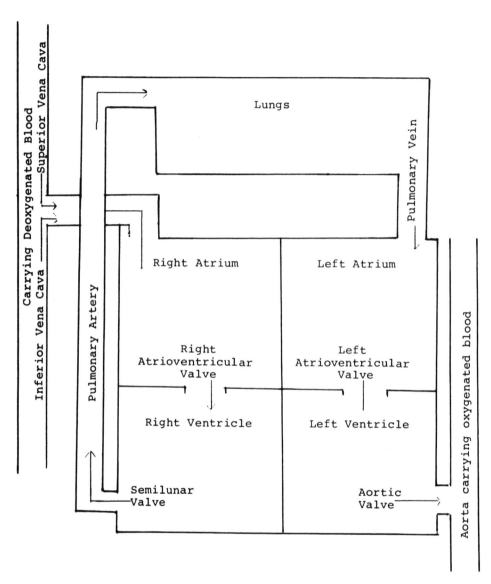

Figure 3–1. Diagram of the Heart

premature or skipped beat occurs when the contraction is early and, because of that, is usually followed by a larger diastole. Because the systole is weak and unnoticed, the individual appears to have missed a beat. This may occur in a normal heart or in one with a pathological condition. It may also result from stress. In a polygraph chart it is seen as an extended diastole followed by a space between cardiocycles, which may then show a larger systole. This is shown in figure 3–2.

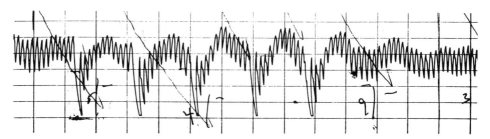

Figure 3–2. Chart Showing Extra Systoles

Average heart rate is about seventy contractions per minute, but it is not unusual to see heart rates in the fifties in people who exercise regularly. Rate also varies with sex; women range from seventy-two to eighty, and men fall between sixty-four and seventy-two. Age is a factor; one-year-olds average a heart rate of about 120, and ten-year-olds average around ninety. Heart rate also tends to increase with each inspiration and decreases as blood pressure rises. In tasks that require attention, heart rate diminishes. In listening to threatening questions while being polygraphed, the individual can experience a rise in blood pressure but a decrease in heart rate to compensate for the blood pressure rise and for attention being paid to the question.

An artery is an elastic muscular tube that conducts blood from the heart. The arterioles are smaller branches of the arteries that are barely visible to the naked eye and lead to the capillaries. They are minute and form a network in the tissues. It is through their walls that the exchange of substances between blood and tissues occurs. The oxygen from blood is transferred to tissues, and waste products including carbon dioxide are taken into the capillaries. Deoxygenated blood is transferred to the venules, which progressively increase in size to become veins as they go from tissues to the heart. They in turn empty into the inferior and superior vena cavae, which enter the right atrium, completing the cycle. This is diagramed in figure 3–3.

In order to obtain a pulse, one touches an artery and can feel and count the contractions of the heart. If an artery is severed, the blood flow will be pulsating from the contractions of the heart that sends blood through the arteries. If a vein is cut there will be a steady flow of blood; the heart's contractions do not return blood through the veins and back to the heart and lungs, but this is brought about through movements of the body. In a soldier who remains at attention for long periods of time, the blood cannot work its way up through the body, and eventually there may be insufficient blood supply to the heart and brain resulting in fainting. Experienced soldiers learn to flex their leg muscles without the movement being perceptible, thereby continuing the blood

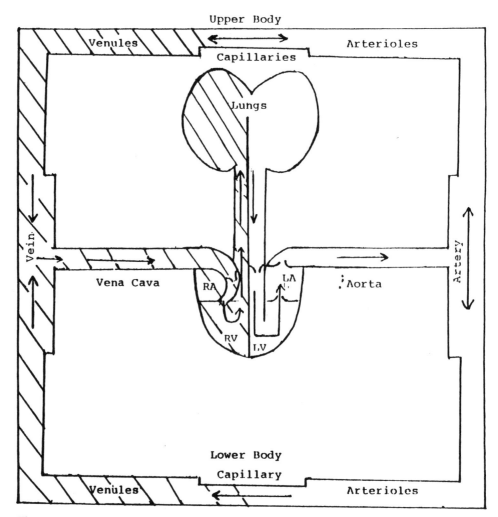

Figure 3–3. Diagram of the Circulatory System

flow. On rare occasions a death results when a person has fainted in a standing or even a sitting position, such as in a telephone booth. What occurs is a veinous pooling of blood that cannot work its way back up to the heart and brain so that the individual eventually dies.

BLOOD PRESSURE

In polygraphy one measures a combination of blood volume and blood pressure. The pressure that the blood exerts within the blood vessels is the blood pressure and depends on a number of factors, including the contraction of the heart, peripheral resistance, elasticity of the arterial walls, and blood volume and viscosity. As blood passes from the arteries to the veins, pressure becomes lower. The elastic arteries closest to the heart show the highest blood pressure, and it is lower in the less elastic arteries closer to the periphery.[4]

The amount of blood discharged from the heart in one minute is the cardiac output. It is dependent on both the rate and force of the contractions. The force is based on the requirements of the body. The rate and force of the contractions are regulated by nerve impulses, chemical substances in the blood, and physical factors such as temperature and pressure within the heart.

The neural control of the heart is determined by impulses transmitted over the afferent (the conduction of nerve impulses from the periphery of the organism toward the central nervous system) and efferent (the conduction of nerve impulses from the cerebral cortex to lower centers but more specifically from the spinal cord and brain stem to muscles and glands) fibers of the cardiac nerves operating through the cardiac center in the medulla oblongata. Although the heart beat is an autonomic action that originates within the heart itself, nervous impulses discharged from the cardiac centers in the brain are able to alter the rate. Nerve impulses controlling the heart are received from the autonomic nervous system. The vagus nerves of the parasympathetic nervous system (PNS) are inhibitory and slow down the contractions of the heart, while accelerator nerves from the sympathetic nervous system (SNS) increase the rate and force of the contractions. The vagus nerve inhibits the heart's action through the liberation of acetylcholine at the nerve endings, while the accelerator nerves release norepinephrine. It is clear that heart action is controlled by both neural and chemical forces.

The diameter of the arteries and arterioles (small arteries), like the heart, is controlled through both neural and chemical action. The smooth muscles of the smaller arteries are supplied by vasoconstrictors that cause the contractions of the muscles and vasodilators that bring about relaxation. This process controls the diameter of the blood vessels and allows for the proper disbursement of blood to the various tissues based on their needs. The vasoconstrictor nerves are associated with the SNS, and stimulation to the vasomotor center in the medulla oblongata causes a contraction of the smooth muscles in the blood vessel walls, which results in a rise in blood pressure. In contrast to that, when the vasodilator center (which also is assumed to be in the medulla oblongata) is stimulated, dilation of the blood vessels occurs resulting in an increased flow of blood to the tissues and a corresponding decrease in blood pressure.

The elasticity of the arteries is mainly responsible for the maintenance of blood pressure. The arteries are generally slightly distended by the blood passing through. With each contraction of the ventricles, the blood discharged into the arterial systems causes a further expansion. At the end of the contraction, the distended walls recoil, forcing the blood forward and thereby maintaining a constant flow of blood through the arteries.

Blood pressure is the pressure exerted by the blood against the walls of the blood vessels in which it is contained. A young adult in good health should have a systolic pressure between 110 and 120 mmHg (mercury) and a diastolic between 65 and 80 mmHg (120/80). Hypertension or high blood pressure necessitates the use of higher amounts of pressure during the testing to obtain a reading when a nonamplified instrument is employed.

THE RESPIRATORY SYSTEM

Two types of respiration occur—external and internal. The former deals with the exchange of gases, the intake of oxygen, and the discharge of carbon dioxide between the organism and the environment. Internal respiration relates to the exchange of gases between the circulatory fluids (blood, lymph, and tissue fluids) and the cells.

A respiratory cycle consists of one inspiration and an expiration. The rate of respiration is influenced by a number of factors, including age, sex, position, and physical disorders. A child of five has a respiratory rate of about 25, a teenager 20, and an adult from 14 to 18. Women tend to have a somewhat more rapid rate. An apnea is a temporary stoppage of breathing, dyspnea is labored breathing, hyperpnea is deep breathing, and polypnea is rapid breathing that would be associated with increased activity or anxiety states. Although respiration is an involuntary and automatic act, it also can be controlled at a conscious level.

The respiratory system is composed of the right and left lungs and a series of passageways. Lungs are essentially elastic bags that open through their passageways to the outer environment. They are housed in the thoracic cavity with the thorax being composed of ribs, sternum (breast bone), and cartilage. At the floor of the thoracic cavity is the diaphragm, which is a muscle that separates the thoracic cavity from the abdominal cavity. During inspiration the diaphragm is flattened and descends, thereby increasing the vertical size of the thoracic cavity. As the diaphragm presses downward against the abdominal muscles, it forces the abdominal wall outward. This abdominal or diaphragmatic respiration is measured by the lower pneumo tube of the polygraph. Although their roles are the same, abdominal respiration presents a different pattern of breathing than occurs in thoracic breathing. As the diaphragm is pressing downward, the chest cavity is enlarged by raising the sternum and ribs, which increases the lateral diameter of the thorax. This breathing is measured by the upper pneumo tube. As the thoracic cavity is enlarged, the reduction in pressure on the lungs allows air to rush in and fill the lungs. When the inspiration stops, the size of the thoracic cavity is reduced. The diaphragm moves upward, and the sternum and ribs are lowered. The recoil of the stretched thoracic cartilage, the weight of the walls of the thorax, along with the recoil of the elastic lungs bring the chest wall back to its former position. This places pressure on the lungs and causes air to be expelled.

Air is taken in through the mouth and nostrils and into the nasal cavity, which occupies the space between the roof of the mouth and the floor of the cranial cavity. It opens to the pharynx, where the air enters the larynx, which contains the vocal cords. It continues through to the trachea or windpipe, which extends downward through the neck into the thorax. Here it terminates by dividing into right and left bronchi that lead to the lungs. On entering the lungs the bronchi continue to divide and gradually become smaller as they branch out. In the bronchi, there are rings of cartilage, but when this is no longer present the tubes are considered bronchioles. Smooth muscle is substituted for the cartilage, which is innervated by constrictor fibers of the vagus nerve and dilator fibers of the sympathetic trunk. The former is parasympathetic and narrows the diameters of the bronchioles, while the sympathetic fibers dilate the diameter allowing more air to be admitted. The diameters are reflexly controlled based on the respiratory needs of the body.

The lungs are the major organs of respiration and allow for the exchange of oxygen and carbon dioxide between the blood and the cells. The pulmonary arteries enter each lung carrying deoxygenated blood from the body. They terminate in a capillary net that allows for the ready diffusion of gases oxygenating the blood and passes it through the pulmonary veins into the left atrium.[5]

It has been seen that neural and chemical changes in the body enable the organism to more effectively cope with stress. The body automatically activates physiologic changes that allow this machine to operate more effectively using resources that are not generally available to it. The bronchioles of the lungs dilate so that more air can be taken in to provide more oxygen, which makes available the increased energy that is needed to cope with a threat. In a similar manner the sweat glands are activated, improving dexterity, locomotion, and even ability to grasp an object. The heart is stimulated to contract more strongly, providing more blood and therefore more nourishment for the entire organism.

THE NERVOUS SYSTEM

The specialized cell of the nervous system is the neuron. Its specific role is conduction, which is the ability to propagate a nerve impulse or electric signal from one point to another. The purpose of a nerve is to carry messages to and from the central nervous system and within it. The neuron is composed of a cell body and two types of cell processes—axons and dendrites. The synapse is the point of functional contact between nerve cells—that is, when the axon of one cell comes in close contact with the dendrite of another neuron. Generally, the nerve impulse travels from the axon of one cell to the dendrite of another cell. When the impulse reaches the synapse, it must bridge the gap at the junction of the nerves. This bridge can be either chemical or electrical, but in humans it is mainly chemical. In addition, synapses can be either inhibitory or excitatory. If the transmission across the synapse is chemical, it is carried out by the release of a substance at the nerve ending, either acetylcholine (which is parasympathetic) or norepinephrine (which is sympathetic). The latter operates to enhance actions associated with activating the fight or flight reactions of the body, while the former brings the organism back to its resting state.[6]

A reflex arc is the simplest neural link from the receptor (a cell with increased irritability to certain stimuli) to the effector (a cell, tissue, or organ that is specialized for some activity such as secretion or contraction), which involves the CNS.[7] The reflex is an involuntary act that is often unconscious as well. It is, however, a purposeful act that is usually necessary for the well-being of the body. Reflexes are either inherent or learned; Pavlov's experiments with salivation is a good example of the latter.

The two major divisions of the nervous system are the central nervous system and the peripheral nervous system. The CNS consists of the brain and spinal cord, while the latter is made up of the autonomic nervous system and the cranial and spinal nerves. Together they act as a switchboard receiving messages from receptors (sensory impulses) and making connections to effector organs such as muscles or glands that are responding mechanisms. The brain interprets sensory impulses received from the sense organs resulting in such sensations as taste and pain. All voluntary acts are initiated by the brain, and all emotions are founded on brain activity. It also is responsible for memory, learning, thought, reasoning, and awareness. The CNS controls all of the activities of the body except for those under chemical control, but even in these, it would appear that the brain can supersede the chemical regulation.

The brain is housed within the cranial cavity and consists of the brain stem, the cerebellum, and the cerebrum. The brain stem is next to the spinal cord, with its lowest portion being the medulla oblongata. It contains the cardiac center, which regulates heart contractions; the respiratory center, which determines respiratory rate; and the vasoconstriction center, which controls the diameter of the blood vessels. The pons, above the medulla, contains tracts that connect the medulla to the higher brain centers. The midbrain is the uppermost section of the brain stem, and it too connects the lower and higher brain centers and plays a role in equilibrium.

The cerebellum regulates and coordinates complex voluntary movements and assists in maintaining equilibrium, posture, and tonus. The diencephalon lies between the midbrain and the cerebral hemispheres. In it is the thalamus, which serves as a relay center for the transmission of afferent impulses from the sense organs to the sensory areas of the cerebral cortex. These are important reflex centers that regulate the organs and structures innervated by the ANS. The hypothalamus contains reflex centers that control body temperature and play a major role in metabolism. It also coordinates nervous and endocrine activities, and together the thalamus, hypothalamus, and subthalamus function in the realm of emotional behavior.

The cerebrum (cerebral hemispheres) is the largest part of the brain. The cerebral cortex is the surface layer of the cerebral hemispheres, and it is here that impulses cause conscious sensation related to vision, hearing, and sensation of touch, pressure, and temperature. It is here that thinking and recall occur. Damage to these areas often seen in stroke patients includes aphasia (loss of language ability) associated with damage to the left side of the brain, paralysis when there is damage to the motor areas, and blindness when there is trauma to the back of the head.

THE AUTONOMIC NERVOUS SYSTEM (ANS)

The ANS is of major importance to the polygraphist, for an understanding of how it operates can help demonstrate how the polygraph technique is effective.

The role of the ANS is to innervate the viscera of the body, the smooth muscles, the glands, and the heart. It has been called the visceral motor system, and because most of its functions are involuntary, it also has been described as the involuntary nervous system. It is a motor system in that it conducts impulses to the effectors (a tissue or organ specialized for some particular form of activity) where it either enhances or inhibits that response. The ANS and the endocrine system control the majority of the internal functions of the organism and serve to maintain homeostasis (internal equilibrium). However, it must be recognized that the brain stem, cerebral cortex, and hypothalamus, which act as an integrator and regulator of the ANS, play a role in controlling ANS activities. The latter explains why there is not always a total unidirectional response in polygraph testing. It is the reason that only some of the measures are indicative of deception, while others actually might be in the opposite direction. There is a relatively low correlation among the various autonomic responses.[8]

There are two branches of the ANS—the parasympathetic nervous systems (PNS) and the sympathetic nervous system (SNS). When the latter is stimulated, a number of the organs are automatically activated, unlike the PNS where the organs operate independently. Because in the SNS the organs essentially act in sympathy with one another, it becomes known as the sympathetic system.

The fibers of the ANS synapse between the spinal cord and the muscles or glands that they innervate. In the SNS the nerve fibers leave the spinal cord from the central area in the thoracic-lumbar region. In the PNS, on the other hand, because the nerve fibers leave the cord at either end, the brain stem and sacral cord, it was named parasympathetic.

The PNS and the SNS have antagonistic effects on the organs; if one system activates a particular organ, the other system inhibits that organ's response. For example, the SNS enhances heart activity, increasing the rate and strength of contractions, but the PNS reduces those actions. In this manner homeostasis is continued. All of the automatic functions are mediated through the release of certain transmitter substances at the termination of their nerve fibers, and the organs that they stimulate are reactive to those chemicals. Acetylcholine is released by PNS fibers and norepinephrine at the SNS nerve endings. The SNS produces activities related to the protection of the individual; it is, in essence, an emergency system that responds to situations involving threat, stress, and fear. It prepares the organism to defend against these threats by providing adequate energy to the working muscles and by removing waste products. In direct contrast to this, the PNS is dominant during states of rest and tranquility. It involves the conservation of energy and the restoration of the organism. During this time, digestion and growth occur, and damaged cells and energy supplies are replaced. It is this stage of anabolism that is the part of metabolism that involves the building or restoration of protoplasm. This phase of the metabolic process is necessary for life. The PNS is generally dominant, but when a threat occurs, autonomically and involuntarily the SNS takes over. Almost immediately, a whole series of physiologic changes take place that assist the body in coping with this threat. This is the catabolic stage, when protoplasm is broken down and energy is expended. The organism prepares for the fight or flight reaction. When the threat is ended, the body through chemical and neural (mainly the vagus nerve) processes almost as quickly returns to its former state. As these physiologic changes occur, either sympathetic or parasympathetic, they are seen on the polygraph chart in the form of changes in the rate and pattern of respiration, in blood pressure and blood volume, in heart rate, and in electrodermal response.

SYMPATHETIC AROUSAL

During emergency situations, there is a generalized discharge of the SNS that includes the firing frequency of the fibers and an activation of the fibers that are at rest. One of the major roles of the SNS is the regulation of vasomotor tone. The arterioles constrict, which results in an increase in peripheral resistance and an increase in blood pressure. Epinephrine (adrenalin) is secreted by the adrenal medulla into the blood, and norepinephrine, which is similar to adrenalin, is released form the sympathetic nerve endings innervating the heart; this increases both heart rate and the strength of contractions. The resulting increased blood flow provides needed nourishment and energy for the organism so that it can operate effectively during a state of stress. A series of changes occur in the arterial system, which channels blood to those systems and organs of the body that require it in order to defend the organism. The blood vessels in the digestive tract and genitalia constrict because these regions of the body are not active during an emergency state. Therefore, their requirement for blood in reduced. In contrast to that, the blood vessels in the skeletal muscles and heart dilate, sending an increased supply of blood and nourishment to those areas to enhance their performance. There is an increased capability for work and a reduced fatigue. Hormones, nutrients, and oxygen are brought to those areas, and waste is removed through an augmented venous return, allowing the individual to run, fight, or climb more effectively. Constriction of the blood vessels in the skin increases the blood flow, which cools the body after muscular exertion. There is also an increase in sweating that aids in this cooling as well. The liver, stimulated by SNS activity, releases glycogen, which increases the blood sugar level and provides more energy, and chemical changes in the blood enhance coagulability.

In the lungs the bronchioles dilate so that there is an increase in the amount of oxygen taken in, allowing for a greater availability of energy through the oxidation of the nutrients. The pupils of the eyes dilate, allowing more light to enter and thereby improving vision. At the same time, changes in the musculature of the eye adjusts it to distant vision. Sweat gland activity in the so-called emotional sweating areas is increased improving locomotion, tactile discrimination, and grasping. The adrenalin secreted into the blood augments all of these reactions.

All of these changes mobilize the organism for action, but once the threat is ended the PNS again becomes dominant.

PARASYMPATHETIC DOMINANCE

Chemical and neural stimulation, with the vagus nerve particularly playing a significant role, brings about parasympathetic dominance. Vagal fibers of the respiratory tract produce constriction of the bronchioles. Vagal activity also slows the contractions of the heart and reduces the strength of these contractions. Through this vagal action, gastrointestinal activity, including salivation, starts again. The blood vessels to the digestive and genital areas dilate just as the arteries to the skeletal and heart muscles constrict, reversing the blood supply. The pupils of the eyes contract, and the eyes once again adjust for near vision. The body is no longer mobilized for defense. Table 3–1 compares these responses.

Table 3–1. Autonomic Nervous System Functioning

Organ	SNS dominant during stress	PNS dominant during relaxation
Eyes:		
Ciliary muscle	Adjusts eyes for distant vision	Adjusts eyes for near vision
Pupil	Dilation; improves vision by allowing more light to enter	Constriction
Lungs	Dilates bronchioles; allows for increased oxygen intake	Constricts bronchioles
Heart	Increases strength of contractions; provides more nourishment for the body	Decreases strength of contractions
	Usually immediately reduces heart rate followed by increase; compensates for blood pressure rise	Returns to resting heart rate
Sweat glands:		
Emotional sweating area	Active; enhance locomotion and tactile discrimination	May cause reabsorption
General sweating area	Reduces body heat associated with activity	
Liver	Secretes glycogen increasing blood sugar level; increases energy	
Blood vessels:		
Peripheral	Constriction; reduce body heat and increase blood pressure	Dilation
Skeletal and cardiac	Provide more blood and nourishment for more efficient operation	Constriction
Blood pressure	Increased	
Adrenal glands	Stimulate secretion of adrenalin; enhance all SNS changes	No effect
Gastrointestinal	Inhibits activity; constricts blood vessels; diverts blood to skeletal muscles; digestion not required during stress	Stimulates digestive processes
Genitalia	Constricts blood vessels; diverts blood to skeletal muscles	Dilates blood vessels

Although the body is an impressive machine, it is not perfect. It is seen in neurotics who suffer from anxiety or panic attacks. They fear something that is neither realistic nor evident. Without an obvious stimulus, they suddenly are afraid and then panicky. They enter a state of SNS dominance, and the pounding of their heart and the difficulty in breathing due to hyperventilation frightens them even more and increases their state of fear, incapacitating them further.

Another example of SNS arousal being a disadvantage is in the case of impotence. A male's concerns about his ability in a sexual encounter could actually cause the very event that he fears. Because an erection is the result of an increased blood supply to the penis, fear of losing that erection will result in sympathetic arousal and cause constriction to the arteries in the genitals and dilation in the blood vessels of the skeletal muscles. The blood supply will be reduced in the penis and increase in the arms and legs, and he will experience a loss of erection.

The final example of the disadvantageous aspect of sympathetic arousal is in a polygraph situation. For here, the examinees' fear that their lies will be detected causes SNS arousal, and instead of it helping them to cope with the threat and getting them out of trouble, the fear accomplishes just the opposite.

PSYCHOPHYSIOLOGIC BASES OF POLYGRAPHY

In 1961 Davis presented three hypotheses to explain the effectiveness of the polygraph technique.[9] The most accepted of these concepts relates to fear of consequences. When a subject recognizes that he or she faces possible imprisonment, financial loss, and personal embarrassment if a deception is discovered, he or she becomes fearful of that outcome. This emotional reaction activates the SNS and the ensuing polygraph changes can be interpreted as indicative of deception. Although this is a logical description of what occurs in most instances, this is not what occurs in laboratory research. In this situation volunteer college students, with little or nothing to lose if their lies are detected, assumedly would have no fear. Despite this, laboratory research has demonstrated an high degree of polygraph accuracy, which indicates that the fear of consequences theory alone cannot explain polygraph effectiveness.

Davis also hypothesized that conflict could play a role in this process. He assumed that moral orientation is learned and predisposes an individual toward truthfulness. However, if someone sees the possibility of avoiding trouble through lying, that person would be tempted to use lying as a way out of difficulty. When faced with these two incompatible responses, a conflict would follow that would result in sympathetic arousal. Psychopaths, however, have little or no conscience and have absolutely no moral problem with deceiving others. In fact, it is quite likely that psychopaths did not learn to be honest but rather to lie quite effectively. In spite of that, there is evidence that demonstrates that psychopaths are amenable to polygraph testing. It is clear from this evidence that the conflict theory alone is not sufficient to explain the accuracy of this procedure.

In a third explanation of why polygraphy is successful, Davis described a conditioned response theory. He indicated that asking questions that were relevant to a criminal act would arouse the same emotional state that the perpetrator experienced during the act itself. If this were true, however, then victims and witnesses would also experience these feelings, which suggests that they also would be seen as deceptive even though they were responding truthfully. Although all three of these hypothesis have merit, it is not believed that one alone can account for all testing situations.

A broader hypothesis is one that indicates that there is a generalized tension, anxiety, or excitement that occurs during polygraphy testing. It would account for polygraph testing in both the laboratory and in real life situations and with psychopaths and nonpsychopaths alike. It is felt, however, that the most plausible concept is that all these emotional states are involves to varying degrees in every examination. In most instances the fear of the consequences predominates, but this would vary with the type of testing, subjects, and perhaps even the case under study.

Although the exact emotion that causes sympathetic arousal during the polygraph approach is not clear, it is evident that the procedures evoke SNS dominance. The art of this process is to create an emotional response, whether fear or conflict, that will occur whenever the examinee lies regardless of whether he or she is innocent or guilty. These emotions will be aroused at the very instant in which the subject hears the question to which he or she is going to respond deceptively. Therefore, reaction might begin after the first few words of the question. The question creates the threat, and the threat in turn causes the emotional reaction that results in the SNS's becoming dominant. The individual's defensive system becomes activated, and physiologic changes will occur that aid the organism in coping with the threat. In order to improve grasping and locomotion, the subject's hands will perspire, which reduces the skin's resistance to electricity and results in an abrupt upward swing of the pen involved with electrodermal activity.

Once again it should be noted that other physiologic functions might be involved in this and the sweating response alone may not cause electrodermal reactions. Changes in the cardiovascular system occur, including the constriction of the arterioles, which increase peripheral resistance and thereby raise blood pressure. A rise in the blood pressure tracings will take place. Secretion of norepinephrine causes the heart to contract more strongly, resulting in an increase in blood volume to the arteries in the muscles of the arm beneath the blood pressure cuff, which also plays a role in raising the cardio tracings. For a reason that is still not clear, a narrowing of the tracings associated with SNS arousal is sometimes seen. Although a more rapid heart rate might be expected, concentrating on some external stimulus (the question) tends to reduce the frequency of the heart beat. Moreover, as blood pressure increases, there is a tendency for heart rate to lessen so that one would be more apt to find a decrease in heart rate with SNS arousal. Although hyperventilation is often associated with fear and anxiety, the immediate respiratory response appears to be a tightening up of the thorax so that deep breathing is less likely to occur, resulting in a suppressed breathing pattern. Once the question has been answered and the threat is over, PNS dominance occurs in order to maintain homeostasis. Through the vagus nerve heart contractions are lessened, reducing blood pressure, and the arteries to the skeletal muscles contract, reducing the blood supply to the arm. The cardio tracings, therefore, drop and return to their previous level. In the sweat glands, the perspiration is apparently reabsorbed, returning the skin's resistance to electricity to its prior state. The electrodermal response returns to its previous base line, but the pen drops more gradually than it rose. It can be assumed that the greater the previous sympathetic arousal the slower the return. This is based on findings that the duration of electrodermal response is as valid a measure of deception as the amplitude. Finally, if the respiration were suppressed, there will likely be a series of deep breaths to make up for the reduced oxygen intake. The changes occur with SNS and PNS dominance, allowing for a highly accurate interpretation of truth or deception.

THE INSTRUMENT AND THE POLYGRAPH SUITE

4

If science bids fair to furnish a fairly effective technique for the exposure of deception, we should not merely welcome it when it comes but stimulate and encourage efforts to speed its coming.

—C.T. McCormick

In a scientific experiment, all variables are held constant with the exception of the one under study. A polygraph examination is much the same; a reaction of truth or deception is the only factor that should influence the tracings. Light, temperature, humidity, noise, and visual distractions are all external variables and must be controlled to the extent that they do not influence the examination in any manner. The testing room should be neutral in color and decor, devoid of any objects that could distract the subject. Recognizing that any noise can cause an artifact in the tracings, the room ideally should be soundproofed. Should any distractions of any nature occur, a notation must be made on the chart of exactly the time when they happened so that any physiologic changes that resulted from the distraction is not mistakingly interpreted as a response to the question being asked at that time.

Although it is not always possible to control internal variables, an attempt should be made to reduce or eliminate any of these that could affect the test results. In an ideal situation, the examinee should not be fatigued and should have had a good night's sleep before the test. He or she should be neither hungry nor thirsty and should have met all needs to eliminate prior to the examination. It is preferable that the subject not take any drugs, but some individuals require certain medications. At no time should the examiner request that the testee refrain from taking prescribed medications because the polygraphist can be held accountable for any negative effect on the subject and accused of practicing medicine without a license. If it is felt important that the medications be delayed until the procedure is completed, this request should be made through the examinee's physician. Pain will cause physiologic responses in the subject, and if it is of a temporary nature, the examination should be delayed until the pain has abated. Individuals with chronic pain may be testable, but some arrangement, such as a finger movement, should be developed so that the examiner is aware of when a sharp pain occurs. The polygrapher should inquire into any illnesses or other areas that might be disturbing the subject at the time. Stress factors, like the loss of a job or an illness in the family, could cause enough of a disturbance to distort the test results. Inevitably, the person to be evaluated is going to be anxious about the test and certainly concerned about the charges being brought against him or her, but other problems might so depress or agitate the subject that the examination will be of secondary importance. Therefore, inquiries into the subject's health and mental state are pertinent.

The examinee should be seated in a comfortable chair facing a blank wall. The examiner should sit at a right angle to the examinee so that movements can be seen but yet far enough forward so that the examinee cannot observe his or her responses on the chart. It should be noted that peripheral vision allows for wide-angle views to the sides and should be considered in arranging seating. Having the testee close his or her eyes may be an effective means of avoiding distractions. No one but the examiner should be in the testing room unless an interpreter is necessary. It would be advantageous to have an examination room that is equipped with a one-way mirror and a sound system if there are occasions when it is necessary to have someone view the process. This would be of value when the procedure needs to be videotaped; when the polygraphist feels that there might be some risk of claims of misconduct; or if an attorney wants to witness the procedure. Laws vary within the states, and permission may be required to tape or have an observer present. These are litigious times, and the polygraphist should practice defensively. Also, one has to meet one examiner who neglected to obtain malpractice insurance and has been sued in order to realize how important this protection is. No one should be tested, for both the examinee's well-being and the polygraphist's safety, whose condition could be worsened in any fashion by the examination.

Most polygraph instrumentation is similar, and the two major manufacturers, Stoelting and Lafayette, are comparable in quality. Elaborate equipment is manufactured for scientific laboratories that have more advanced instrumentation and more sensors. This equipment, however, is not portable and is prohibitively expensive for field workers. The usual field equipment includes measures of respiration, blood volume/blood pressure, heart rate, and the electrodermal skin response. Additional sensors such as the cardioactivity monitor, heart rate monitor, and plethysmograph are sometimes employed along with the primary measures. The instruments very from three- to five-pen models, with the larger instruments having the advantage of measuring more areas of physiologic functioning. The equipment may be mechanical or electronically enhanced. In the latter, the examiner can increase or decrease the sensitivity of the response for improved interpretability. In the cardio unit, for example, an individual who is very obese or who suffers from hypertension might require a good deal of pressure in the blood pressure cuff before an adequate tracing can be obtained. Because great pressure on the arm causes discomfort, it might result in a distortion of the tracings or force a shortening of the test because this pressure can not be tolerated for an extended period of time. Employing the amplified cardio, good tracings can be achieved at low pressure, thereby eliminating problems of this nature. Amplification of the pneumograph, however, is rarely required because the amplitude can be adjusted through tightening or loosening the pneumographic tubes about the examinee's chest and abdomen. Figures 4–1 and 4–2 show the polygraph instrumentation.

Figure 4–1. An Administration of a Polygraph Examination

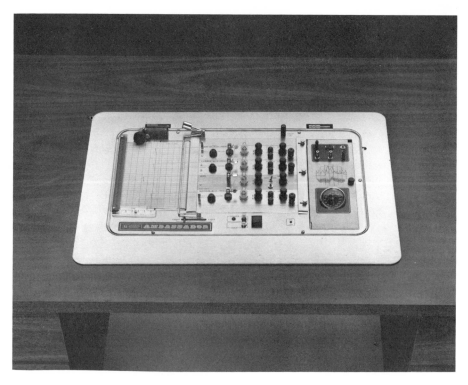

Figure 4–2. Polygraph Instrument

THE PNEUMOGRAPH

The pneumograph consists of one or two corrugated rubber bellows positioned across the individual's upper abdomen and chest and attached behind the back with a beaded chain. The chest tube is placed at about nipple level in men and above the swell of the breast in women. If only one pneumograph tube is used, thoracic (chest) breathing generally provides the better measure in women and abdominal breathing in men. The pneumograph is connected to the recording module through rubber tubing that moves the pen and provides a graphic representation of the person's respiration rate and pattern. Breathing in causes the pen to rise, and the greater the inspiration the larger the amplitude of the tracing. An expiration, of course, causes the opposite reaction, whereas a stoppage of breathing (apnea) is shown as a straight horizontal line that continues as long as the respiration stops. The chart paper has vertical lines at five- or ten-second intervals, and by counting each rise in the tracings, respiration rate can be readily calculated.

The pneumograph vent is located on the top panel, and in its open position allows outside air to enter the system. When it is not in operation it is kept open to avoid damage to the system. During the recording mode, the vent must be closed, keeping the air captive in there. On the electronically enhanced model, there is a sensitivity control that allows the polygraphist to adjust the amplitude of the recording. If the tracing produced is too small, amplitude can be readily increased by raising the sensitivity. If, on the other hand, the response is too large—so that the pens touch the stops or conflict with the movements of the other pens, preventing a completed curve from being expressed on the chart—sensitivity can be reduced. A centering control is present in both the mechanical and electronic models to adjust the placement of the tracing on the chart and to ensure that the pens are operating within their own tracing realm.

THE CARDIOGRAPH

This measure is composed of a blood pressure cuff similar to the instrument employed by a physician in medical examinations. It contains an inflatable bladder that is held in place against the brachial artery of the upper arm by the cuff. The center of the cuff should cover the inner arm approximately several inches above the elbow. If the subject complains of too much tenderness or if the arm is too large for a good recording to be made, the forearm can be used. Rubber tubing connects the cuff bladder to the recording system. A hand pump bulb that is part of the system pumps air into the cuff bladder, placing pressure on the arm. The same pressure enters the sphygmomanometer, which provides a measure of the pressure. When the heart contracts, blood is spurted out into the aorta and through the various arteries of the body. As the blood goes through the brachial artery and under the blood pressure cuff, the distension of the artery presses against the bladder, forcing a proportionate amount of air through the tubing, which in turn causes an upward movement of the pen. Following each contraction of the heart, there is a resting state that reduces the pressure and results in a downward swing of the pen. As the wave of blood passes beyond the cuff, the artery and the arm return to their normal size and the pressure in the bladder is reduced. Each rise is equivalent to a pulse beat so that one can easily determine pulse rate by counting the number of upward swings of the pen for each minute of chart paper. The dicrotic notch (discussed in chapter 3) can be seen as the slight rise and drop that occurs during the descending cycle. The contraction of the heart and the upward swing of the pen is the systolic, while the heart at rest (seen as the downward stroke of the pen) is the diastolic. As with the pneumograph, when the cardio vent is in its open position, outside air enters and leaves the system. The blood pressure cuff then easily can be affixed to the arm. The instrument is operable, however, only when the system is closed, preventing outside air from entering.

The bladder is pumped up on the electronically amplified cardio to 60 to 70 mmHg of pressure. (Raskin has reported that the amplified cardio operates most effectively at 70 mmHg of pressure, but Max Wastl, Sr., of Lafayette Instruments, recommends 60 mmHg.) The sensitivity control is then adjusted to obtain an amplitude of about three-quarters of an inch. In the mechanical cardio, the pressure in the bladder, and therefore in the arm, must be increased in order to obtain an adequate amplitude for accurate interpretation. As has just been indicated, in individuals with hypertension, the pressure might have to be increased to 90 or 100 mmHg of pressure. There would seem to be little doubt at this time that the electronically enhanced cardio has numerous advantages over the mechanical version of this sensor.

A thumb transducer is also manufactured, which serves the same purpose as the blood pressure cuff without placing any tension on the arm. It may replace or be used in addition to the cuff. Because these tracings are essentially the same, it is preferable to use a different sensor rather than duplicate the tracing. Appropriate placement of the dicrotic notch should be at about the center of the vertical swing of the cardio tracing. The notch can be lowered by increasing the pressure or raised to the appropriate position by reducing the pressure.

THE ELECTRODERMAL RESPONSE (EDR)

The skin's resistance to electricity is measured through the use of two electrodes, which generally are attached to the finger tips of the index and ring fingers. Positioning the electrodes in this manner, with one finger between, prevents contact being made between electrodes. The electrodes are placed on the opposing hand to which the blood pressure cuff is affixed. A wire then connects the electrodes to the electrodermal response (EDR) unit. It operates in either a manual or automatic mode. The latter causes the pen to be brought back to a base position after each deflection, resulting in ease of scoring because each question can be asked when the pen is at approximately the same base line. Comparisons of amplitude are also readily made. The disadvantage, however, is that it restricts the freedom of movement of the pen and reactions are forced into a rather narrow response pattern. In the manual centering, the range of the reaction is seen in much more detail as the pen swings below the artificial base line and the amplitude is maintained for longer periods of time. Although manual centering provides more information, it causes difficulty in regulating and comparing responses because the pen is much more active. Despite this, manual control is the preferred mode.

The sensitivity control is employed by starting at a low level and then telling the subject that his or her hand will be touched to determine reactivity. There should be an EDR response at the point when the subject is informed of this and when he or she has actually been touched. If the response is too large, sensitivity is reduced, and it is increased if there is an insufficient reaction. A rise of several inches is adequate. It should be noted that the level of response can be changed during the test if it is too large or too small. There is a tendency for the reaction to diminish with testing in some individuals. If the sensitivity is changed in the middle of a specific test, the change should be clearly marked; it never should be done at a point when questions asked under different sensitivity levels will be compared. If a comparison is to be made between questions 4 and 5 and also between 6 and 7, altering the sensitivity should follow the response to question 5. It is preferable to make this change during the actual testing rather than lose the value of the EDR because the individual has ceased responding enough to obtain a scorable reaction. (This problem will become clearer after a reading of the various types of questions in chapter 5.)

As in the pneumo and cardio sensors, a centering control exists. The EDR pen, however, is somewhat longer than those in the other measures. Because the EDR responses have wider swings of movement, the EDR pen might become entangled with the other pens if it were their size. This slightly complicates the scoring procedure because the larger pen means that the GSR reaction on the chart will be seen at about five to seven seconds of chart time earlier than that of the other sensors. The examiner should mark the beginning of the EDR response rather than estimate where the reaction occurred because there will always be times when the response precedes the question and should not be scored.

The psychogalvanic reflex is demonstrated when a weak electric current is passed through the fingers. With a galvanometer in the circuit, the skin's resistance to this electricity can be measured. An upward movement of the pen is indicative of an increased flow of current due to a decrease in the skin's resistance to electricity. As was indicated in chapter 3, it has been hypothesized that the sweating associated with sympathetic arousal causes the reduction in resistance.

THE CARDIO ACTIVITY MONITOR (CAM)

The cardio activity monitor (CAM) monitors heart rate and blood pressure changes through the placement of a transducer on the thumb or wrist. Like the EDR it should not be used on the same arm as the cardio. The amount of pressure applied and the placement will vary the response pattern. It should be about one-fourth to one-half inch from the tip of the finger on the palmar side. Pressure is adequate if the notch is at about the center of the tracing. If the notch is too low, the pressure should be reduced, and if too high, increased. A sensitivity control allows the amplitude to be adjusted to its appropriate size, between one-fourth and three-fourths of an inch. The centering control serves to maintain the tracing at its proper chart position.

The CAM is capable of monitoring the individual's cardiovascular activity for long periods of time without the discomfort that the blood pressure cuff produces. In measuring the activity in the distal blood vessels of the fingers, it studies the opposite effect as the cardiograph. In stress, the blood is transported from the peripheral area of the body in order to increase the blood supply in the larger skeletal muscles. Therefore, the cardiograph responds to an increased flow of blood to the arm, whereas the CAM measures the blood being drawn from the fingers and hand. In contrast to the cardio tracings, which demonstrate an upward trend with sympathetic arousal, the CAM shows a downward movement.

THE PLETHYSMOGRAPH

The effectiveness of this approach is determined by its capacity to measure blood volume in the thumb or middle finger. The tissue has varying degrees of optical opacity, which are affected by the quantities of blood in the area and changes due to pressure pulse. This is accomplished by directing a light of constant intensity through a segment of tissue in the finger. Changes in blood flow are then measured by a sensor and transmitted through an amplifier. A sensitivity control allows the examiner to maintain an amplitude between one-fourth and three-fourths of an inch, and a centering control keeps the tracing within its proper chart position.

This device consists of a finger transducer, which contains the sensor and light. A wire connects it to the appropriate module on the instrument itself. The tracing obtained is much like the cardio in pattern.

THE KYMOGRAPH

The kymograph controls the chart paper flow through a motor that drives the chart paper at a rate of six inches per minute. Knowing this allows for a computation of heart and breathing rate and provides the examiner with a means of knowing and controlling the amount of time between questions.

THE INKING SYSTEM

There are two basic inking systems, and the most common procedures use an ink flow. There are various types, but in each case, the system is sealed so that transporting can be carried out while the instrument is fully linked. In some systems different color ink can be used for the different sensors. The flow of ink can be adjusted to affect the thickness of the tracings. There are disadvantages to this approach in that on occasions the pens will become clogged, some leak-

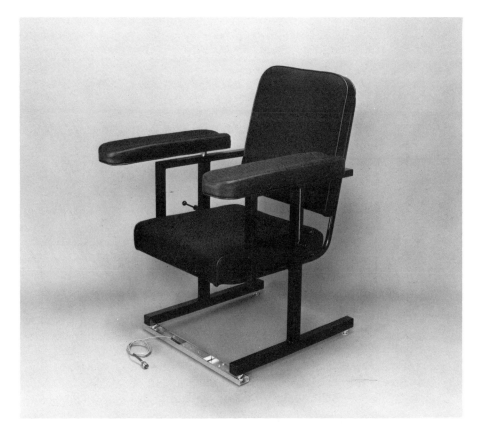

Figure 4–3. A Motion Chair for Evaluating Movement Countermeasures

age and blurring of the tracings might occur, and maintenance in the form of cleaning the pens, bottles, and tubing is required. A second system operates through the use of an electric stylus pen, which produces a tracing when the heated tip of the pen moves across a chemically treated chart paper. This is much more maintenance free, but the cost of both the thermal writing system and the chart paper is greater.

CHART MARKER

A variety of stimulus markers have been developed that allow the examiner to write on the chart by either touching a button or squeezing a bulb exactly where the question is asked and the response occurs. Because the EDR pen is longer, stimulus markers show where the subject responds on all measures with the exception of EDR. The polygraphist has either to assume that the EDR reaction was about five to seven seconds earlier than where the chart markings were indicated or to mark it separately.

THE MOTION CHAIR

A recent addition to the polygraph instrumentation is a device used to detect countermeasures through body movements. By attaching a transducer to the front or back legs of the polygraph chair, even minor movements than cannot be detected by an observer can be seen on the polygraph chart. In view of the findings that physical countermeasures have been demonstrated to be effective, this is an important addition to the polygraph instrumentation. Figure 4–3 shows the motion chair.

VIDEO RECORDS

Videotapes or even audiotapes are rarely made of polygraph examinations although the practice is advisable in cases that are of great significance and will be part of a major courtroom battle. If video equipment is employed, it should be set up in a manner that will not disturb the subject during actual testing. The camera should have a clear view of the subject, the examiner, the instrument, and the chart. Obviously, the tape will be studied for voice inflection, adjustments of the instruments, and the verbal interchange with the subject. Any expressive movements or verbalizations that could be seen as threatening or overly reassuring will be subject to scrutiny and questioning.

POLYGRAPH TEST PROCEDURE I: INFORMATION

GATHERING AND THE PRETEST PHASE

5

The most difficult lie to detect is the one that we want to believe the most.
—Stan Abrams

Every examination should be conducted as if it were going to be admitted into evidence and subject to the scrutiny of an expert witness from the opposing side. It must be assumed that the technique, question formulation, tracings, and scoring will be rigidly critiqued by another polygraphist. Each test can significantly affect someone's life but also can influence the examiner's reputation in the community.

In evaluating each case, it is important to operate independently from the influence of those who have something to gain or lose from the results. If other polygraphists have already tested the subject, they have investment in having similar findings obtained during the second evaluation. Attorneys, too, are not above trying to influence the examiner in order to gain some assistance in winning their case. It should be noted that if a private examiner employed by the defense is biased by others to the extent of finding a deceptive person truthful, the examiner may hurt the lawyer's case. Assured that his or her client is able to pass an examination, the lawyer might agree to a stipulated test administered by another polygraphist. If the subject then fails the stipulated test, that failure is admitted into evidence, and the defendant is in considerable difficulty. The examiner's reputation suffers and the attorney would have grave doubts about referring further individuals to the examiner for testing. Moreover, the prosecutor would not be likely to accept the examiner's opinions in the future. This in turn would mean that few defense attorneys in the community would find any value in referring clients to the polygraphist. When a police examiner misdiagnoses a subject, he or she also loses the respect and trust of the prosecutor's office and of fellow police officers and might receive fewer referrals.

The ability to avoid the influence of others is a valuable trait required of polygraphists. Not only must the examiner remain free of the influence of other professionals involved in the case, but he or she has to be strong enough to cope with any subject, regardless of personality or position. Without being abusive, it is necessary that the examiner remain in complete control of the testing situation and not permit anyone to dictate how the test will be conducted. An effective polygraphist creates an air of professionalism that mixes good common sense, intelligence, sophistication, and good verbal ability with an ability to deal with people from all levels of life. The purpose should not be to relax the innocent and create fear in the guilty but rather to develop in both a sense of fear that a lie may be detected. Ideally, the set that is developed leads the innocent to be as concerned that deception on the control questions will be detected as the guilty are afraid that their deceit to the relevant questions will be discovered.

A polygraph test is like a chess game in which specific moves are planned well in advance, but the examiner must be creative and flexible enough to alter his or her approach if an obstacle is met. Moreover, every move that the examiner makes should serve a purpose, whether it is physical positioning or providing information to the subject. It is important to create a picture of objectivity, capability, being in charge, and above all, having the ability to ascertain if the examinee is responding truthfully or deceptively.

The polygraph procedure can be divided into four distinct phases: data gathering, pretest interviewing, actual testing, and posttest interviewing (the latter two phases are discussed in chapter 6).

DATA GATHERING

The first aspect of the test process generally has not been treated as a separate entity but is sufficiently important to warrant this. Insufficient or inaccurate data can be damaging to both attaining an accurate finding and to fostering the credibility of the expert in court. In regard to the latter, an opposing attorney who learns that certain information is not available will make an issue of it and in so doing will weaken the examiner's testimony.

Complete details must be gathered on both the case in question and the person to be tested. Details of the examinee's medical state should be known prior to the testing to determine whether he or she is, in fact, testable and whether the examinee should discontinue certain medications around the time of the examination. The polygraphist must never directly request the subject to postpone use of a specific drug but must do this through the subject's physician. Doing otherwise places the examiner in a position of risk, with the possible result ranging from a lawsuit to a charge of practicing medicine without a license. Medical conditions that would preclude testing must be considered on the basis of danger to the subject and to the examiner. A good rule of thumb is that no one should ever be examined whose condition, whether physical or psychological, could be worsened by the testing process. This occurrence would be rather rare, but the examiner should practice defensively by always obtaining a physician's written approval for the test to be administered in questionable cases. Epileptics should not be tested unless their convulsions are controlled by medications, and cardiac patients whose conditions are so severe as to warrant caution need to be avoided. Most other conditions will not be adversely affected by either the stress of the examination or the minor physical pressure of the blood pressure cuff. Another consideration, however, is the risk to the polygraphist; in these litigious times, the examiner must be wary of being sued. For example, when testing a woman who is pregnant, the danger to the subject or the fetus is almost nonexistent, but should she miscarry months later for reasons other than the examination, she could initiate a suit against the examiner. Anyone can sue anyone else for almost anything, and attorneys can be found who are willing to take such a case, just as experts are available to testify for any side.

Prior to the examination date, some information on the individual's psychiatric background should be obtained. If a history of significant symptoms or hospitalization exists, these data should be obtained in the form of medical reports so that the severity of the condition can be assessed. Likewise, details of educational and work background provide evidence of intellectual deficits that might make testing less than accurate.

The examiner should examine complete reports related to the act in question before the test date. In a criminal case the police records should include the statements of the victim, the accused, the witnesses, and any information from such experts as pathologists or arson investigators. Certain specifics such as dates, addresses, and charges should be checked for accuracy. Typographical errors or sloppy reporting can invalidate the testing if inaccurate material is included in the questions. A separate statement written up by the examinee prior to the test date can be helpful in obtaining a broader picture of the situation.

The attorney, whether for the defense or prosecution, certainly has a right to provide a list of questions to be asked, but the polygraphist is the expert, and the questions to be used and their wording rests with him. Some prosecutors and law enforcement officers make demands of the police polygraphist that appear like orders. In a tactful manner the examiner must explain how the test will be invalidated if employed in an inappropriate manner.

In testing for defense attorneys, it is imperative to determine in advance of the examination whether the attorneys want an admission if their client is found to be deceptive. Although some attorneys want a confession because it aids them in the plea bargaining process, the majority feel that an admission weakens their case. Examinations for the defense are almost always ex parte tests—that is, no one else will learn of the results but the attorney and his client. To ensure that the findings remain confidential and that the examiner is serving as the lawyer's agent, the appointment should be made by the lawyer's office and the bill should be sent to the lawyer not the client. The attorney should be made aware that he or she is responsible for the fee and will be charged even if the client does not appear for the examination. At least twenty-four-hour notice of cancellation should be required.

It has been found helpful in some instances to have the referring lawyer inform his or her client that a urinalysis probably will be carried out. This considerably reduces the likelihood that the examinee will employ drugs as a countermeasure. A urine sample can be taken on each subject and then disposed of if no problems are evident in the test results. In a few questionable instances, the urine sample can be sent to a laboratory for evaluation. Using this routinely, however, becomes prohibitively expensive.

PRETEST INTERVIEW

The most important part of the entire test process in the pretest interview, for the validity of the procedure hinges on how effectively it is conducted. Numerous functions are served, and each one is significant.

Rapport must be established, allaying the examinee's anger, suspicion, and generalized anxiety. In part, this can be accomplished by the examiner's presenting himself or herself as being highly objective with an interest only in learning the truth. Trust can be developed with an assurance that there will be no surprise or trick questions and an explanation of the test procedure that reduces the fear of the unknown while enhancing the fear of a lie being detected. The explanation might be somewhat over the subject's head but will impress the examinee with the examiner's expertise and allow him or her to get a feel for the effectiveness of the approach. It has been found that an explanation of the approach can be introduced best through a description of the physiologic bases of the procedure such as following:

The polygraph is not a lie detector. It is an instrument that operates off of what is called the autonomic nervous system. "Autonomic" means automatic or involuntary, so it deals with those aspects of the body that cannot be controlled. It is helpful to us because the individual being examined is unable to control those parts of the body. There are two branches to the autonomic nervous system. The first one has to do with growth and development, and the second one is an emergency system. These two parts operate in opposition to one another, which means that only one (usually the part that has to do with growth) is in control at a time. The emergency system becomes dominant only when there is some threat to an individual and he or she becomes fearful. For example, if you are walking down the street and a man suddenly approaches you and pulls out a knife, you will become afraid. That message will go to the brain, and the brain in turn will send a message back to the autonomic nervous system to put the emergency system into control. When that happens a series of physiologic changes takes place that helps you cope with that situation. Your heart contracts more quickly and strongly, which sends more blood throughout the body and provides it with nourishment so it can function more effectively. Your liver secretes sugar, giving you more energy, and the pupils of your eyes dilate so you can see better. The palms of your hands perspire so that you can grasp things more effectively, just as a baseball player spits on his hands to get a better grip on a baseball bat. These and other changes occur, allowing you to run faster, hit harder, or lift more so that you can get out of that dangerous situation.

   The polygraph test measures a similar response. If you tell the truth, you will function at your normal level. If you come to a question to which you are going to lie, you will become afraid of being caught in that lie. As soon as you become afraid, your body automatically shifts into the emergency system. There is no way that you can stop it. Then all of these changes will take place, and I will be able to see them on the polygraph chart.

The examiner should indicate that nervousness in this situation is normal and that everyone who takes this test is nervous and does not operate at a normal level.

Your pulse rate is usually about seventy but now is probably about ninety. That is the base line that we will be functioning from. Therefore, if you are telling the truth you will stay at that level, but if you lie, your pulse will probably go up to one hundred twenty.

At this point, it has been found of value to show the subject a good sample of a stim test, saying something like this:

This will give you some idea of what a polygraph chart looks like. What I did with this subject was to give him six cards numbered from twenty to twenty-five. I had him choose one of the cards, and then on the test I asked him if he chose a twenty, twenty-one, and so on. However, I told him to respond no to every single question, including the question about the card that he selected, which meant that he lied on one question. Do you understand?

For some individuals this explanation is too complicated and must be explained again until they can comprehend it. The subject is then shown the large changes in the GSR and the cardio that very clearly demonstrates deception on the card number where the subject lied. No mention is made of respiration because when the individual becomes aware that respiration will be measured, he consciously or unconsciously tends to control it. The subject is then presented with the analogy that the test is similar to fingerprinting someone:

Each person has a unique polygraph pattern. Your response to deception will be quite different from this man's. Each person is different, and the purpose of this test is to find out what you look like when you tell a lie. I'll do the same thing with you, and once I have your lie pattern, it will be easy to determine if you are lying or telling the truth on the test itself. Even nervousness won't make a difference.

The explanation of how the polygraph test works and the example of the stim test should serve to increase the fears of the guilty while reducing the anxiety of the innocent. Later in the examination, both the truthful and deceptive will be oriented toward a fear associated with deception.

The first phase of the pretest interview is devoted to developing rapport, and the second explains the polygraph process and, more important, enhances the subject's fear of being caught in a lie. The third purpose of the initial interview is to learn more about the subject and what he or she knows about the case in question. Once the latter is accomplished, questions to be asked can be developed.

Although a considerable amount of data have already been gathered, new material can be obtained from the subject. The subject's knowledge of the details of the case might be found to vary considerably from the information already received. While the questions are being formulated, the examinee is informed that the instrument does not measure gray, only black and white. It cannot deal with shades of truthfulness, and therefore the individual must respond to each question with a definite yes or no with absolutely no doubt as to the answer. If, for example, it is a case of alleged sexual child abuse and the critical issue is whether the individual fondled the child's vaginal area, other nonsexual contacts have to be eliminated. Bathing, applying medication, and accidental touching during wrestling have to be excluded. When this information is presented to the subject, it is very likely that for the guilty, the door to obtaining an admission will be opened. Without undue pressure, he might begin to admit many of the so-called accidental contacts. Whether innocent or guilty, the questions can then be phrased much more precisely to eliminate the areas that might have caused a false positive reaction. The question could be constructed to read: "Other than the one time that you applied medication to Betty, have you ever inserted your finger into her vaginal area?" On occasion, attorneys will present the examinee with a series of questions that they feel need to be answered. It has been found helpful to inform the subject that all results must be included in the report, not only the results of questions that he passes. "Therefore, it would be wise to tell me in advance which questions you would prefer I eliminate. If you cannot pass them, let's not even include them. We'll just concentrate on those you can pass." The guilty person frequently eliminates a number of lesser issues, which is, of course, an admission of guilt. In all likelihood, he will fail the other items, but it simplifies the test and allows for an admission without pressure. The rejection of those questions must be included in the report or else the results could be misleading.

Obtaining all of the subject's knowledge about the case not only assists the examiner in developing the questions but also determines the type of test that can be employed. Discussing the acts of which the individual has been accused affords the polygraphist the opportunity of studying the examinee's responses. Not only will the examinee provide information by what he or she says verbally, but considerable data can be obtained through an awareness of the subject's facial expression, movements, speech, and demeanor in general. Vocabulary, even in the uneducated, allows for an estimate of the person's intellectual ability. By comparing the subject to others whom the examiner has seen, to associates, and even to oneself, he or she can be placed at some approximate level of ability. Emotional state can be ascertained by his or her reaction to the testing situation. Degree of assertiveness can be measured by how much he or she attempts to control the situation in contrast to being passive. Anxiety will be evidenced by such signs as a dry mouth, constant leg movements, clammy hands, stuttering, and a tremor. One must not assume that such signs of tension and fear are indicative of guilt. Knowing what defenses are being used helps considerably in knowing the subject. The Bible-carrying alleged rapist, the Boy Scout leader who loves children and who is accused of child abuse, and the thief who attempts to blame others for his situation provide the examiner with meaningful insights into these people.

Other information is obtained more directly and should be part of a questionnaire that remains as part of the record. Appendix A provides an example of this. Of particular importance are those areas that query the subject about educational background, time in the armed services, medical and psychiatric problems, police record, and work history. Based on the information made available on the individual and the case, a decision can be made as to which test procedure to use. Although there are many specific types of tests that can be administered, they all fall within three major categories: the relevant-irrelevant approach, the control question technique, and the guilty knowledge test.

In the relevant-irrelevant (R-I) approach a series of neutral (irrelevant questions) and emotional questions are compared with critical items (relevant) like, "Did you shoot John Smith?" (This is a simplified version of a procedure that will be discussed in detail in chapter 10 by Paul Minor.) The control question technique

(CQT) employs irrelevant and relevant questions but includes control questions as well. These are assumed lies garnered from the subject during the pretest interview and employed as a basis of comparison with the relevant questions to assist the examiner make a decision regarding the subject's guilt or innocence.

The guilty knowledge test or peak of tension (POT) procedure is significantly different from other tests in that it requires that certain crime data not be available to anyone but the perpetrator and possibly the investigators. This means that innocent suspects must not have access to this information. Unfortunately, this is a relatively rare occurrence because most crime details are released through the news media, attorneys, or investigators. An example of this procedure would be a situation in which a shooting occurred with four possible suspects, all of whom denied any knowledge of the homicide except what had been reported in the newspaper. Because they indicated that they did not know the caliber of the weapon, each subject was asked:

1. Do you know if John Smith was shot with a .22?
2. Do you know if John Smith was shot with a .25?
3. Do you know if John Smith was shot with a .38?
4. Do you know if John Smith was shot with a .44?
5. Do you know if John Smith was shot with a .45?

Innocent subjects were expected to respond to each question in much the same manner because they had neither guilty knowledge nor any idea at all as to which question to feel guilty about. In contract to that, the guilty individual is very likely to demonstrate a very specific and definite response to the key item. (This approach is discussed chapter 7.) Various types of questions are employed in the R-I and CQT tests.

POLYGRAPHY QUESTION TYPES
IRRELEVANT QUESTIONS

Irrelevant questions are benign questions that are factual in nature and easily answered without any thought or stress. Queries related to age, place of birth, and name are typical of irrelevant questions. As in all polygraph questions, they must be phrased so that they can be answered with yes or no. On rare occasions, these questions are not as neutral as they seem because an objectively straightforward nonemotional question might have significance for the person tested. For example, a person's marital status, divorced or widowed, could well have considerable emotional impact on the individual.

Irrelevant questions provide a picture of the individual's normal response pattern during the stress associated with taking the test. Therefore, they allow for a comparison with the key items. Because there typically is a reaction to the first question simply because of its position, a pertinent question could not be employed there because of the difficulty in interpreting the tracings.

An irrelevant question also can be used to bring the subject's physiologic level back down to its base line after a reaction has occurred.

RELEVANT QUESTIONS

The relevant question relates to the issue at hand. It is the critical item in the test. Unlike the irrelevant question, which is highly likely to be truthful, and the control question, which is very likely to be deceptive, the relevant question can go either way. Law enforcement examinations generally result in higher percentages of truthful findings because they tend to examine a number of suspects in each case, while in private testing, more deception is reported. The latter is due to the fact that the police will not make an arrest without fairly clear evidence and prosecutors will not take the accused to court unless they have a strong case. Therefore, a large percentage of those examined by private companies will have committed the acts of which they have been accused.

This question should be formulated in a manner that is short and to the point. Extra verbiage tends to make the query more cumbersome. It should be completely understandable to the examinee and therefore must be developed at a level that is consistent with his or her intelligence. The polygraphist must never assume that the subject understands the vocabulary but should go over the sentence with him or her. In sexual cases, words like "vagina" may have to be replaced with street language because these are the only terms with which the subject is familiar. Words that are so obvious to the examiner, even something like "anus," may have a completely different meaning for the examinee. The questions must be completely unambiguous so that there is no way that they can be confused with a different situation. "Did you rob the Safeway store?" is not a sufficiently clear question because the subject could have robbed a Safeway store in the past but not the one under investigation. A possibility could exist that his denial might result in a deceptive finding despite the fact that he was responding truthfully to that question. Another aspect of this can been seen when the individual is in fact guilty but attempts to use an ambiguous question to appear to be innocent: "Did you force an object into Betty's vagina for sexual reasons?" In many sexual deviants, sex and hostility are blended together. The subject in this instance might have been able to convince himself that he did not do it for sexual reasons but to hurt the victim. If he could accomplish this, he might be found truthful in his response to that question. Another weakness of this question is that it asks two questions in one: "Did you force the object into her vagina?" and "Did you do it for sexual reasons?" The subject could truthfully answer yes to the first and no to the second. The result of ambiguous questions of this nature could be an inconclusive reaction or a false negative. Anytime the wording of the question is vague enough to allow the subject to convince himself or herself of some alternate meaning, a false negative could result. Some rapists force their victims to say that they wanted it and are enjoying it. If the question asked was "Did you rape Jane Jones?" there is the slightest of possibilities that the testee could rationalize that it was not rape because Jones said she wanted it. Although it is highly unlikely that the subject could appear truthful in denying the act, the question should be concise as possible. It is conceivable that an individual who drove a getaway car or acted as a lookout might be able to rationalize that he did not rob the bank. Again, this is quite unlikely, but it is better to avoid providing the opportunity for the examinee attempting this by making the questions narrow, unambiguous, concise, concrete, specific, and understandable to the subject: "On June 4 did you drive the getaway car in the Portland First National Bank robbery?"

It is important that the issue involved be clear. Backster gives an example of a situation in which several men kicked a victim to death. "Did you kill John Smith?" is a poor question to ask in this case because the subject does not really know if he killed the individual.

Another important point to recognize is that there is conflict between issues if they exist in the same test. An example of this is a test that deals with two different robberies, the second one involving a shooting. The subject is likely to react more strongly to questions about the second robbery because he has more to lose if he is discovered to have participated in that crime. Therefore, he may be found deceptive to that question but truthful in his response to the first robbery despite the fact that he was involved in both. This is the result of the competition between responses. Although deceptive on both, the tendency would be for more fear to be aroused on the more significant issue, thereby masking the reaction to the first robbery. Another example of this competition is when two relevant questions are asked in a test such as "Do you know who shot John Smith?" and "Did you shoot John Smith?" It is expected that someone who has guilty knowledge but did not commit the act will respond to the first query but not the second. On the other hand, the guilty person should react to both questions. However, it would not be unusual if the subject were to respond only to the second item to the extent that he or she might appear truthful in his or her answer to the first question. Although this may appear to be illogical, it is due to the great significance of the second question and its tendency to draw the emotional responses away from the other questions.

The examiner must recognize that the relevant question is a threat to the guilty and innocent alike. Although the former fears that a lie will be detected, the innocent is afraid that the examiner will make an error. Because of this threat, there is a risk that the truthful person will appear deceptive. Every effort should be made to guard against this by making the control questions as equally intense as the relevant items. This technique will be discussed shortly. It should also be recognized that many other factors can cause an emotional reaction to the question other than lying. Inflections in the examiner's voice for example, can affect the examinee's physiologic response on the tracings. Lykken has suggested that another examiner who does not know the correct answer on a guilty knowledge test read the questions. In that way there would not be an unconscious emphasis on the correct key. The wording of a question should be done carefully to avoid emotionally laden words that would in themselves cause a physiologic response. The wording on both the control and relevant questions should be toned down. "Did you participate in the killing of John Smith?" rather than "Did you participate in the strangling of Smith?" "Did you force sex on Betty Jones?" rather than "Did you force your penis into Betty Jones' vagina?" In no case should strong words be used in the controls and not in the relevant or vice versa. If a difference exists, the examiner will predetermine where the greater response will occur.

THE INTENT QUESTION

Another area that deserves some consideration is that of the intent question. The general view of polygraphists is that this approach should be avoided if possible. If, however, there is no other way to ask the question, it is acceptable. An intent question does not deal with a concrete issue but rather an ideational matter. For example, an individual is arrested on a shoplifting charge for having stolen a package of five cigars. He states that he did not intend to take the item but absent mindedly put them in his pocket. Obviously, he cannot be asked if he took them because he admits that. Therefore, he is asked questions related to whether he planned to take them or whether he knew that he had taken them as he left the store. The risk here is that there is a slight possibility that the subject might talk himself into believing that it was accidental and thereby beat the test. On the other hand, an innocent person might be so concerned that he might have been aware of taking the cigars that he might be found deceptive. A survey of polygraphists indicated that it was not felt that the guilty could rationalize away their theft nor that the innocent would appear deceptive.[1] This writer agrees with the former but has some concerns about the latter. It is difficult to believe that a man burglarizing a house could talk himself into believing that he simply went in there to get out of the rain. However, it is more likely that a man who is accused of fondling his daughter sexually, but who is innocent of the charge, might become so worried about whether he was stimulated while applying medication that he would demonstrate a deceptive response. Although there is no clear evidence for this, the examiner must be careful of the wording of questions dealing with intent to commit an act rather then commission of the act itself.

THE CONTROL QUESTION

This question is an assumed lie and its response is compared with responses to the relevant questions. It is as important as the relevant item, for if it is not effective then neither is the relevant question.

It is developed during the pretest phase of the examination by indicating to the subject that additional information is required that relates to his or her moral values. Developing it in this manner motivates the examinee to respond in the negative to these queries because he wants to create a good impression. This holds for the innocent and guilty alike. The questions should be broad enough so that the polygraphist is almost certain that the subject is responding deceptively if he denies the act, such as "Have you ever stolen anything?" Everyone has at some time taken a pen from work. These inquiries should also deal with acts that one can be reasonably certain that almost everyone committed, such as, "Did you ever hurt anyone?" Because a no response is a necessity, if the examinee responds yes, further probing must be carried out until the subject responds in that manner. If he states that everyone has stolen something as a child, he then is asked, "You've never stolen anything as an adult have you?" The inflection in the polygraphist's voice should be with some disbelief to foster a no response. The examinee who admits to taking something should be questioned as to whether he or she has ever stolen anything of value. The word "value" should be left vague so that the subject will always have some doubt in mind. If the subject admits to stealing, another ploy is to try to find out how many times. Then the question can be worded, "Excluding those two times, have you ever stolen anything in your life?"

The control question ideally should be in the same general area as the relevant items. Therefore, if it is a rape case, the controls should relate to sex, and if it is a burglary, they should be in the realm of stealing. Some of the literature recommends that euphemisms be used in the control questions, like, "Did you ever take anything that didn't belong to you?" instead of using the word "steal." The emotional effect of the words in the control questions must match those in the key questions. If the word "steal" is employed in the relevant, it must be part of the controls as well.

Reid first developed the control questions in 1947 because he was obtaining many inconclusive findings with the R-I approach.[2] His assumption was that if an individual were lying in response to the control questions, he or she would demonstrate greater physiologic reactivity to that question than to the relevant item if he or she answered truthfully. If, however, the subject responded deceptively to both questions, a greater physiologic response would be seen on the relevant question because it would hold the greater threat. The examiners who employ the R-I technique criticize this theory on the grounds that one does not have any idea of how much or how little effect the control question will have on the subject. Some significant experience in the individual's life could result in a heightened reaction to the control question despite the fact that he or she also lied on the relevant item. In turn, those who use the control question approach feel that comparing a critical item with an irrelevant question results in difficulty in interpreting the results. An innocent person with a great deal of physiologic reactivity would show large responses to the key items making him appear to be deceptive. In contrast to that, a guilty individual who tends to be flat physiologically, might seem to be truthful in her response to the control questions.

The criticisms of both of these groups cannot be taken lightly, and it is evident that some weaknesses lie in both approaches. It is apparent that a person who responds truthfully to the relevant question does not show as great a reaction to his or her deception on the control question as the reaction to the relevant question by the individual who lies to that question. The control question does not have the same effect that the relevant question does, and therefore there is some tendency toward obtaining false positives. (This will be discussed in more detail in chapter 8.)

Cleve Backster used the concept of psychological set to explain the control question technique. People are literally bombarded by stimuli and could not function if all were attended to. Therefore, perception is selective and based on such variables as interest, need, and even constitutional factors. Novelty, complexity, suddenness, intensity, or relevance to a person's needs determine awareness. Backster indicated that an individual's attention is involuntarily channeled to whatever holds the greatest immediate threat to his or her well-being.[3] Therefore, if the subject is lying in response to the control question and truthful to the relevant question, he or she will be fearful that the lie to the control will be detected. Despite concerns about such things as the examiner misinterpreting a truthful response to the relevant question, the subject's set will be on the control item. The examinee will then demonstrate greater physiologic reactivity to that question than to the relevant question. In contrast to this, if the examinee is responding deceptively to both questions, his or her set will be to the relevant item because the detection of the lie on that question is of greater threat than the discovery of deception on the control. Accordingly, greater physiologic response will be found on the relevant items. It can be expected that the innocent will demonstrate larger physiologic changes to the control questions, while the guilty will react more to the relevant items. Generalizing from the work of Barland, the greater the difference between the two, the more confidence one can have in the accuracy of the results.[4]

Some disagreement exists among examiners in regard to the manner in which the controls are presented. Reid's original approach included the use of a broad control such as, "Have you ever stolen anything in your life?" The control question in this case would overlap with the relevant question because it would cover the present theft as well. It was assumed, however, that a guilty person would react more to this direct question, "Did you rob the Safeway store on January 3?" than to the broad general control question described above. Backster developed a bracketed control that specifically separated it from the relevant issue. If the robbery in question occurred when the subject was forty years of age, Backster would recommend a control such as, "Before the age of thirty-five, did you ever steal anything?" Any type of exclusion would serve the same purpose. Therefore, if this act occurred at a time when the suspect was a civilian, he might be asked, "Did you ever steal anything while you were in the army?"

There are several areas of difficulty in regard to the control questions. They must be of equal power to the relevant items. This is difficult to accomplish because the relevant question, is a significant threat for both the innocent and the guilty. It becomes imperative that the examinee be made to feel that the questions are equally important. Too often subjects see only the relevant items as being significant in the test. (Chapter 6 describes a method to make the controls as important as the key questions.)

A second problem occurs on those rare occasions when a subject feels that inquiry into issues other than the case at hand is an invasion of privacy. This writer has found that the most effective means of coping with this is to emphasize that one manner of determining whether a subject did or did not commit a crime is to know what the subject's morals are in that area. Knowing that allows the examiner to determine if the subject was involved in what he or she has been accused. If the subject continues to refuse to give this information, the choice is to employ an R-I technique or to simply indicate that the subject cannot be tested because he or she is uncooperative.

The final area of difficulty is associated with the fact that more people are becoming knowledgeable about the control question technique. A chapter in Lykkin's book *A Tremor in the Blood* describes how to "beat the test," and prison libraries often have copies of polygraph textbooks.[5] In addition, there are pamphlets that have been published that specifically deal with countermeasures. In view of this, the examiner has to attempt to learn what the subject knows about polygraph. It is also important to note that new approaches need to be developed to counteract this problem. Some examples of control questions are provided below.

SAMPLE CONTROL QUESTIONS

SEXUAL CASES

1. Have you ever used any force of any kind to get a woman to do something sexual?

2. Have you ever taken part in an unnatural sex act?

3. Have you ever thought of picking up a hitchhiker for sexual reasons?

4. Have you ever had fantasies about raping a woman?

CHILD SEXUAL ABUSE

1. Have you ever looked at a child under the age of eighteen and had sexual thoughts?

2. Have you ever had sexual fantasies about a child under the age of eighteen?

3. Have you ever looked at a child under the age of eighteen and wanted to touch her in a sexual area?

4. Did you ever look at a child under eighteen and want to see her nude?

THEFT

1. Have you ever stolen anything?

2. Have you ever stolen from an employer?

3. Have you ever cheated anyone out of something of value?

4. Have you ever ripped someone off who trusted you?

VIOLENCE

1. Have you ever wanted to see anyone dead?

2. Did you ever hurt anyone?

3. Did you ever want to hurt someone badly?

4. Did you ever want to do something to get even with someone?

LYING

1. Did you ever lie to anyone in authority?

2. Did you ever lie to someone who trusted you?

3. Have you ever lied to a real friend?

4. Did you ever lie in court?

THE GUILT COMPLEX QUESTIONS

This particular approach appears to have fallen into disuse. In a survey conducted in 1978, the overall opinion was that it needlessly complicated the test procedure and simply was not employed to any degree.[6] It was developed by Reid in 1947 and was misnamed because it related much less to guilt than fear or anxiety. Its purpose was to detect those individuals who would appear to be deceptive despite not having committed the act. Reid indicated that when the subject responds strongly to both the control and relevant items or to the relevant question but his or her behavior makes guilt doubtful, the guilt complex test should be administered. The examinee is apprised that he or she is to be tested on another issue as well as the case in question. The subject must be convinced that it is a real situation and that he or she is a real suspect. The polygraphist must be certain that a crime like the fictitious crime could not have been committed by the subject so that there is absolutely no possibility of deception being found because the subject actually committed the act and is lying about it. If the examinee responds in a deceptive manner when he or she denies having been involved in this bogus crime in the guilt complex test, it might indicate that the examinee is not testable and possibly innocent of the original accusation. If, however, the subject does not react deceptively on the guilt complex, test, deception can be assumed on the real test. Reid also suggested that this can be an effective lever in interrogation by showing the subject how he or she passed in the guilt complex test and failed on the actual examination.

THE THROW-AWAY RELEVANT QUESTION

Backster employed a broad relevant question early in the test to draw off some of the subject's emotional reaction to the issue under study. He might ask, "Do you intend to answer every question about the robbery of the First National Bank on June 4 truthfully?" The response on the chart was neither evaluated nor scored. Although in agreement with the possible value of this technique, the writer has found that a slight variation in the wording allows it to serve a double purpose. Employing Backster's wording, the subject's response of yes is deceptive only if he or she plans on lying to the relevant questions. By altering the question so that it reads, "Are you going to answer every one of my questions truthfully?" a yes response from either the guilty or innocent will be deceptive since the former will be lying on the relevant and controls and the latter to the controls. Not only does this serve to reduce some of the reaction to the critical questions, but it provides an indication of the subject's physiologic responses when he or she is lying. Although the stim test does not accomplish this, asked in this manner, the throw-away relevant does.

THE SYMPTOMATIC QUESTION

Another question developed by Backster is the symptomatic. Its purpose is to determine if the examinee is so concerned about some other matter, possibly a more significant crime that he or she has committed, that the emotional reaction is drawn away from the relevant question. This conceivably could result in a deceptive individual appearing to be truthful. "Are you afraid I'll ask a question that we didn't discuss?" should bring out any excessive amount of concern in this area. If a strong reaction is shown, this can be discussed with the subject and the subject can be given some degree of reassurance that no question other than those already discussed with him will be asked. However, it must be pointed out that any time any additional emphasis is placed on a question, even in the form of reassurance, it might result in a greater reaction.

VARIATIONS ON THE CONTROL QUESTION

Several variations of the control questions technique are utilized that allow for more variety in testing procedures and may evoke more of an emotional response from the subject.

THE SILENT ANSWER TEST (SAT). In this approach, the examinee is told to think the correct answer rather than say it aloud. Reid developed this technique to open the door to the use of countermeasures that might cause an even larger response in this test as well as the subsequent examination.

THE ZONE OF COMPARISON TEST (ZOC). This is an approach developed by Backster to maintain a single issue examination. Two relevant questions normally deal with the issue in question, which is quite different from other procedures that tend to delve into a number of issues within in a particular investigation. A Reid technique, for example, might ask the following relevant questions in a single test.[7]

> Last Saturday night did you shoot John Jones?
>
> Did you kill John Jones?
>
> Did you steal John Jones's watch last Saturday night?
>
> Do you know who shot John Jones?

THE SKY TEST. This is another Backster approach in which he added the following three questions to his ZOC test:

> Do you suspect someone of having killed John Jones?
>
> Do you know for sure who killed John Jones?
>
> Did you kill John Jones?

THE YES TEST. This procedure was developed by Reid as a means to cope with those individuals who attempt to avoid detection of a lie by distorting their polygraph tracings. The test is administered without the control questions and the subject is instructed to respond yes to every question. Individuals who had previously lied when they responded no will attempt to distort their tracings in an attempt at making their yes answers appear to be lies.

THE MIXED QUESTION TEST (MQT). The order of presentation of the questions is changed to guard against the possibility of a subject's reacting to a question because of its position once he or she learns the order of presentation. According to Reid and Inbau, it also serves to increase responsivity. These tests will be discussed in more detail in the chapters to follow.

Throughout this chapter, the idea of a draining off of tension, anxiety, or emotion has been mentioned. It can be assumed that the greater the threat, the greater the fear of detection and the stronger the sympathetic nervous system arousal. The various questions can be pictured in terms of a competition among them to draw these reactions. Various extraneous factors, such as inflection, loudness, or surprise, can affect these responses, but these would be extrinsic to the test and should not be part of it. Drawing power should be derived only from the threat associated with the question itself. That, of course, is the whole idea of the control question technique where a competition exists between the control and relevant items. This, however, occurs in other situations as well, sometimes to the detriment of the examiner. As already indicated, if two separate and distinct issues are ever inappropriately included in the same test, the more potent question may draw some of the emotional reaction from the other. This may occur to the extent that, even though deceptive on both, the subject might appear to be truthful on the weaker of the two.

The specific ways of developing tests in order to most effectively draw the emotion into the appropriate questions will be dealt with in the following chapters when the major schools of thought are presented. A starting point, however, is this typical control question test:

Irrelevant	1. Is your first name John?
Throw-away relevant	2. Are you going to answer every one of my questions truthfully?
Symptomatic	3. Are you afraid I'll ask a question that we didn't discuss?
Control	4. Prior to this year, have you ever used any force at all to get a female to do something sexual?
Relevant	5. On July 4 did you force Annie Ross to have sex with you?
Control	6. Between the ages of twenty and thirty-five did you ever take part in any unusual sex acts?
Relevant	7. Regarding Annie Ross, did you use force to get her to have sex with you on July 4?
Irrelevant	8. Are you thirty-six years old?

POLYGRAPH TEST PROCEDURE II: TESTING, SCORING,

AND THE POSTTEST INTERVIEW

6

If falsehood like truth, had only one face, we would be in better shape. For we would take as certain the opposite of what the liar said. But the reverse of truth has a hundred thousand shapes and a limitless field.

—Michel Montaigne

Properly establishing rapport, explaining the procedure, developing the questions, and stimulating the subject should take between a half an hour and an hour and a half depending on the complexity of the case. If more time is required, it might be preferable to delay the examination to avoid oversensitizing the examinee. The actual testing will take less time than the pretest phase. Despite attempts at reducing generalized anxiety, it persists in guilty and innocent alike. Informing the individual of this might reassure him or her.

TESTING

Although the majority of examiners who use a stim test prefer to position it after the first test, the writer feels that it is more appropriately administered first.

Because the examinee has been told that the test's purpose is to determine the pattern of tracings when he or she responds deceptively and to ascertain whether the examinee is a fit subject for testing, it appears more logical to test him or her on this procedure prior to the actual examination. Moreover, this permits the polygraphist to separate this test from the chart and show it to the subject demonstrating how easily a lie is detected. This is more effective than simply informing him of the number on which the subject lied.

The individual is given a series of cards numbered from twenty to twenty-five, for example, or is told to write a number between twenty and twenty-five on a sheet of paper. If the former approach is being used, the examiner should be certain that the subject actually looks at the number of the card. The examinee then is told to place the card in a pocket or even sit on it so that it is not available to the polygraphist or a distraction to the examinee. The various sensors are then placed on the person in accordance with the description presented in chapter 4. As the pneumotube is raised to place the beaded portion behind the subject's back, one should be aware of whether the subject leans forward and raises his arms to assist the examiner. Likewise, it should be noted if the subject extends the fingers when EDR electrodes are going to be applied. People who have been previously tested will usually unconsciously respond in this manner, whereas individuals who have never experienced this are unsure of how the sensors will be positioned on them.

The blood pressure cuff is placed on the person after the pneumotube. A mechanical cardio might have to be positioned on the lower arm if the individual is overly obese or suffers from hypertension. High levels of pressure can be tolerated more readily in the lower arm. This should not be of concern with an amplified cardio. Lastly, the finger electrodes are affixed to the subject, with the approximate sensitivity being estimated by informing the subject that his or her arm will be touched to determine reactivity. A rise in EDR will occur at both the announcement that the subject is going to be touched and at the actual contact. Sensitivity can be raised or lowered after the first question of the stim test; the response to that question is usually rather large but tends to settle down after that question is completed. Once EDR sensitivity is ascertained, blood pressure is pumped up to the appropriate level. The cuff is then kneaded to circulate the air more equally throughout the system. Because this reduces blood pressure, it is necessary to pump additional air into the cuff to reach the amplitude required. The pens are then centered so that each pen operates within its own field and does not conflict with the other pens or lose tracing data because the pens are striking the stops.

The subject is instructed to respond no to every number on the list including the one actually chosen. Only rarely does someone not understand these directions, but occasionally an individual will attempt to thwart the testing process by responding in the affirmative to the number that he or she has selected. Once the stim test is completed, the chart can be evaluated, and then the examiner can show the subject where and how the deception was found. The polygraphist cannot rely on the subject's word but must check the number. Should the examiner be in error in selecting the number chosen, it is important to explain this. The subject is informed that the purpose of the test is to determine what his or her lie pattern is. If the subject were to have been examined without having done this preliminary testing, the charts might have been inaccurately interpreted, just as occurred with the number. Observing what the examinee looks like when he or she lies will allow for the accurate interpretation of the remaining test results. The examiner must recognize, as previously indicated, that it is not the stim test that provides an indication of the subject's response to lying, but the question, "Are you going to answer every one of my questions truthfully?"

If the examiner has accurately detected the lie on the stim test, the subject can be reassured by, "You can relax now knowing how easy it is to determine when you are responding truthfully." It is not necessary to mention that a lie can be discovered just as readily because that is obvious and every person who is going to lie will be aware of it.

At this stage, it is important to inform the subject that he or she must be completely truthful to every question throughout the remainder of the examination.[1] Lying about any question on the test will be distinctly to his or her disadvantage. This simple statement clearly develops the set that Backster has described. The guilty will continue to be concerned about their deception to the relevant items, but the innocent who have been told that a lie to any question will be harmful to their situation focus their attention on the controls.

Too often, examinees assume that only the relevant questions are significant. Moreover, innocent subjects feel threatened by the possibility that the polygraphist may err in diagnosis and therefore direct their attention toward the relevant items. If they think in this manner, there is a possibility that they will react more strongly to those key items in contrast to the controls. In fact, research has shown that there is a greater tendency toward errors of a false positive nature on control question techniques.[2] Considering this, it is extremely important to impress on every subject the importance of being truthful in response to every question.

Presenting these data to subjects after the control questions have been formulated makes it difficult for them to change their answers to the controls, for that would be an admission of having lied to the examiner.

Lykken[3] has argued that the control question technique is not logical because inevitably the relevant question is much more intense than the controls for both the guilty and innocent. Approaching the test in the manner described eliminates this criticism because the content of the questions is less important than the concept of lying. Whether the innocent individual stole as an adolescent is not significant; what is important is that he or she is lying about it and this deception might be detected by the examiner. If it is, it will certainly hurt the subject's cause. On the other hand, although the guilty will be threatened by having their lies discovered on both the controls and relevants, the risk factor on the latter inevitably remains greater. Therefore, this approach does not in any way reduce the guilty's reaction to the critical items but does enhance the response of the innocent to the controls.

One final advantage in employing the procedure is that because the content is not important, it is not imperative for the control and relevant questions to be in the same specific area. Therefore, if the examiner has difficulty finding acceptable controls in the area of stealing, he or she could acceptably broaden out into other areas. Generally, however, the examiner should keep the controls and relevant with in the same realm.

In the private sector, it has been found effective to approach the control question technique in the following manner:

If you pass this test, the charges against you will very likely be dropped, but the prosecutor will probably have the police examiner check your charts. If I find you truthful, the police examiner will also because scoring the test is straightforward and easily accomplished. But you must be truthful to every single question. If you lie on just one, all of this will have been a completely wasted effort that will hurt your situation rather than help it.

Presenting the test in this manner also diminished the strength of the argument that might be raised in court of Orne's concept of the friendly examiner.[4] Orne assumed that because the results of a test administered by a private examiner that were indicative of deception would be discarded, the deceptive subject would have little to fear and might pass the test. However, when the subject is told that passing the test will very likely result in the dropping of charges, he or she has a great deal to lose by not passing the test. The examiner should not make this statement, of course, if the prosecution does not typically drop the charges. The subject is informed that he or she must answer every question with a yes or no, not "yes, sir" or anything of that nature. Each response should be immediate, and any delays should be pointed out to the subject and discontinued because delays offer the possibility of subjects' employing such countermeasures as biofeedback, relaxation techniques, or self-hypnosis in an attempt to avert or even cause a reaction. The subject also again is cautioned about movements.

Prior to the administration of the first control question tests, the examinee's subjective findings at the time he or she lied on the stim test should be discussed:

Whatever you felt when you lied to the number will be magnified if you are going to lie anyplace within the actual test. You'll feel your pulse beating more strongly, more quickly against the blood pressure cuff. You'll feel your mouth momentarily grow dry so that it will be a little difficult to answer and there will be some sensations of tightness in your stomach. If you aren't lying anyplace in the test, there will be little reaction of this nature.

Once a subject has been well stimulated, a significant difference between the control and relevant questions should be seen on the first test. If the reactions are not as clear as needed, before the second test the polygraphist can say,

I told you that I would not make any changes in the test unless I told you in advance, and I told you that I would tell you why I was making those changes so that you could understand everything that I was doing. Now I'm going to repeat the test in exactly the same way. The reason for the repetition is to obtain additional data to score, but also, people who are telling the truth to every question begin to relax after a time and their tracings start to flatten out. People who are lying, no matter where they are lying, react even more each time. That's the reason for repeating the test, so that I can more easily determine who is lying and who isn't.

Quite obviously, the purpose of this statement is to stimulate in both the innocent and the guilty alike the fear that a lie will be detected. Before the third test, if it is necessary, the examinee is informed that the questions will be exactly the same, only the order will be different.

The reason for changing the order is that for people who are telling the truth, it doesn't matter where the question is, but for someone who is lying, the combination of the lie and surprise because the questions are in a different position multiply one another so that the response of someone who is lying is much greater. This is the best test and so we save it for last. This will tell us if you are lying anyplace on the test.

Once again, this is a device employed to stimulate the subject to enhance his or her responses.

During the test process, appropriate chart markings have to be made in order to accurately determine truthfulness or deception. Markings must be meaningful enough for another examiner to read. The examiner has to know where each question was asked and answered and whether any other interfering factors occurred that would reflect the subject's functioning at a particular question. An examinee will recognize a question in most instances after the first few words of the question has been read. Therefore, physiologic changes in response to that question can occur before the question is completed and certainly before the examinee responds. It is therefore important to know exactly where the question begins and ends, what the subject's answer was, and where it occurred. A horizontal line should start at a point on the chart at exactly where the polygraphist begins the question and end it where the polygraphist stops speaking. It has become customary to end with a vertical line. A plus for a yes and a minus for a no is placed at exactly where the subject responds to the questions. The number of the question is placed inside the two-sided figure indicating the number of the question. These markings are generally placed below the cardio tracings at the bottom of the page. A mechanical marker makes a horizontal line that also shows the question timing, and a dot indicates the exact spot at which the question was answered. The examiner has to write the number and indicate beneath the dot whether it was a yes or no response.

At the beginning of the test the chart should clearly indicate the name of the subject, the date and time that the test was started, and the type of test being administered. Before each set of tracings, the sensitivity level should be noted for each sensor. In addition, before the cardio tracings, pressure should be indicated, and before the EDR a sign indicating whether it was administered under automatic or manual mode. If any sensors other than the usual are employed, this should be written down at those specific tracings so that another examiner evaluating the charts will know if it is a plethysmograph, CAM, or movement monitor. Prior to each individual test, there should be an indication of the type and number of the test. For example, "CQTI C1 for control question technique, test 1, chart 1." The second test of this series would be "CQTI C2," and if it were to be a silent answer test, the symbol "SAT" would be added. "MQT" would be noted for the mixed question technique. At the very end of the chart, the time should be written so that there are clear notations of the start and finish of the test. All of these markings should be clear enough for another polygraphist to interpret their meaning and readily understood what has occurred throughout the testing, whether an extraneous noise occurred, the subject coughed, or the examiner inadvertently misworded a question. It is a good practice to have the subject sign the chart at the termination of the testing.

Some examiners prefer to cut the chart paper after each individual test, but this writer feels that there is less room for mistrust if chart paper is kept intact from the beginning to the end of the examination. This precludes any concern that a particular test might have been discarded because the findings did not lead to the desired conclusion.

There is no question an unethical examiner can cause a chart to appear truthful or deceptive by manipulating the situation in some manner. The inflection of the polygraphist's voice will affect the subject's physiologic response as much as an overdiscussion of the control question can result in a deceptive person appearing truthful. The number on the questions can be changed so that the relevant question will appear to be control questions, and even sensitivity and centering can be manipulated during the test to appear to produce a particular response. Other than relying on the ethics of the examiner, only videotaping the entire process can guard against this deception and prove to the courts that it did not occur.

The writer prefers to administer the test three times, with the first two times being identical and the third administration being a mixed question technique (MQT). For example, the first and second series might be:

1. Is your true first name Robert?

2. Are you going to answer everyone of my questions truthfully?

3. Are you afraid I'll ask a question that we didn't discuss?

4. Excluding what you told me and prior to this year, did you ever attempt to defraud anyone?

5. Regarding the insurance claim you filed on the May 5 burglary of your house, were all of the items that you listed actually stolen?

6. Prior to the age of forty, did you ever cheat anyone out of anything?

7. Were all of those items listed on your insurance claim actually stolen from your house on May 5?

8. Other than the 10 mg of Valium, have you used any drugs or medications since midnight?

9. Did you obtain a master's degree from PSU?

In the third series, the following order would be used 9, 2, 6, 5, 4, 7. If no response has been obtained to questions 3 and 8, there is no reason to repeat them. Changing the position of control questions 4 and 6 allows the examiner to compare each relevant item with a different control so that relevant 5 is compared with control 4 the first two times and with control 6 in the third testing. Relevant 7, of course, is compared with control 6 twice and the control 4 on the last testing.

It is important to allow about a fifteen- to twenty-second pause after the subject's response and the start of the next question. As indicated earlier, starting a question while the EDR tracing is rising or falling, when a rise or fall in the cardio base line is occurring, or when a significant change in breathing like a deep breath or suppression is taking place is not appropriate. More energy is required to raise an EDR or cardio that is dropping than one that is moving on a level line. For an appropriate comparison between questions, all of the sensors should be operating on this essentially horizontal track. If the delay between questions becomes too long while waiting for one of the sensors to flatten out, it is necessary to ask an irrelevant question; otherwise the delay in and of itself might cause a response.

Just as in the pretest phase of the examination (which should not be an interrogation nor accusatory in any fashion because it is likely to cause an emotional reaction that might result in false positive findings), no accusatory statements should be made between the tests. Any implication of this nature is very likely to cause a response to the relevant questions because of the accusation and not deception. In fact, even an emphasis on one set of questions, like the controls, will cause response to intensify. Therefore, the examiner cannot discuss the controls unless equal time is spent on the relevant and vice versa. Only when the testing is ended should any interrogation take place.

SCORING

When the testing is completed, the tracings are interpreted and scored. A numerical scoring system provides an objective measurable evaluation of the differences in response between the control and relevant questions. By forcing an actual measurement of the changes that occur within the tracings of each sensor, the polygraphist can avoid almost all biasing effects. Moreover, it ensures a high level of agreement between examiners who score the same chart. This, of course, is a measure of reliability, while validity is an indication of accuracy. Numerical scoring unquestionably increases both validity and reliability and should be employed with every examination that is administered.

In 1963 Backster developed the numerical scoring system, and its use has expanded throughout the polygraph community. Various systems have been developed that are, in part, simplified versions of the original procedure. It would have been ideal for the sake of standardizing the procedure if only one process were used, but different schools of thought have developed, and, in their views, improved the approach. There is a fair amount of reliability among the various techniques.

CHART INTERPRETATION

There is a considerable degree of agreement among the different schools of thought as to when changes in the tracings are indicative of deception, but there is some disagreement as to which sensors are the most valuable in detecting deception. Reid and Inbau indicated that respiration was of most value followed by EDR and then cardio.[5] This writer ranks effectiveness in the following order—EDR, cardio, heart rate monitor, and respiration,[6] and Barland and Raskin[7] have reported EDR to be the most valuable measure.

ELECTRODERMAL RESPONSE

The EDR is undoubtedly the measure that is the easiest to measure and therefore most readily scored. Backster has indicated that only amplitude should be scored and not the duration of the reaction. He hypothesized that a control question requires extended thought because of the broad and general nature of the question. In contrast to this, the subject immediately knows whether he or she carried out the act that is being queried about on the relevant question. Backster assumes that the more thought required the greater the duration of the response. Therefore, he felt that it would not be a fair comparison between the two question types. The federal approach, however, recommends that both duration and amplitude be measured. In an unpublished study I found that duration was of equal value to amplitude and recommend that both be used in the scoring. When evaluating the EDR, it is important to know exactly when the EDR response was initiated. At times it occurs before the question or too long after the question has been answered. Any reaction prior to the question should not be scored; in fact, the question should not have been asked at that time because the EDR was already rising. It can be argued that the subject has learned the order of the questions and is reacting because he or she knows the next question that is going to be asked, but it could also be an extraneous thought that caused the response. To avoid the risk of error, it is preferable not to score it. Any response that occurs later than five seconds after the subject has answered the question also should not be scored. The examinee is quite capable of recognizing a question after he or she has heard the first few words, and it is not unusual for a reaction to begin at that point. A response can be appropriately scored if it occurs after the first few words of the question until about five seconds after the subject's answer.

Basically, two types of changes occur in the tracings—reaction and relief. The former is associated with some threat to the organism that causes an emotional response resulting in sympathetic arousal. The physiologic changes that occur can be objectively measured to the degree that a comparison can be made between relevant and control questions. An ideal situation would be what Backster described as an either-or response in which the individual reacts to either the relevant or the control but not both. More frequently, there is a greater reaction to one than the other. Despite a subject's innocence, it is unlikely that all fears related to the relevant questions will be alleviated. Because of that, some reaction to these queries will persist.

If a reaction can be categorized as sympathetic, then relief can be classified as parasympathetic. The body returns to its balanced state (homeostasis), or parasympathetic dominance might return it temporarily to a state beyond homeostasis so that is has to recover from this as well. For example, a guitar string lightly plucked returns to its normal state, but if it is pulled with more force, when it is released it will go beyond its normal position only to rebound from there to its resting state.

Prior to stimulation, the EDR tracing generally demonstrates a horizontal movement. Once a threatening question is asked, a reaction occurs as demonstrated by a rise in the tracings (amplitude). Relief is the return of the tracing to its base line or even below it.

A determination of reaction is made by literally measuring the height of the rise and its duration until it returns to its original baseline. The difference between these measures on the relevant and control questions is calculated. If the difference in amplitude is four times or more as great a score of 3 is given, three times as large is a 2, and one-half to twice as large is a 1. The total EDR score cannot total more than 3 because it must be equivalent to the other sensors. Therefore, when duration is scored, it cannot add points beyond a total of 3. It can add or reduce points in the same proportions as amplitude—twice as long a duration being a score of 1 and so on. Rises or double saddles occur when the tracing rises, drops, and rises again. These are scored as part of duration.

The score is prefixed with a plus or minus sign for truthfulness or deception, respectively. If the control shows a large reaction, it is scored plus, while it is marked minus if the relevant is greater. It is scored a zero if the reactions are essentially the same for both questions. There are seven possible scores for each question on the EDR—ranging from +3, +2, +1, 0 −1, −2, and −3.

Although most numerical scoring systems use this seven-point range, some employ a three-point procedure of +1, 0, and −1. The weakness of this approach is that it is less sensitive because it does not take into account the degree of variability between questions. An extreme difference in EDR between the two questions would be evaluated in the same manner as a minor difference. Figure 6–1 through 6–4 are examples of EDR reactions and their scoring.

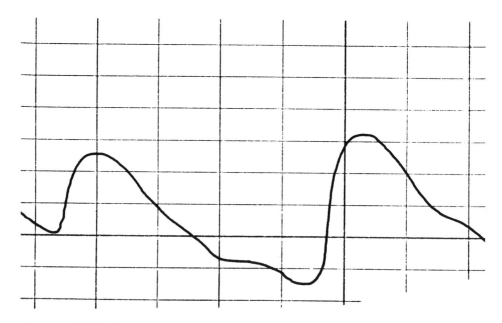

Figure 6–1. EDR Comparing Amplitude

Figure 6–2. EDR Comparing Amplitude and Duration

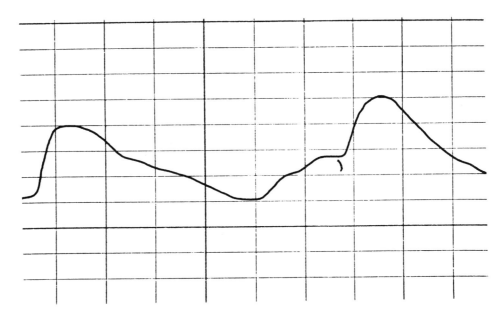

Figure 6–3. EDR Where Amplitude and Duration Are Equal

Figure 6–4. EDR Comparing Reaction to No Reaction

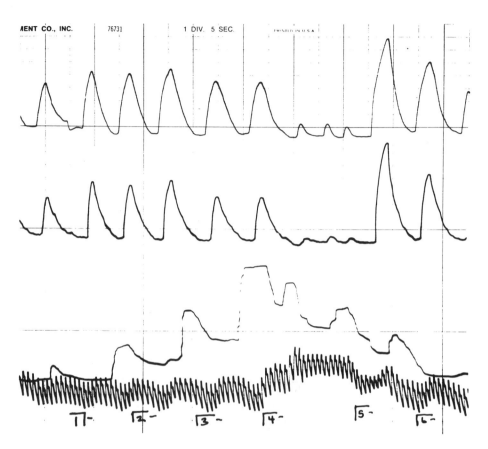

Figure 6–5. POT Showing Typical Peak-Type Pattern

In figure 6–1 a score of −1 is obtained because the relevant question on the right has an amplitude about twice as great as the control question on the left.

In figure 6–2 a score of −2 is given because the response to question 5 not only has an amplitude twice that of question 4 but a duration that is twice as long as well. Recognize that the reaction starts about five seconds before the markings because of the longer pen.

In figure 6–3 a score of 0 is earned because no significant difference exists between either amplitude or duration.

When no reaction occurs in one question compared to reaction in another, the examiner must use a system similar to that employed with cardio and pneumo scoring. Instead of being based on numerical differences, the system must be based on an arbitrary minor, moderate, or major categorization. In figure 6–4 neither reaction is as small as to be seen as minor for a score of 1, nor so large as to be considered major for a score of 3. Therefore, relevant question 5 is scored as −2.

In the POT test, the patterns in figure 6–5 through 6–7 are indicative of reaction to the key question 4. In figure 6–5 the rise in cardio, the suppression in pneumo, and the peaking effect at question 4 all are strongly indicative of guilty knowledge.

Fairly consistent reactions are seen to each stimulus question until question 4, when deceptive responses are seen in all three channels in figure 6–6.

In figure 6–7 pneumo shows a long apnea, whereas only a slight rise in cardio is seen. The EDR demonstrates a consistently large reaction until after the lie is completed and like a sigh of relief the EDR drops.

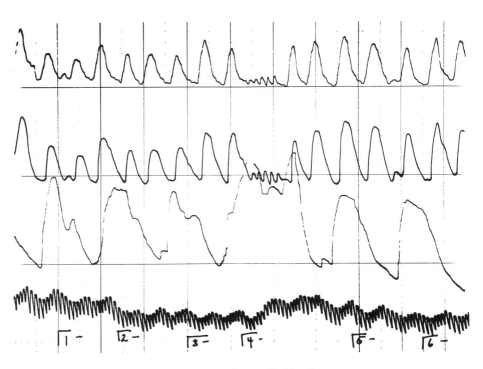

Figure 6–6. POT Showing a Larger Reaction to the Key Item

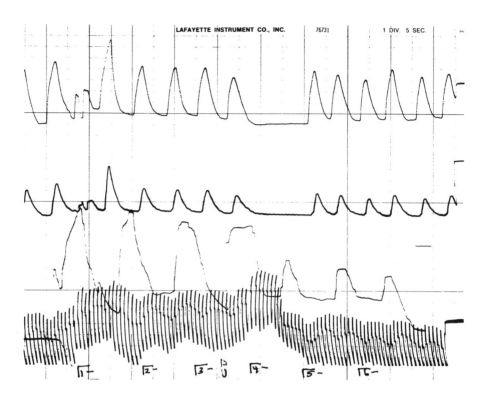

Figure 6–7. POT Showing Large Reactions until the Key Followed by Diminished Response

CARDIO

In this measure, reaction is shown when there is a rise in the base line; a narrowing of the tracings from base to ceiling; an upward change in the position of the dicrotic notch; and either an increase or decrease in the heart rate. Relief can be evidenced in a corresponding drop in the base line, a widening of the tracings, a drop in the dicrotic notch, and an increase in heart rate. Th position of the dicrotic notch is the best means of measuring the rise and fall of the cardio tracings because the tips of both the base line and ceiling tend to be rather erratic. When the dicrotic notch cannot be used, then the base line change is the preferable measure. Scoring rests on a minor, moderate, and major difference between the questions with the scores for each being 1, 2, and 3, respectively. Thus, if no change occurred on the control and a minor reaction were present on the relevant, the score would be − 1. If a major change were present on the control and a minor change on the relevant, the score would be +2. Figure 6–8 through 6–12 are examples of changes in the cardio that are indicative or reaction and relief.

In figure 6–8 the amplitude and duration between questions 4 and 5 are essentially the same resulting in a score of 0.

In figure 6–9 moderate rises in the cardio occur in both questions 6 and 7, but the increase in relevant question 7 is somewhat larger resulting in a score of −1.

In figure 6–10 control question 4 demonstrates a greater reaction than relevant question 5, but not large enough to be scored more than a +1.

In figure 6–11 a major reaction can be seen in relevant question 9, but compared to the moderate response on question 8, it can be scored only as - −1. Note the narrowing of the tracings at the reaction in question 9, which is often indicative of deception followed by relief and which is seen as a widening of the tracings.

The extreme erratic responses shown in figure 6–12 are unsophisticated attempts at employing countermeasures. The movements are blatantly obvious and therefore of no value to the subject.

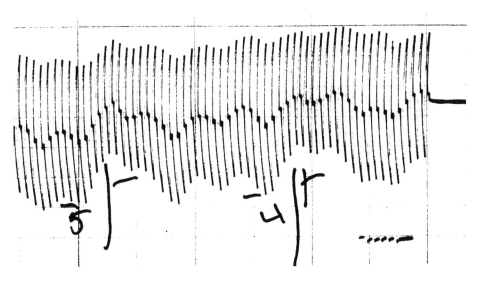

Figure 6–8. Cardio Showing Minor Differences in Reaction

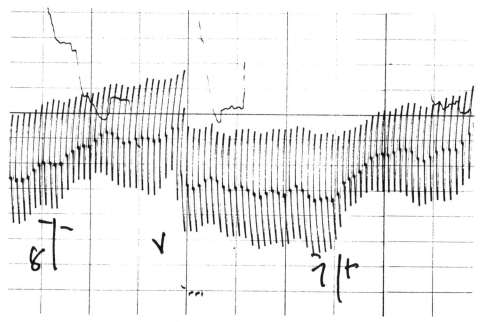

Figure 6–9. Cardio Showing Moderate Changes

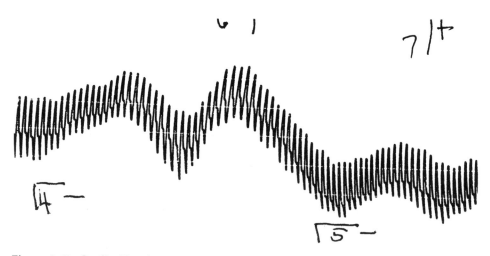

Figure 6–10. Cardio Showing Moderate Rise Compared to Minor Rise

RESPIRATION

Changes in respiration can be readily noted. There is, however, much more conscious control that the subject can bring to bear on this physiologic function as compared to the others. Moreover, changes in respiration can dramatically affect cardio and EDR. A deep breath, for example, might result in a decided

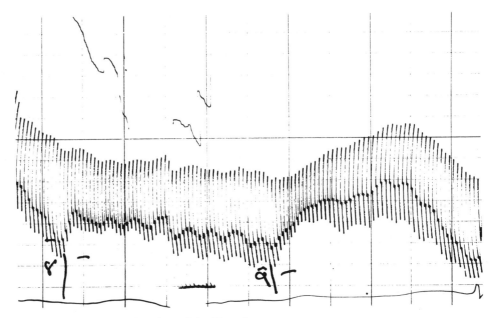

Figure 6–11. Cardio Showing Major Reactions

rise in each of these areas. The examiner has to be particularly aware of breathing changes and evaluate whether these are countermeasures. Because a deep breath affects the tracings, if this begins to occur, it is important for the examiner to discontinue this by emphasizing the effect of movement rather than breathing: "Every time you take a deep breath you cause your whole body to move, which affects the tracings. You will have to stop these movements, or I won't be able to get an accurate reading."

Reactions indicative of deception are suppressed breathing, apnea (stoppage of breathing), base-line changes, stair steps, and a change in the breathing pattern. Relief would be seen in hyperventilation (rapid breathing), deeper breathing, and a drop in base line after a rise. Scoring, like cardio, is based on the seven-point system using the minimum, moderate, and major categories. Figures 6–13 through 6–17 are examples of reactions, relief, and scoring.

Although no significant changes can be seen in the control questions on the left in figure 6–13, the relevant question on the right demonstrates a suppression that can be scored − 1.

A significant base line change is seen in figure 6–14. It is seen as extreme and extended. This is viewed as being at a score of 3 if no reaction occurs on the opposing question. Too often EDR is more readily scored as a 3 because the

Figure 6–12. Countermeasures Attempted in Cardio

examiner can measure and find the reaction on one to be four times as large as the other. In both pneumo and cardio the difference is more judgmental, so that a 3 is rarely obtained. If scores of 3 are to be obtained on EDR, they should be equally obtainable on the other measures.

In figure 6–15 an apnea can be seen followed by relief—the need to take in additional oxygen after the temporary deprivation. Assuming that there is no reaction on the opposing question, it would be scored 2.

In figure 6–16 and 6–17 two separate stair-step patterns are shown. In figure 6–16 the pattern is below the ceiling of the pneumo pattern and in Backster's view would be considered a suppression and scored accordingly. There is debate on the second pattern seen in figure 6–17 where the stair exceeds the ceiling. Backster would see this as a relief and not score it, but other examiners score a stair

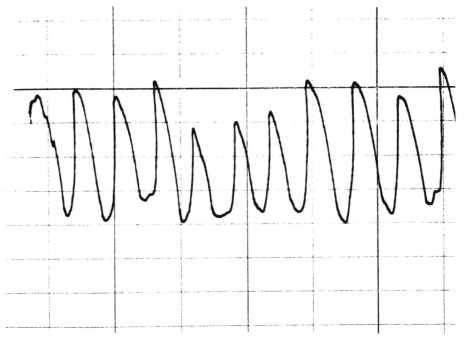

Figure 6–13. Pneumo Showing Suppressed Breathing

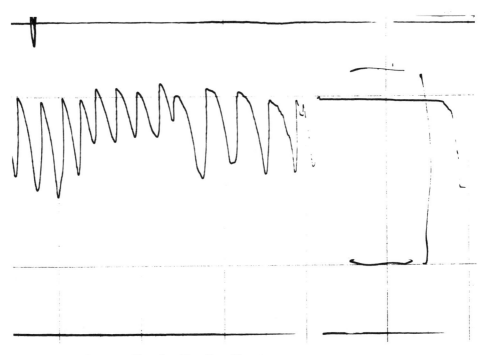

Figure 6–14. Pneumo Showing Baseline Changes

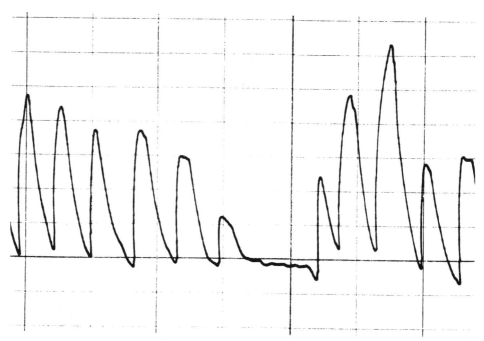

Figure 6–15. Pneumo Showing an Apnea

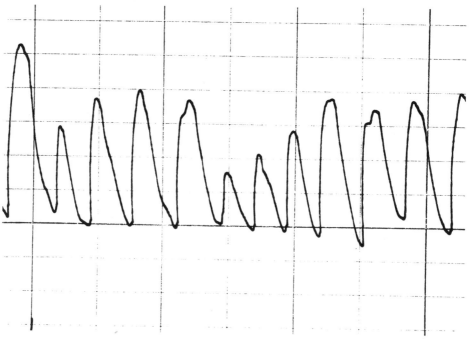

Figure 6–16. Pneumo Showing Stairsteps

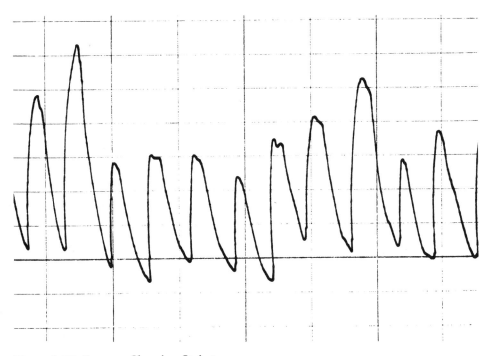

Figure 6–17. Pneumo Showing Stairsteps

step as indication of deceptive whenever it occurs. Because the writer has seen no research that indicates that a stair step is a sign of deception, the view taken is that it should be scored only when the breathing is suppressed.

POSTTEST INTERVIEW

The American Polygraph Association's Ethics and Standards indicate that at the completion of a test, the polygraphist must provide the subject with the results of the examination. Partly, this is to provide the person who failed with the opportunity to explain why deception was found. Although in most instances this will encourage the examinee to provide a series of excuses for his or her deceptions, on occasion legitimate reasons are forthcoming. A service station attendant denied any involvement in a station robbery, but deceptive findings were obtained during a test. After the test the attendant admitted that although he had not been involved in the robbery, he had routinely stashed away some money just in case a robbery occurred. His pocketing of that money caused him to appear to be deceptive. When the questions were reworded to "Except for the $200 that you hid away, did . . . ," he easily passed the test. In an instance of embezzlement, a suspect who failed later admitted to taking several hundred dollars but not the $10,000 that was missing. Rewording the question to read,

"Other than the $200 that you took from the bank, are you responsible for having taken any of the missing $10,000?" resulted in a truthful chart. There is no doubt that the examinee needs to be questioned as to possible reasons for failing the examination.

There are times when attorneys do not want their clients to know when they fail and certainly do not want clients questioned as to the reason for their failures. These lawyers do not want an admission because they feel that this information would place them at a disadvantage in defending their clients. Despite this, if there is any risk that some other factor might have caused the deceptive findings, it is the examiner's responsibility to question the examinee further and retest him or her if appropriate.

The polygraph is an effective tool in eliciting a confession. Asking the individual who was found deceptive whether he or she lied on the control questions and then pressing for an admission of these lies is an advantage. Showing the subject how clear it was on the charts that he or she lied enables the examiner to point out that there was even a larger reaction to the relevant questions. The charts then become an effective lever to obtaining an admission. The same approach can be used with the stim test.

Even without using a comparison, showing the subject obvious reactions in response to the control questions opens the door to obtaining additional data. Added to this is all the information that the examiner previously provided the subject related to deceptive reactions not caused by the instrument or by the examiner but by him or her.

The polygraph is only an instrument like a thermometer; it simply registers what is happening inside of you. These signs of deception are coming from you, from your head and your body—not the instrument and not me. You can't say that I'm wrong or the instrument is wrong; it's you that is saying that you are lying.

THE GUILTY KNOWLEDGE OR PEAK OF TENSION TEST

7

In man there exists the potential to deceive and be deceived, to bias and be biased, and to corrupt and be corrupted. However, it is through science that the law can discover the means to overcome these imperfections and achieve justice.

—Stan Abrams

The peak of tension test (POT) was developed by Leonarde Keeler.[1] Although it is unquestionably one of the most effective polygraph procedures, its use is limited to those situations in which only guilty suspects and not innocent suspects have access to specific crime information. Unfortunately, this is a relatively rare occurrence because in most instances this information is readily available through the attorneys involved, the news media, and even the investigating officers. Lykken, however, feels that this approach is greatly underused by polygraphists and recommends a way of increasing its usage.[2] He has suggested that the polygraphist should be part of the initial investigation in order to become more aware of material that can be employed as a key, but also so that he can protect the secrecy of these data. In this manner it will very specifically not be made available to the press and can become part of the guilty knowledge test (GKT).

Two types of POT procedures exist—a known solution peak and a searching peak. In the former, both the perpetrator and the examiner know the critical crime issues, while in the searching peak, only the person with guilty knowledge is aware of it. These might include cases in which money is hidden, accomplices are in hiding, or bodies are buried. Although it is unusual to have the opportunity to administer such an examination, results can be dramatic. A case in point involved a polygraphist with the Oregon State Police who was investigating a theft.[3] It was learned that the suspect's wife had mysteriously disappeared but he claimed that she had returned to her family in Mexico. When a control question technique showed him to be responding deceptively in this matter, a POT test was administered to determine if the location of the body could be discovered. The first searching peak asked the following questions:

1. Is your wife's body in the river?

2. Is your wife's body by the railroad tracks?

3. Is your wife's body in the potato field?

4. Is your wife's body by the farm buildings?

5. Is your wife's body by the house?

When strong reactions occurred in response to question 4, the man was presented with another series of questions worded in a similar manner but relating to the specific farm buildings. Large responses were found to questions associated with the shed. While spectators waited in suspense, a bulldozer cleared the area around the building where the body eventually was found. (An interesting sidelight on this case was that although the body had been buried for a considerable period of time, the combination of soil and climate in that region of Washington had mummified the body; the victim looked about as she had when her husband buried her months before.)

The searching or probing peak can also be employed to make a determination of the subject's degree of participation in a particular act. When an individual has been apprehended stealing from an employer and is suspected to have taken other items, the searching peak can be used. Starting with an overly high estimate and working downward, the following questions can be asked:

1. During the time that you worked at McCormick's, did you take more than $5,000?

2. During the time that you worked at McCormick's, did you take more than $4,000?

3. During the time that you worked at McCormick's, did you take more than $3,000?

4. During the time that you worked at McCormick's, did you take more than $2,000?

5. During the time that you worked at McCormick's, did you take more than $1,000?

6. During the time that you worked at McCormick's, did you take more than $500?

It is very unlikely that the individual actually would know how much money had been stolen but probably could make a reasonably accurate estimate. Knowing that the amount had not been $5,000 or $4,000, the subject would not react to these questions. If the subject started doubting at $3,000 and was unsure if that were the amount, a reaction would most likely be demonstrated at that point.

In both the known solution and searching peak, it is preferable to develop the questions prior to seeing the subject. Revisions then readily can be made during the examination if new information is obtained from the examinee. In the known solution peak, question formulation requires some concentrated effort and can be carried out more effectively outside of the time constraints of the testing situation. The questions must be developed in a manner in which no item stands out from any of the others in that any one of them could be the critical item. To accomplish this, each question has to be of equal magnitude, from the same general category, and worded in a like manner. In regard to the magnitude or intensity, all of the stimuli have to be at a similar level. A minor jewelry piece cannot be combined with valuable gems anymore than a three-carat diamond can be part of a test that includes an opal, onyx, and amethyst. The examinee's attention would be immediately drawn toward the diamond, thereby distorting the test results. In a homicide case, the examiner can list various weapons, but four different types of guns would not be combined with a knife, anymore than a series of single-word items would be included with a two- or three-word description. For example:

1. Was the victim wearing loafers?

2. Was the victim wearing jeans?

3. Was the victim wearing a white sweater?

4. Was the victim wearing a blouse?

5. Was the victim wearing leotards?

It is important that the critical items must be something that would be remembered by the guilty person. Lykken[4] has used a bank robbery as an example in which he would have a picture of the bank teller combined with pictures of dissimilar looking people and have the various suspects take a POT test based on the photographs. Unfortunately, eyewitnesses have notoriously poor recall, and if the teller cannot be expected to remember the bank robber, how could he accurately recall her? It is evident that a poor selection of a POT test could result in a guilty person's appearing to be innocent. In fact, there is a greater likelihood of obtaining false negative results in using this approach.[5]

Another event that can cause a false negative reaction is when an accomplice pockets valuable items so that the examinee does not know about the missing diamond bracelet. It is also conceivable that the subject does not know the caliber of a handgun used by an accomplice in a shooting. Another factor that can complicate a GKT is the fact that victims of a burglary or robbery might exaggerate their losses in order to file a fraudulent insurance claim. The examiner must also be wary when dealing with specific amounts of money because the guilty individual might not have counted it, the victim might have increased the amount, or the accomplice might have taken more than his or her share. Another reason for finding a guilty individual innocent is when the subject reacts to one of the neutral stimuli because it relates to some crime committed in the past.

It can be seen that there are some obvious risks to the use of this approach. A false positive result also can occur if the examiner inadvertently cues the subject to the critical question by his or her facial expression or inflection. On the other hand, a false negative finding might result if the guilty person is not aware of the critical item or reacts to a neutral item because it has significance to him or her. Therefore, the examiner should not rely on the GKT alone but should employ a control question test along with it.[6]

A number of separate POT tests should be employed. The more tests in which an examinee responds to the critical item and the greater this response, the more certainty the polygraphist can have in his or her results. In a burglary case, point of entry, objects taken, and unique factors such as a dog barking, an alarm sounding, or a baby crying could be developed into specific tests.

Arther has recommended the use of seven questions, with the critical item positioned somewhere in the center area. The first question would be neutral because of the tendency for examinees to respond to it simply because of its position. The second item could be a false key. In 1959 Arther[7] developed a control question for a known solution peak. This was accomplished by employing a neutral question that very much appeared to be the key item. He used the example of "Was the jewelry taken from . . . a jewelry box?" When no obvious key question exists, he suggests that during the pretest the examiner should emphasize the false key by discussing that question a bit more, altering tone or loudness, or gesturing in some manner to make that particular question stand out. The subject with guilty knowledge should show a greater response to the critical item as in contrast to any of the neutral questions or the false key. One would expect that the innocent would react to the false key rather than the critical question. The following is an example of a known solution probe:

Regarding the jewelry that was stolen at 500 Main Street on May 4, do you know whether

1. a bracelet was taken?	Neutral item
2. a diamond ring was taken?	False key
3. a watch was taken?	Neutral item
4. a pendant was taken?	Neutral item
5. a necklace was taken?	Critical item
6. a brooch was taken?	Neutral item
7. a choker was taken?	Neutral item

Although Reid[8] indicated that it is not necessary for the examiner to review the specific questions with the examinee in advance in a GKT, Arther presents them to the subject in advance but in a different order than they will be given during the test. In both instances, there is the advantage of surprise reactions that might enhance the results. Employing the latter approach, however, provides the examiner with the opportunity of going over the questions with the subject; it is also of value to ascertain whether the subject is having difficulty with any of the questions. At this point the examinee might be able to talk about any disturbing items. If a neutral question is disturbing, it can be left in the test or employed as a false key, but if the critical item is a problem, the subject must be questioned to determine whether this is only a dodge to avoid the examination.

After the first test, which again will be in a different order than already presented to the subject, the two or three remaining tests will be in the same order. This allows for a possible peaking effect. This response can be enhanced through the pretest description of this procedure. As indicated earlier in chapter 5, it is advisable to have a sample chart of a stim test to show to the subject. In this instance, it should demonstrate a classical peak-like reaction. The responses on the GSR and cardio should increase with each question until the critical item is reached, and here the greatest reaction should occur. After that, the responses should diminish. An effective polygraphist presents this information in a somewhat dramatic and flowing style that not only explains what occurs physiologically but reinforces the validity of the techniques. Emphasis has to be placed on the growing anxiety as the lie is approached, until finally, at the deception itself, the bodily reactions peak. Blood pressure rises, heart rate increases to the extent that one can feel one's pulse throbbing against the blood pressure cuff, and the palms perspire, causing the EDR to rise. Once the lie is over, like a sigh of relief, all of the physiologic processes relax returning to normal or even less than normal. The fear is over.

Arther indicated that the examiner should be aware of the subject's behavior as the questions are being asked.[9] He states that almost all of those with guilty knowledge will show a physical gesture or a change in voice as the critical item is read, whereas the innocent will respond in a like manner to the false key.

Lykken has varied this procedure, approaching it more from a laboratory than from a crime situation.[10] He reported that the effectiveness of this procedure can be increased by employing ten or more questions. He then scores one point each time the key item demonstrates a greater reaction than the neutral questions. In a single test administered one time, individuals with guilty knowledge generally obtain a score of 8, whereas the innocent receive a 3. Employing a cut-off point of 5, he found that only 1 percent of the innocent and 3 percent of the guilty could be inaccurately scored.

To further enhance the accuracy of the approach, he recommended placing the critical item in a different position each time the test was administered. To avoid inadvertent cuing of the subject to the key item, he suggested having the questions read by someone who did not know the key item. Lykken also tests his series of questions in advance with known innocent subjects to be certain that there is nothing in the test that would cause them to respond inappropriately. As Arther had already recommended, he felt that more accuracy could be achieved if the subject were not to simply answer no but instead to repeat the last portion of the question:

> No, I don't know if a ring was taken.
> No, I don't know if a bracelet was taken.

When the subject responds merely with no, he or she has the opportunity to use countermeasures such as not listening to the question or thinking of something else. The possibility of successfully avoiding the question would be reduced when the subject has to concentrate on the question enough to repeat it. Lykken recognized that a subject who is going to employ countermeasures probably will choose a specific neutral question and attempt pain or movement responses to it. If large responses are obtained on a question other than the false key, one should check the reactions to the key item to determine whether a response is occurring there as well.

This particular polygraph approach has definite strengths but some weaknesses as well. If the examiner is careful, most of the risks in this technique can be eliminated. Examiners grow accustomed to not using it because there are few situations when it can be employed, therefore it is not used to the extent that it should be.

Finally, it is an effective lever in obtaining an admission. Once the subject sees a sample stim test prior to the examination, he or she understands the principle involved. If the examinee is found to have guilty knowledge, he or she should be shown the chart, pointing out where he or she peaked. Then the subject has to be made aware that the only reason a reaction could have taken place at that point is that the subject information that he or she has not shared. From there, the door to a confession is open.

THE BACKSTER ZONE OF COMPARISON

8

It is incumbent upon any examiner to utilize whatever means he is exposed to if it directs him toward a more professional method of chart interpretation.

—Cleve Backster

It has been said whoever takes pen to paper writes about himself. In no polygraph approach is this more apparent than in the work of Cleve Backster. His work is creative, complicated, and with a strong emphasis on details. The student of his method is bombarded with definitions, rules, descriptive terms, and even a note pack that prescribes how to conduct the entire testing process. It is both a compulsively organized system and ever changing as new ideas are developed and incorporated into the method. The emphasis on rules and numbering systems is an attempt to create a highly standardized and objective approach in which a decision of truth or deception is based solely on the charts. This is in direct contrast to a global interpretation that incorporates the case facts and the behavior of the subject to draw a conclusion.

Backster described the competition between the control and the relevant questions in terms of a psychological set or orientation. This orientation was broadened to include the interaction of a variety of factors, including outside issues. A subject establishes a set toward the stimulus that holds the greatest threat to his or her well-being. The subject involuntarily focuses on that set while tuning out other stimuli. In Backster's terms, the subject's response to other stimuli is dampened. The psychological set of the guilty person is directed toward the relevant questions, for those clearly pose the greatest threat. If deception to these items is discovered, the subject faces possible financial loss, imprisonment, or even personal embarrassment. The innocent individual focuses attention on the control items out of fear that lies to these questions will be detected. In an anticlimax dampening effect there is a reduction in both emotional and physiologic reactions to other less threatening stimuli. Therefore, an individual could be lying in response to these key questions but react deceptively to only one of them because the one is much more threatening than the others. In the same manner, overall verification questions such as, "Did you lie to any question on this test?" might show little reactivity because it is anticlimactic to the query, "Did you shoot John Smith?" A similar dampening effect might occur in questions such as "Do you intend to answer all of my questions truthfully?"

In what Backster has termed the superdampening effect, the orientation of the examinee is directed toward the fear that a possibility exists that another and probably more serious crime will be discovered. Because of that, reactions to both the control and relevant questions will be diminished. Backster developed the symptomatic question, "Are you afraid I'll ask a question that we didn't discuss?" to guard against this possibility.

"Zone of comparison" is the term Backster employs to indicate a block of time that contains a question that will affect a particular group of individuals. A relevant question will affect the guilty, a control question will affect the innocent, and an outside issue or symptomatic question will cause a reaction in those who are more concerned about some issue other than the case under study. Using a color system, Backster has labeled these as red, green, and black zones, respectively. Yellow is indicative of neutral or irrelevant question areas. Yellow/red is a sacrifice relevant that is not scored, and red/yellow is a relevant item that is scored but because of some factor, like a mixed issue, must be interpreted with caution. The TRI-zone approach is basically a comparison of reactions among the control, relevant, and outside issue zones of influence. Each zone is influenced through a specific stimulus question, and the response to that can be objectively measured. Consequently, the relevant question causes a reaction in the guilty, the control question results in a response in the innocent, and the symptomatic question stimulates a response in those who are concerned about some outside issue. A lack of reaction should occur to the other two areas in each case. In essence, there is a competition among the three zones, and the area that presents the greatest threat will cause the greatest physiologic change to occur, whereas in the other two areas the responses will be dampened. Therefore, the tracings can be expected to show one of the following:

1. **Tracing average:** the portion of the tracings that shows no evidence of a reaction:

2. **Reaction tracing:** the portion of the tracings that shows a reaction:

3. **Relief tracing:** the portion of the tracings in which there is a recovery from a reaction such as hyperventilation in the breathing or an increase in amplitude and rate in the cardio:

4. **Tracing distortion:** Distortion in the tracings due to such factors as movement or a response to noise.

Indications of deception in breathing include suppression. This requires a distinct reduction in amplitude for three or more cycles. Base-line arousal also requires a rise of at least three cycles. An apnea is viewed as an indication of deception if it is supported by three signs of deception in the tracings because of the ease of which this could be utilized as a countermeasure. The final sign of lying is a slowing of the exhalation rate.

For cardio, blood pressure arousal, amplitude reduction in the upper limbs, and rate reduction are all considered to be signs of deception. Electrodermal response (EDR) is measured by a rise of the tracings. As indicated in a previous chapter, Backster does not consider duration or a number of rises as indicative of deception.

The Backster scoring system employs his concept of spot analysis. This is the evaluation of each sensor on each relevant question as it compares to its control question. Seven scores ranging from a +3 to 0 and 0 to −3 are possible. He also labels these numerical scores TT, T, T?, D?, D, and DD. A comparison between the intensity of responses of control and relevant questions is not sufficient in itself. In order to achieve a +3 (TT) or −3 (DD), an upgrade is required. For example, on the EDR not only must the amplitude of one exceed that of the other by being an excess of four times as great, but other rules must be met. Question spacing must be between twenty-five and thirty seconds and no artifacts must exist. A T requires that the control have at least three times as large an amplitude as the relevant, and twice as great a reaction on the relevant is needed for a TT? In cardio and pneumo, unlike the EDR, one cannot score by measuring with the same exactness. Therefore, scoring must be evaluated in terms of minor or major differences. As in the EDR, a 3 can be obtained only through upgrading, which means a purity of responses must exist. It must meet all of the rules laid out by Backster.

Backster has developed a numerical means for measuring whether the proper selection of a target issue has been made. This is based on the adequacy of case information, degree of threat to the guilty, and clarity of the issue under study. Together, these provide the examiner with an estimate of the validity of the findings.

1. **Adequacy of case information:** The information concerning the case must be sufficiently accurate and detailed enough to formulate an adequate series of questions.

2. **Strength of issue:** How much the examinee has to gain or lose determines the intensity of the issue. A subject who faces a long prison term should he or she be found guilty is assumed to display more concern during the polygraph test than someone facing a minor charge. Therefore, the findings will be more valid.

3. **Distinction of issue:** Case data vary in clarity. An example would be a rape case in which neither force nor threat were employed but the victim acquiesced out of fear. Therefore, the victim believes it was a case of rape, but the perpetrator believes it was voluntary. A case of this nature would be quite low in distinctions in contrast to a straightforward armed robbery.

Each of these is rated on a 1 to 5 scale ranging from least to most. The lower the total score the less certainty the examiner can have in the validity of the test results. Even a high truthful score, for example, would be diminished in value if the low scores were obtained in other areas. Expanding his numerical evaluation procedure, Backster awards a possible high score of 25, 40, and 35 to the three areas, respectively, so that one can obtain a total of 100. The cut-off is arbitrarily set at 50; any score below 50 causes the test results to be questionable, whereas a score over 50 is indicative of an adequate test situation. The higher the score, the greater assurance one can have that the results of the test are valid. Table 8–1 shows Backster's scoring procedure.

Other aspects of quality control that are important to the examiner in evaluating charts are listed by Backster. These are pertinent when presenting data in court to indicate the degree that the charts can be accepted or in testifying as an expert for or against another's charts.

Table 8–1. Backster's Method for Determining Individual Test Validity

	1	2	3	4	5
Adequacy	5	10	15	20	25
Strength	8	16	24	32	40
Distinctions	7	14	21	28	35

CHART AUTHENTICATION

Authenticity of the charts should be demonstrated. This can be accomplished most effectively through the use of a video recording, but this is prohibitively expensive, except in major cases. Another method is to be certain that the charts are signed by the subject and perhaps even witnessed by some other non-involved person. It is unusual for this question to be raised by the court, particularly if the polygraphist has an established reputation.

TECHNICAL IDENTIFICATION

By this Backster means using an accepted technique and not a procedure that is unique to an individual or, in his terms, experimental. In most scientific fields a variety of approaches can be employed, and to be acceptable in court the process used does not have to be the procedure used by most specialists in that field. A minority approach can be employed as long as a significant number of people use the approach and there is scientific evidence as to its effectiveness, validity, and reliability.

INSTRUMENTATION

In this category, Backster includes the use of appropriate chart markings, tracings that are readily interpretable, and no evidence for the use of counter-measures.

NUMERICAL EVALUATION

Numerical scoring enhances objectivity, and this, in turn, increases both validity and reliability. The more objective the scoring system employed, the more an examiner can rely on its findings. The scoring system should not be unique to the individual but one that is employed by a significant number of polygraphists. In an ideal situation, another examiner should blindly score the charts to determine if there is agreement in the findings.

CASE INFORMATION REVIEW

The information on the case should be adequate and accurate, and the area under polygraph study should be of major significance to the case. Along with this, the questions should be appropriate for the specific area under investigation.

QUESTION FORMULATION

All questions should be developed in a manner that falls within the accepted parameters that have been previously discussed. In this Backster emphasizes that there should not be too many relevant questions in the same test and they should not be in consecutive order. Not using a sacrifice relevant is detrimental as is mixing issues. The latter is significant because of the dampening effect. Mixing issues, however, is acceptable when the case situation is not clear enough to employ a YOU-Phase single issue test. When this is the case, a SKY or exploratory test can be utilized. These procedures will be discussed shortly. Compound relevant questions—that is, those asking two questions at the same time, such as, "Did you stab and kill John Smith?"—also would be viewed as weakening the test.

The control questions should be reviewed with the subject to the same extent as the relevant questions. All of the questions must be reviewed word for word with the subject for a number of reasons. There is no diagnostic value to an unreviewed question because the surprise or resentment experienced by the examinee will cause a distortion of the tracings. Reviewing the questions also allows the examiner to determine if the individual understands the question and the vocabulary used.

A time bar is required with the first control question dealing with the first portion of the subject's life and the second control dealing with the second portion of his life. The cutoff point is, of course, prior to the time of the commission of the alleged act. The controls should be in the same general area as the issue under study and should be positioned next to the relevant to which it will be compared. Backster also warned of employing too strong a control. For example, questions such as, "Have you ever used force in getting a female to do something sexual?" might overpower the relevant items because of a past history of violent rapes that the suspect is concerned about being uncovered. If an examinee responds yes to a control question, the response cannot be utilized as a reaction, for changing an answer in itself could cause the reaction. However, it can be scored for a lack of response if the relevant shows a greater reaction.

Backster believes there should be two symptomatic questions such as, "Are you afraid I'll ask a question that we didn't discuss?" Neutral questions with any possibility of causing arousal should not be employed, nor should there be an excessive use of the irrelevant question.

EXAMINER CONCLUSIONS

The findings drawn should be justified by the charts and a decision be based solely on this.

Table 8–2. Scoring for Backster's YOU Phase Test

YOU phase: two relevant questions

	Truthful	Inconclusive	Deceptive
2 charts	+5 and higher	+4 to −8	−9 and higher
3 charts	+7 and higher	+6 to −12	−13 and higher
4 charts	+9 and higher	+8 to −16	−17 and higher

YOU phase: three relevant questions

	Truthful	Inconclusive	Deceptive
2 charts	+7 and higher	+6 to −12	−13 and higher
3 charts	+10 and higher	+9 to −18	−19 and higher
4 charts	+13 and higher	+12 to −24	−25 and higher

TEST PROCEDURES

YOU PHASE (DID YOU YOURSELF)

This particular approach deals exclusively with a single issue regarding direct involvement in a specific case. Although the wording of the relevant questions varies, they have essentially the same meaning. Either a two- or three-relevant question series can be employed. The following is an example of the two-relevant-question YOU phrase test.

Irrelevant	Are you twenty-two years of age?
Sacrifice relevant	Do you intend to answer truthfully every question about the burglary?
Symptomatic	Are you completely convinced that I will not ask you a question during this test that has not already been discussed?
Control	Before the age of thirty, did you steal anything?
Relevant	Did you participate in the burglary at Walnut and Johnson Streets on May 5?
Control	Between the ages of thirty and forty did you ever steal anything?
Relevant	Regarding the burglary on May 5 at the house on Walnut and Johnson, did you take part in it?
Symptomatic	Is there something else you are afraid I will ask you about, even though I told you I wouldn't?

On the second administration of the test, the relevant questions are transposed to deal with any possibility of a spot responder. That is an individual who reacts to a question because of its position in the test rather than its content.

To make a determination of truth or deception, the following scores are employed. It should be noted that in contrast to some other techniques, the more a test is repeated or the addition of a relevant question results in a higher score being required to determine either truth of deception. Because there is a tendency to have a greater risk of false positives on the control question technique, Backster has skewed the control line so that a lesser score is required to pass a test as in contrast to failing. This is shown in table 8–2.

THE SKY TEST

The SKY test is employed as with the exploratory test when a clear single issue is not available. The SKY test allows a comparison of the three areas: (1) Do you suspect someone, (2) do you know for sure who did it, and (3) did you do it?

Irrelevant	Were you born in the United States?
Symptomatic	Do you believe me when I promise you I won't ask a question that we haven't gone over?
Sacrifice relevant	Regarding the sexual assault on Betsy Smith on May 4, do you intend to answer truthfully each question about it?
Suspect	Regarding the sexual assault on Betsy Smith, do you suspect anyone in particular of doing it?
Know	Regarding the sexual assault on Betsy Smith, do you know for sure who did it?
Control	Between the ages of fifteen and twenty-five did you ever think of forcing sex on a female?
Did you	Regarding the sexual assault on Betsy Smith on May 5, did you do it?
Control	Between the ages of twenty-five and forty did you ever use force of any kind to get a female to do something sexual?
Symptomatic	Even though I promised you I wouldn't, are you afraid I'll ask you a question we haven't gone over?

The scoring procedure for the SKY test is shown in table 8–3. The scoring is vertical in that it is done on a question-by-question basis. Therefore, it is for a single relevant question. When a YOU phase test is employed, two administrations of the test with two like relevant questions in each test is of course the equivalent of four administrations of the same question because in the SKY test and exploratory test each question is dealt with separately and four administra-

Table 8–3. Scoring of Exploratory and SKY Single Relevant Question

	Truthful	Inconclusive	Deceptive
1 chart	+2 or higher	+1 to −2	−3 or higher
2 charts	+3 or higher	+2 to −4	−5 or higher
3 charts	+4 or higher	+3 to −6	−7 or higher
4 charts	+5 or higher	+4 to −8	−9 or higher

Table 8–4. A Comparison of the YOU Phase, SKY, and Exploratory Test

	Irrelevant	Symptomatic	Sacrifice relevant	Control	Relevant	Control	Relevant	Control	Relevant	Symptomatic
Backster Zone comparison YOU phase test	y 13	b 25	y/r 39	g 46	r 33	g 47	r 35	g 48	r 37 (opt)	b 26
Backster Zone comparison SKY test	y 13	b 25	y/r 39	g 31 -S-	r/y 32 -K-	g 47	r 33 -Y-	g 48	r/y 34	b 26
Backster Zone comparison Exploratory test	y 13	b 25	y/r 39 (42)	g 46	r/y 43	g 47	r/y 44	g 48	r/y 45	b 26

Color key	Type of question
Y Yellow	Irrelevant
B Black	Symptomatic
G Green	Control
R Red	Relevant
YR Yellow/red	Sacrifice relevant
RY Red/yellow	Mixed question relevant, secondary relevant

tions of the test would be required to be comparable to the number of repetitions on the YOU phase.

EXPLORATORY TEST

The exploratory test was developed to allow for the same capability as the Reid mixed general question test while having the controls positioned next to each relevant question. It is employed when the data is not clear enough for a single issue test.

Table 8–4 compares the YOU phase, SKY, and exploratory tests. Backster utilizes a question numbering system that permits the examiner to identify the type of question based on the number employed. For example, 46, 47, and 48 are control questions.

The significant weakness in this approach is the lack of scientific research to demonstrate the validity for many of these findings. Although Backster has reported that these data are the result of evaluating thousands of test protocols, this in itself does not guarantee objectivity. Ideally, the rules for interpretation, the scoring, and the principles should be experimentally evaluated.

THE REID CONTROL QUESTION TECHNIQUE

9

Brian C. Jayne

We profess no infallibility for the polygraph technique, properly employed [it] possesses a degree of accuracy commensurate with, and even superior to, most of the presently approved forms of evidence, scientific as well as unscientific, that feature in criminal and civil trials.

—John E. Reid

John E. Reid developed the control question technique in 1947 because of his experiences at the Chicago crime laboratory with the relevant-irrelevant technique. Specifically, he found that the R-I technique produced an unacceptable error rate and relied, to a great extent, on interrogation in formulating opinions of the subject's truthfulness. In addition to developing the control question technique, Reid, by himself or with others, also made the following contributions to the polygraph field:

1. Used card test for stimulation purposes only;
2. Added a second pneumograph recording to the polygraph instrument;
3. Developed and patented a muscle movement recorder for the polygraph instrument;
4. Developed the silent answer test;
5. Developed the guilt complex test;
6. Developed the yes test;
7. Researched and incorporated behavior-provoking questions into the pretest interview;
8. Founded Reid College of Detection of Deception, a six-month post-graduate school to train polygraph examiners;
9. Was instrumental in writing the first state detection of deception licensing law that required a college degree.

THE REID DETECTION OF DECEPTION PHILOSOPHY

The Reid technique differentiates between a polygraph operator and a detection of deception examiner. A polygraph operator relies exclusively on chart recordings in rendering an opinion of truth or deception. A detection of deception examiner, however, is trained not only in detecting deception through physiological indexes but also through factual analysis and behavioral analysis. Therefore, the Reid control question technique relies on three interrelated assessments of a subject in formulating an opinion of truth or deception. This approach has been termed a global approach.[1]

"Factual analysis" refers to forming a probability of truthfulness based on evaluating a suspect's opportunity, access, motives, psychosocial background, and physical and circumstantial evidence. Research shows that, compared to college students not trained in factual analysis, detection of deception examiners trained in factual analysis display a high degree of accuracy in predicting the truthfulness of suspects based strictly on factual assessment.[2]

Behavioral analysis involves assessments of the subject's verbal and nonverbal behavior during the course of the examination. Similar to factual analysis, research indicates that examiners trained in behavior analysis can validly identify a subject's truthfulness based on behavioral observations.[3]

Incorporating factual and behavioral analysis into the diagnostic process increases the examiner's accuracy in the opinion, and guards against false positive test results. Table 9–1 illustrates different combinations of independent assessments and the resulting opinion of truth or deception.

Table 9–1. Global Response Evaluation

Factual	Behavioral	Chart	Opinion
Truthful	Truthful	Truthful	Truthful
Deceptive	Deceptive	Deceptive	Deceptive
Truthful	Truthful	Deceptive	Inconclusive
Deceptive	Deceptive	Truthful	Truthful

As can be seen in the table, global evaluation is not used to reverse chart indications. However, this process may lead the examiner to question the validity of deceptive test reactions. Although this presentation of global evaluation is oversimplified, the principle is that a polygraph examiner must acknowledge the possibility of errors within the technique. Global evaluation allows the examiner to identify the probability that the test outcome falls either within the 90 to 95 percent range of accurate results or, conversely, within the 5 to 10 percent range of inaccurate results. When all assessments are consistent, the examiner statistically has an accuracy higher than the highest accuracy of any individual test result.[4] When inconsistencies within the assessments do exist, the examiner may render an inconclusive opinion or employ certain procedures in an attempt to resolve the inconsistencies. These could involve obtaining additional investigative information, reevaluating the suspect's behavior, using specialized test procedures, or reexamining the subject using additional or different test questions during the reexamination.

The remainder of this chapter provides a brief description of the Reid control question technique. It is not a complete representation of all aspects of the technique and does not represent procedures that must be followed in every case situation.

THE PRETEST INTERVIEW

The pretest interview within the Reid control question technique is a nonaccusatory structured interview that generally lasts between thirty and forty minutes. The subject is not attached to the polygraph instrument during this interview so as not to inhibit nonverbal behavior. To document information obtained during the interview, the examiner writes down the questions asked of the subject, and the subject's verbal and nonverbal responses to the questions. The interview serves six main purposes:

1. Clinical assessment of factors that could affect the validity of the examination results as well as the subject's suitability for the examination;

2. Analyzing the subject's verbal and nonverbal behavior;

3. Defining and clarifying the issue under investigation;

4. Introducing and formulating the control questions;

5. Conditioning the subject for the examination;

6. Formulating and final review of all test questions.

CLINICAL ASSESSMENT

Although most polygraph examiners are not trained in or licensed to diagnose mental or medical conditions, an important aspect of the training an examiner receives is to be familiar with medical and psychiatric diagnoses, as well as the symptoms accompanying those conditions. During the pretest interview a clinical assessment of the subject is accomplished through observations, questioning, and a review of the information on a medical history sheet that is completed by the subject prior to the examination (see appendix A).

One assessment the examiner makes is the subject's emotional and behavioral affect. Obviously the examiner is interested in symptoms or diagnosis of depression, anxiety disorders, or psychosis. The subject's intelligence and comprehension are also evaluated. From this assessment the examiner may determine that the subject is unsuitable for the examination or may realize going into the chart recording phase of the examination that the subject is at a higher risk for inconclusive test results.

The subject's medical condition is also evaluated to determine whether a liability risk might be incurred in administering the examination (such as subjects who are pregnant or have heart conditions or pulmonary disease). This information also allows the examiner to account for unusual recording such as arrhythmias from a subject with a heart condition or forced respiration from the emphysemic. If the subject is taking any medications, the examiner obtains relevant information about the medication to assist in establishing the subject's suitability as well as possible effects the medication may have on the subject's physiological responsivity.

The examiner also elicits information from the subject with respect to intrinsic emotional states that have a known effect on polygraph validity. Examples of these would include anger, prior bad experiences with the polygraph, feelings of responsibility regarding the issue under investigation, and a general negative attitude toward the investigation. If such intrinsic emotional states are present, the examiner will attempt to resolve those feelings and take them into consideration during chart interpretation. In some situations, the examiner may incorporate a special question within the test for diagnostic purposes. For example, in a case where the subject experiences feelings of responsibility about the crime, the examiner may ask as a test question, "Are you personally responsible for [crime]?" and develop this question. More so than to the specific relevant questions dealing with committing the crime, this would be indicative of the subject's truthfulness to the relevant questions.

BEHAVIORAL ANALYSIS

During the pretest interview specific questions are asked to elicit verbal and nonverbal behavior indicative of the subject's truthfulness.[5] Examples of these questions follow:

1. **"What will your polygraph results be today?"** Many truthful subjects will be confident and direct in their responses to this question. For example, "I will do just fine," or "It better show I am telling the truth." On the other hand, the deceptive subject may delay responding and qualify an answer, such as, "Well, I hope it will come out all right," or "I don't know. I've never had one before."

2. **"What do you think should happen to the person who did [crime]?"** The truthful subject will typically offer a reasonably harsh punishment for the guilty party such as, "Well, for sure he should be arrested and sent to jail." The deceptive subject, conversely, is typically more forgiving in his answer, such as, "I think it is important to find out why he did it before any decision is made."

There are about thirty such behavioral provoking questions the examiner chooses from during the course of the pretest interview. The questions are tailored to the particular investigation and are interspersed with fact analysis questions and questions specifically designed for clinical assessment.

Nonverbal behavior that occurs consistently on cue to key questions is also noted by the examiner. Examples of significant behavior would be breaks of gaze, grooming behavior (dusting pants, running fingers through hair), adaptor behavior (the hands coming in contact with different parts of the body), the use of illustrators (hand and arm gestures that accompany speech), and leg behavior (crossed legs, bouncing feet, retracted feet). An important concept in evaluating nonverbal behavior is to establish the subject's normal behavior during non-threatening questions and using that behavior as a baseline for comparison when key questions are asked. Another factor that affects the validity of behavioral analysis is identifying the consistency and timing of the subject's behavior.

In addition to asking specific behavior-provoking questions and observing the verbal and nonverbal responses to those questions, the examiner notes the subject's posture during the course of the interview. Truthful subjects tend to be frontally aligned in the chair and will evidence free and natural movements of changes in posture. The deceptive subject, on the other hand, often is rigid in the chair and may assume a leaning posture with his head supported with the palm. Barriers such as crossed legs and arms would be another posture often associated with deceptive subjects than truthful subjects.

Although most subjects will display some truthful and some deceptive behavior during the pretest interview, the examiner evaluates the preponderance of behavior with respect to final analysis. The examiner is able to form a definite opinion of truthfulness or deception based on behavioral analysis with approximately 75 percent of subjects examined. The accuracy of identifying deceptive subjects through behavior analysis is approximately 75 percent, whereas the accuracy for identifying truthful subjects is approximately 80 percent.[6]

DEFINING AND CLARIFYING THE ISSUE UNDER INVESTIGATION

In order for a polygraph subject to form a proper psychological set during an examination requires a clear understanding of the issue under investigation. Therefore the examiner will define exactly what the purpose of the examination is and allow the subject an opportunity to go over his alibi and suspicions he may have and discuss his connection with the victim or crime scene. The examiner also questions the subject about similar acts that the subject may have on his mind. For example, in an investigation regarding a sexual assault of a woman named Vicki that occurred on March 15 at Boyd Park, the examiner would ask the subject whether he had sexual relations with anyone on March 15, whether he ever had sex with a woman named Vicki, and whether he ever had sexual relationships with someone in Boyd Park. If the subject acknowledges similar occurrences to the issue under investigation, the examiner would adjust the relevant questions to make certain that the unrelated acts do not overlap with the same issue under investigation. Of equal importance, by discussing these similar occurrences, the examiner is able to reassure the subject that the issue of the examination deals only with the particular offense occurring on the date in question and with the victim in question.

Another aspect of clarifying the issue under investigation is to have the subject define certain words that will be used in relevant questions. Contact verbs such as "hit," "strike," "punch," "kick," or "slap" should be defined by the subject before they are used in a relevant question. If this is not done, the subject may attach a different meaning to the verb than does the examiner. Sexual terms for the male and female sex organs and sexual intercourse should also be defined by the subject if the terms are used in relevant questions. If a location or specific name is used in a relevant question, the examiner must establish that the subject knows where the location is or that the subject is familiar with the name used.

INTRODUCTION AND FORMULATING THE CONTROL QUESTIONS

A control question is a question of similar nature to the issue under investigation and one to which the subject, in all probability, will lie or at least have some doubt about the truthfulness of an answer.[7] Empirically it is observed that a truthful subject exhibits greater autonomic arousal to the control question than the relevant questions and, conversely, that a deceptive subject exhibits greater autonomic arousal to the relevant questions than the control questions. A theoretical explanation for this response discrimination is that a polygraph subject responds to test questions as a function of a perceived threat to a goal and not as a function of the magnitude of a lie.[8] In other words, the truthful subject enters the examination with a belief and expectancy of being reported as telling the truth to the issue under investigation. The control question threatens that goal—not because the subject is lying to the question but rather because of the implication a response to the question holds with respect to the subject's goal of the examination.

The deceptive subject, on the other hand, enters the examination with a desire and expectancy not to be identified as lying about the issue under investigation. The control question is formulated to be broad in scope, time, and content and therefore does not threaten the deceptive subject's goal of the examination nearly as much as the specifically worded relevant questions do. The control question, therefore, is a special question because it is perceived differently by a truthful subject than by a deceptive subject. To accomplish this perceptual distinction requires expertise on the examiner's part in selecting the proper area for the control question, introducing the control question to the subject, and finally formulating the control questions.

The selection of the control question is dependent on the subject's perception of the issue under investigation. In an employee theft case, for example, the subject may perceive the act as stealing, doing something against company policy, doing something dishonest, cheating the company out of money, or violating the law. During the pretest interview the examiner attempts to elicit the subject's perception of the issue under investigation to select an area for the control question. For example, if the previously mentioned subject was asked, "Tell me why you wouldn't steal this money," and the subject responded, "Because it is against the law," the examiner may select a control question dealing with violating laws. If, on the other hand, the subject responded, "I've got a wife and family to feed and I can't risk losing my job," the examiner may develop a control question dealing with violating company policies or doing things for which the subject could be fired.

Because the examiner can never be certain of the subject's perception of the issue under investigation, the Reid control question technique uses two control questions that usually address different possible perceptions of the issue under investigation. The control question that addresses the most likely perception is asked at question 6 and the control question that addresses a second possible perception is asked at question 11.

The control question is introduced in such a manner as to appear to be a natural extension of the issue under investigation. Ideally, the subject should perceive the control question as instrumental in determining whether he or she is telling the truth to the issue under investigation. This perceptual process, however, must occur within the subject and not be influenced by the examiner's statements. For example, the examiner does not explain why the control question is asked (such as, "This question will tell me whether or not you are the type of person who could do this)." Such a statement could influence the subject's perception of the control question, which lies at the very heart of the diagnosis. At a fundamental level, the control question polygraph technique identifies whether or not the subject attaches significance to the control question or, on the other hand, if the subject considers the control question insignificant. This perception therefore must be generated from within the subject and not be influenced through the examiner. The following dialogue is an example of how a control question may be introduced during the pretest interview:

E: Joe, have you ever been questioned before about missing money?

S: No, this is the only time.

E: Have you ever worked around money before this?

S: Sure, I have—in my last two jobs.

E: Joe, is there any time you have stolen a deposit? Now, I know you said you didn't take this deposit, but in any job have you taken a deposit?

S: No way.

E: Well, would there be any money you've ever taken from an employer for yourself?

S: Not that I can remember.

E: How about from outside of a job, have you ever taken money from parents, or a friend, or maybe gone into someone's locker at school and taken money?

S: Well, when I was younger, I did take some change from my dad's wallet.

E: Besides that money, is there anything else you can remember stealing from anywhere?

S: Sure, I mean, I've shoplifted candy.

The examiner at this point has introduced a control question dealing with stealing things in the subject's life. The general procedure is to start out with very specific questions closely related to the issue under investigation and continually broaden the area of inquiry until the examiner reaches the area that will be developed as a control question. To make certain that the subject understands the question and that the question holds a possible significant meaning to the subject, the examiner attempts to elicit two or three admissions and then discourages the subject from making any further admissions by asking negative questions, making the subject's admission sound significant, or asking a double question, part of which is true, and the other part which is false. For example, continuing with the previous dialogue:

E: Now, you mentioned that you stole money from your father and that you shoplifted. When was the last time you shoplifted?

S: Years ago—maybe when I was in grade school.

E: So that was the only time you stole candy, right? (negative question)

S: Yeah, that's really all I remember.

E: How much money did you steal from your father, Joe?

S: Just a couple of dollars.

E: And that was the last time you stole money. You didn't take any money from employers or deposits? (double question)

S: I can't really remember stealing anything else.

E: That would be in your whole life right?

S: Yeah, I think so.

E: Joe, what do you think should happen to the person who stole this deposit? (returning to issue under investigation)

During the development of the control question the examiner pays close attention to the subject's behavior to make certain that the subject is exhibiting some doubt about the truthfulness of his or her answer. If the subject appears confident in denying the control question or fails to understand the implication of the question, it will not function as intended. Also to assist in the perception of the control question, the control questions are introduced approximately two-thirds of the way through the pretest interview, and after the control question is introduced, the examiner returns to specific questions about the issue under investigation.

When formulating the control question, the examiner makes the question as broad as possible. This serves three distinct purposes. First, the control question should include the time of the offense so the truthful subject can attribute a response to the control question as being a threat to his goal of the examination. In the above example, the final formulation for the control question would be, "Besides the candy and $2 you told me about, did you ever steal anything else in your life?" Because this question overlaps with the time of the offense ("Did you ever . . ."), the truthful subject can attribute a response to this question as threatening to his or her goal. In other words, the truthful subject is concerned that the examiner may interpret a response to the control question to mean that the subject stole the missing deposit. The second purpose for making control question broad is to increase the probability that the subject will be lying to the control question. But perhaps the most overlooked reason for making the control question broad is to diminish its significance for the deceptive subject. Because the control question covers stealing anything in the subject's entire life, the deceptive subject can easily attribute a response to the control question to something other than the deposit that he or she stole, having the effect of making the question nonthreatening to his or her goal. It would therefore be incorrect to ask control questions such as, "Did you ever steal any money in your life?" or "In the last three years did you steal anything of value?"

CONDITIONING THE SUBJECT FOR THE EXAMINATION

Conditioning a subject for a polygraph examination actually starts before the individual arrives at the examiner's office. Accordingly, the writer has distributed pamphlets about the proper use of the polygraph to his clients. The one for business clients is reproduced in appendix B. In addition to this information, prior to the examination subjects are given a written description of the procedures and their legal rights as a polygraph subject. This document is reproduced in appendix C.

Despite these procedures, some subjects will still be apprehensive, apathetic, resentful, defeated, angry, or suspicious at the onset of the examination. The examiner typically addresses these conditions during the pretest interview and first attempts to identify the source for the emotional state. Once the source for the emotional state is identified, the examiner will attempt to alleviate the state through educating the subject, reassuring the subject, or sympathizing with the subject.

With respect to education, the examiner may explain to the subject exactly what the examination consists of in terms of instrumentation, the length of the examination, the laws relating to polygraph, or research findings. If the subject asks specific questions, the examiner is open in answering them, but at the same time may respond in such a way as to condition the subject. For example, if the apprehensive subject asks how accurate the test is, the examiner might respond, "If you are telling the truth today, I will be able to clearly demonstrate that."

Reassurance may involve a simple statement that the subject's nervousness will not affect the validity of the test or that the test will not be physically painful. In some situations the examiner may reassure the subject with respect to the confidentiality of pretest statements. For example, a subject who is very concerned that a suspect may learn of the suspicions harbored about them by the subject should be reassured that the examiner will not report those suspicions to that person. Especially in employee theft investigations, it may be necessary to reassure a long-term employee of the purpose for the examination. For example, the examiner may explain that the employer asked the particular employee to take the examination first because the employee is well respected and is setting an example for other employees.

Sympathizing with the subject is a very effective technique in alleviating intense emotional states. For example, a subject who is clearly angry about the way the police spoke to him before the test could be told, "I don't blame you at all for being angry. I would be too." The subject should be encouraged to vent his anger or resentment, and the examiner should help the subject justify his feelings, while carefully directing the subject to more positive feelings such as how relieved he will feel after the examination or how he will be able to use the examination results to support his allegations.

For subjects who are apathetic or distant during the pretest interview, the examiner may try to draw the subject out with a question like, "You don't seem to care very much about this examination," or, "You seem a little preoccupied today. Is there something on your mind other than this examination?" If a source for the emotional state can be identified, the examiner can deal with it directly. Frequently an apathetic demeanor is indicative of a deceptive subject who believes the examination results will not be used against him because he is such good friends with his employer or that he taking the test privately for his defense attorney. Conversely, the subject who appears preoccupied may be depressed or simply concerned about whether her husband will remember to pick up the kids from school.

At the completion of the pretest interview, the examiner typically steps out of the laboratory and formulates test questions. On returning to the lab, the examiner reviews all of the test questions with the subject. The order of review does not separate the relevant from the control questions. For example, the questions are usually reviewed in the following sequence: relevant, relevant, control, relevant, control, irrelevant, irrelevant, irrelevant, irrelevant. The subject is instructed to answer each question as he or she will during the actual tests and also encouraged to discuss any questions for clarification purposes. If the examiner is uncertain as to the subject's comprehension of a question, or the issue under investigation is particularly complex, such as a past intent issue, the examiner reads the question and asks the subject to repeat, in his own words, what the question means to him. When this procedure is used it, is important that the examiner elicits the subject's understanding for all of the relevant questions as well as the control questions. To do otherwise may focus the subject's attention to one question type.

In conclusion, the pretest interview is an intricate part of the Reid procedure. From making clinical assessment to properly conditioning the subject for the examination, the entire validity and reliability of chart interpretation depends on the competency of the pretest interview. Regardless of an examiner's ability to formulate test questions or interpret polygraph records, if the pretest interview is inadequate, little confidence can be placed in any subsequent opinion rendered by the examiner.

QUESTION FORMULATION

Before discussing relevant question formulation, it is appropriate to briefly comment on the irrelevant questions asked in the Reid control question technique. Each Reid examination contains four basic irrelevant questions asked at positions 1, 2, 4, and 7. The irrelevant questions are known truths and formulated not to stimulate sympathetic autonomic arousal (they certainly can stimulate a parasympathetic recovery response). Therefore the irrelevant questions should not appear humorous, embarrassing, threatening, or confusing. The questions also should appear to have a logical point of origin so if the subject asks why they are asked, the examiner can respond that they identify elements of the examination, such as the subject's name, age, and location of the test. The irrelevant questions typically used follow:

1. Do some people call you [a name the subject acknowledges people call him]?
2. Are you over [two to five years younger than the age the subject gives the examiner]?
3. Are you in [city] right now?
4. Did you ever go to school?

If the city has emotional significance to the subject (such as, the subject states, "I hate Chicago"), the question would be changed perhaps to the state in which the examination was administered. Similarly, if the subject has a very high or low educational level, the last question may become stimulating and would be changed to perhaps, "Is today [day of the week]?"

Some of the reasons for asking irrelevant questions in the Reid technique follow:

1. To establish normal physiology;
2. To acclimate the subject to the test;
3. To provide a place for relief responses;
4. To separate emotional responses;
5. To provide a place for instrument adjustments;

6. To invite the deceptive subject to engage in acts of purposeful noncooperation by distorting physiological responses to the irrelevant questions.

Before formulating any relevant questions, the examiner must determine what issue will be investigated during the examination. Although the Reid technique is flexible enough to investigate multiple issues under certain circumstances (screening examinations, general theft investigations), this discussion will deal only with the specific issue examination. All specific issue examinations have a principal issue that can be defined as a statement that will resolve a particular event. Therefore, in a homicide investigation where the victim was killed with a .22 caliber handgun while watching television, the principal issue is whether or not the subject killed the victim. There are two subcategories of principal issues: The first is a diametrically opposed issue, and the second is a past intent issue.

A diametrically opposed issue exists when the subject's knowledge confirms a principal issue. In other words, the subject who is telling the truth about his or her knowledge is necessarily also telling the truth about the principal issue and vice versa. An example of a diametrically opposed issue is a bank robbery involving two suspects, one of whom shot a security guard. Suspect A says that suspect B shot the guard, and subject B says that suspect A shot the guard. Another example would be a situation where a police officer pulls over a vehicle and suspects that the driver and passenger switched places. Both suspects are saying that suspect A was driving, and therefore when testing suspect A he is either telling the truth when he admits driving himself and denies that suspect B was driving, or he is lying about driving himself and also about suspect B not driving.

With diametrically opposed issues we have found that it is important to address both the suspect's principal involvement as well as his or her claimed knowledge in the relevant questions. For many years we experienced a high percentage of inconclusive charts on this type of issue until we addressed both issues during the examination. Specifically, we address the principal issue in the first two relevant questions (such as, "On March 3, 1988, did you shoot a security guard at the National Bank of Chicago?" and "Did you kill that security guard?"). The subject's knowledge is addressed in the third relevant question (for example, "On March 3, 1988, did Harry shoot that security guard at the National Bank of Chicago?").

A past intent issue is considered suitable provided that the examiner can redescribe the intent through physical actions or prior knowledge. For example, in a shoplifting investigation where the subject claims to have absentmindedly put sunglasses in her purse and walked out of the store without paying for them, the examiner could ask, "Did you put those sunglasses in your purse to steal them?" and "At the time you left the store did you know those sunglasses were in your purse?" Because the word "intend" is ambiguous and has degree of meaning, it is suggested to avoid relevant questions containing the word "intend" (such as, "Did you intend to shoplift those sunglasses?").

There are several issues that are generally considered undesirable for the Reid technique. Specifically, these are collateral issues, future intent issues, and opinion issues.

A collateral issue tends to support but does not resolve a principal issue. Examples of collateral issues would be, "Do you own a .22 caliber handgun?"; "Last Friday were you inside [victim's] living room?"; and "Did you see [victim] last Friday evening?" Not only do collateral issues fail to resolve a particular crime, but they are weak relevant questions that potentially may not threaten the deceptive subject's goal of the examination and thereby result in a false negative test result. Investigating collateral issues may also result in a false positive conclusion if, for example, the subject lies about being with the victim on the day of the homicide even though he or she was in no way connected with the killing.

Questions that address the future intent of the subject are improper to use in a validity conducted polygraph examination because no subject can predict the future. Examples of future intent issues include, "Do you plan on working for this company for more than one year?" or "Do you plan on stealing from this company?" These questions investigate the subject's beliefs, which can change at any time. The nature of a psychological set, the premise for the polygraph technique, is that it is formed around past experiences and present knowledge. Therefore the examiner can have no confidence in the validity of evaluating autonomic arousal, or the lack of arousal, occurring to questions that investigate future actions.

Opinion issues, similar to future intent issues, investigate a subjective belief and are not considered suitable for the Reid technique. Examples of questions that investigate an opinion are, "Did Mary have sex with you voluntarily?"; "Did you touch Julie's vagina for sexual gratification?"; and "Were you driving too fast for conditions?" Each of these questions involve the subject's placing a value on certain words "voluntarily," "gratification," "too fast") that can be cognitively manipulated through rationalization mechanisms.

Provided a suitable issue has been selected, the examiner will formulate three or four relevant questions and two control questions to investigate that issue. The relevant questions are asked at positions 3, 5, 8, and 9. After an issue has been selected, the first consideration in formulating relevant questions is to select the verb used within the question to describe the act. The following list indicates preferred verbs under different categories:

Arson	Set, start, burn, light
Burglary	Steal, break into, pry open
Complicity	Know, help, plan, arrange, pay
Drugs	Use, smoke, inject, sell, receive, give
Force	Describe nature of force, such as, point knife at, hold gun to choke, say, tell
Homicide	Kill, shoot, stab, cut, choke, poison, hit
Robbery	Steal, hold up, point gun, say
Sexual	Have (sexual intercourse with), put (penis in mouth), touch (bare vagina), show (bare penis)
Theft	Steal, falsify records
Victim	Make up a story, falsify report

Question 3 is the most descriptive account of the crime and usually includes a date and location. Examples of question 3 for different principal issues follow:

On January 4, 1988, did you start the fire in the stockroom of Jay's Liquor Store?

Last weekend did you steal a 1987 Chevrolet Celebrity from the parking lot on Wells Street in Chicago?

During March 1988 did you have sexual intercourse with Linda Johnson in the back seat of a car?

Question 5 generally addresses the same act as question 3, but in an abbreviated form. Examples of question 5 include the following:

Did you set the fire at Jay's Liquor Store?

Did you steal that 1987 Chevrolet stationwagon?

Did you have sexual intercourse with Linda Johnson?

Question 8 is usually reserved for an evidence-connecting question. This question attempts to recreate, in the deceptive subject's mind, some emotional recollection of committing the crime. For example,

On January 4, 1988, did you light an accelerant inside Jay's Liquor Store?

Did you break the driver's window on that 1987 Chevrolet Celebrity?

Did you put your penis in Linda Johnson's vagina?

Question 9 is used when the subject may have been an accomplice in the crime, may have guilty knowledge, or may have committed similar acts as those under investigation. If these possibilities are improbable from evaluation of case facts, question 9 often is not asked. When question 9 is asked, it may function as a secondary relevant question because it addresses a weaker issue than the other relevant questions, resulting in little automatic arousal to the question even though the subject is not telling the truth to it. On the other hand, question 9 may be used diagnostically as a control question to report a subject as telling the truth to the principal issue if the subject is responding consistently more so to this question than the questions addressing principal involvement. The following are examples of possible secondary relevant questions:

Do you know who started that fire in Jay's Liquor Store?

Did you help anyone steal that Chevrolet stationwagon?

Did you steal any money from the National Bank of Chicago?

(The principal issue involves a specific theft of a deposit.)

The final question type under consideration is the formulation of the control questions. As previously mentioned, the selection of the control question depends on the subject's perception of the issue under investigation. Although the control questions themselves should be formulated as broadly as possible with respect to the time, scope, and content, the subject's admissions to the control questions should be excluded as specifically as possible.

The general rule is that if the subject makes three or fewer admissions to a control question, the admissions are listed separately. For example, a subject who admits shoplifting a magazine, stealing six cans of soda from a former employer, and stealing a $10 bill from his college roommate would be asked the following control question:

Besides the magazine, six cans of soda, and $10 you told me about, did you ever steal anything else in your life?

If the subject makes more than three admissions to the control question, the examiner should attempt to group the admission in some manner. For example, a subject who states that he has lied to a principal about why he was absent from school, lied to a police officer about his age, lied to his wife about an affair, and lied to his boss about leaving early, should be asked the following control question:

Besides the four times you told me about, did you ever tell any other lies in your life to get out of trouble?

As a last resort, in cases where the subject's admissions cannot be categorized, the examiner should simply preface the control question with, "Besides what you told me about . . ." At no time should the examiner make blanket exclusions to a control question, such as, "Besides for money, did you ever steal anything else in your life?"

For some subjects, despite the examiner's efforts to elicit an admission to a control question, the subject will maintain that he or she has never done what the question addresses. In these situations the examiner should ask first, "Have you ever tried to do [issue]?" If the subject still denies trying to engage in the behavior, he or she should be asked, "Have you ever thought about doing [issue]?"

Regardless of the subject's answer to these follow-up questions, the control question would maintain its original form—that is, "Did you ever in your life do anything you could be arrested for?" The exception to this rule is the subject who fails to evidence any verbal or nonverbal concern toward the control question. For example, a sixty-five-year-old subject who is asked a control question about stealing in his life may very well be lying to the question when he denies any theft, but the implication between his last theft and the issue under investigation is so obscure that he may not perceive any threat to the question. In this situation, the examiner would identify behaviorally his lack of concern to the control question and select a control question more suitable to his bearing, perhaps one dealing with doing things he regretted in his life.

TEST TYPES

There are six different test types used in the Reid control question technique. Each of these will be discussed individually, and then the rationale for selecting test sequences will be presented. In the Reid technique, a test represents a single reading of the test questions to the subject during which time the subject's physiology is being recorded. A polygraph chart consists of a series of individual tests, and an examination includes the pretest interview and chart recordings. The examination is completed at such time that the examiner renders an opinion of truth or deception, and therefore an interrogation is not considered part of the examination procedure.

STRAIGHT-THROUGH TEST (ST)

The straight-through test consists of all the irrelevant, relevant and control questions asked in sequential order. Specifically, the test order is

1(1)-2(1)-3(R)-4(I)-5(R)-6(C)-7(I)-8(R)-9(R)-11(C)

The examiner's instructions for the first straight-through test are as follows:

Joe, this first test will consist of all of the questions we just reviewed. I want you to listen to each question as I read it and answer truthfully just yes or no to each one as soon as I finish reading the question. Each of the tests I will be conducting today takes about three minutes to complete. It is important that you sit up straight in the chair with your feet flat on the floor, eyes open, looking straight ahead at the wall.

The straight-through test is administered in the first and third position of the examination. The first time the test is given the subject does not know the order of the questions.

STIMULATION CARD TEST (CT)

The possible second test in an examination is the stimulation test. The purpose for this test is to affect the subject's responsivity and increase question discrimination.[9] The card test is also administered to invite the deceptive subject to engage in acts of purposeful noncooperation by distorting their tracings during the test.[10] The instructions for the stimulation test are as follows:

Joe, this next test is a standardization test I run on everyone. I have a set of cards here and I want you to select one card from the deck, look at it, memorize the number on it, but don't tell me what number you picked. Now, put that card back in the deck. What I am going to do is to go through this deck and ask whether or not you picked each card in it, and I want you to say no to every card I call out, even the one that you picked. So on this test I am asking you to lie to me. Now the reason I run a test like this is to see what it looks like when you tell the truth and when you don't. This test will also tell me whether or not the instrument is properly adjusted for you, so remember to answer no to every card I call out—even the one you picked.

The previous instructions apply to a blind card test, where the examiner allows the subject to believe that he or she does not know which card the subject selected. The reasons the examiner should know which card the subject selected before running the test is to take precautions against a subject who engages in acts of purposeful noncooperation that will render the charts uninterpretable or who lies about which card he or she selected from the deck.

Under some circumstances it is advisable to administer a known card test, where the subject is instructed to turn the card over and it is clear at the outset of the test that the examiner knows which card the subject selected. A known card test should be administered for subjects of lower intelligence where comprehending the test instructions may be a problem or with a subject who has expressed suspicions toward the examiner or the technique.

The sequence in which the cards are asked to the subject is as follows where (I) represents cards that are not in the deck and (R) represents the card the subject selected.

(I)-(I)-(R)-(I)-(R) (cooperative subject)

(I)-(I)-(R)-(I)-(R)-(I)-(R) (subject who distorts the tracings)

The reason the examiner calls out the numbers not in the deck is to make certain that if the subject states that the examiner made an error in picking out the subject's card, the examiner can evaluate whether or not an error was actually made. Frequently, when the examiner asks the subject to say which card the subject did pick, the deceptive subject names one of the other numbers called out, which, of course, is not possible because those numbers are not in the deck.

Although the stimulation test alone may increase response discrimination, the statement that the examiner makes following the stimulation test has a significant effect on the subject's responsivity. The following are recommended examiner responses based on the subject's responsivity on the first straight-through test.

1. **Hyporesponsive** (minimal changes in any parameter to either relevant or control questions): "Joe, you are showing very dramatic responses to card 4; that must be the one you picked.

2. **Hyperresponsive** (general erratic records probably due to nervous tension): "Joe, the only card you are responding to is number 4; that must be the one you picked. You are a good subject for the polygraph technique; when you tell the truth it is very obvious, and when you don't tell the truth it is equally apparent.

3. **Noncooperative subjects** (the subject may distort respiration frequency or cause false blood pressure rises, move the fingers on which the GSR electrodes are placed, and so on): "Joe, did I call out the card you picked? Was it number 4?

These procedures are designed to provide instant feedback to the subject in an effort to clarify chart interpretation. Through this technique the hyporesponsive subject is led to believe that he or she is responsive to the technique and therefore becomes more concerned about deception to either the relevant or control questions. The hyperresponsive subject, on the other hand, becomes more stable in his or her responses as the examiner reassuringly states that he is a good polygraph subject. Finally, the subject who is distorting his or her tracings is essentially told that those efforts are not obvious enough and should be increased on subsequent charts.

Following the stimulation card test the examiner leaves the subject alone in the laboratory for a few minutes. Before leaving, however, the examiner instructs the subject to think about all of the questions on the test and to let the examiner know if there are any questions that should be changed. The effect of the stimulation test as well as the statements following it are to motivate the subject to form a clearer development of concern over either the relevant or the control questions. The particular value of the stimulation test is the positive effect it has on the truthful subject who focuses attention on the control questions on subsequent tests.

When the examiner returns to the lab, a second straight-through test is administered with the subject fully aware of the sequence of the test questions. The examiner emphasizes to the subject that the questions will be asked in the same order as the first test. The reason for this is to reduce general nervous tension due to the uncertainty of not knowing which question will be asked next and to observe peak of tension type responses that may occur to either an anticipated relevant or control question.

Following the second straight-through test, the examiner has a choice of three possible tests, depending on the nature of the subject's responses on the earlier tests.

MIXED QUESTION TEST (MQT)

The mixed question test consists of the same questions asked on the straight-through test, but the questions are asked in a different order, with some of them repeated. The mixed question test serves several different functions within the Reid technique:

1. Checks for "spot responder" wherein some truthful subjects exhibit significant autonomic arousal to the first relevant question asked during a test;

2. Allows for a variety of direct comparisons between relevant and control questions:

3. Stimulates the subject for better response discrimination. The stimulation comes from the test instructions that state that some questions may be repeated. The implication for the truthful subject is that he or she has responded to control questions on earlier tests and for the deceptive subject that he or she has responded to relevant questions on earlier tests.

The instructions for the mixed question test are as follows:

This next test will be a little different. I will ask the same questions, but this time I am going to change the order of the questions. Some of the questions will not be asked at all.

The typical order for the mixed question test, where three relevant questions are asked, is

        7-8-2-3-6-1-5-11-8-6

        I-R-I-R-C-I-R-C-R-C

If four relevant questions are asked, the examiner may use the following sequences:

        7-9-1-3-6-5-11-2-3-6-(8-11)

        I-R-I-R-C-R-C-I-R-C-(R-C)

        7-8-4-9-6-5-11-2-3-6-(8-11)

        I-R-I-R-C-R-C-I-R-C-(R-C)

As illustrated, the question order for the mixed question test is not predetermined but rather is selected based on the subject's previous responses.

THE SILENT ANSWER TEST (SAT)

The silent answer test consists of a straight-through test sequence wherein the subject is instructed to merely think the truthful answer to each question. The SAT has a stimulation effect on the subject's responsivity and also eliminates answer distortions from obese subjects or those suffering from pulmonary disease.[11]

THE YES TEST (YT)

When a subject has engaged in purposeful acts of noncooperation to distort the chart recordings, or the examiner suspects that the subject may be engaging in such acts, a yes test is conducted to confirm whether or not the subject's apparent acts of noncooperation are indeed purposeful. The instructions for the yes test are as follows:

This next test will be different from the other ones. For one thing, I am not going to ask you these two questions [the examiner reads the control questions], but all the other questions will be asked. The thing that will be different about this test is that I want you to answer yes to all of the questions I ask, even the ones you answered no to before. The reason I run a test like this is that I have recorded what it looks like when you answer no to some of the questions, and I just want to see what it looks like when you answer yes. One answer is the truth and the other answer isn't.

For victims or witnesses who have been answering yes to the relevant questions on previous tests, the examiner can administer a no test. In this event the subject is instructed to answer no to all of the test questions and the irrelevant questions are changed to make them known truths when the subject answers them no.

The sequence for the yes test is

1-2-3-4-5-7-8-4-9-2

I-I-R-I-R-I-R-I-R-I

The reason the control questions are not asked during a yes test is to eliminate the possibility that the subject's prior acts of noncooperation were the result of concern to the control questions.

THE GUILT COMPLEX TEST

The guilt complex test actually consists of a series of tests in which the subject is questioned about a fictitious crime. The guilt complex test follows the normal testing sequence. Typically the examiner would return to the laboratory following chart interpretation and advise the subject that he received a call from the client indicating that the subject is being suspected of another similar act. The examiner then describes the fictitious crime and questions the subject about it. Although the fictitious crime should be similar in nature to the actual principal issue, it should be of slightly less significance. The subject, of course, is led to believe that the fictitious crime is real.[12]

Relevant questions are formulated to address the fictitious crime and a straight-through test using these guilt complex questions (GCQ) is conducted. If the subject is exhibiting responses to the GCQ, the examiner may continue with a MQT using the GCQ along with the original relevant questions in the following sequence:

I-I-GC8-R8-I-GC3-R3-C6-GC5-R5-C11

Some circumstances that may warrant that a guilt complex test be administered include

1. When the subject's behavior or factual analysis indicates truthfulness but the polygraph charts indicate deception;
2. When the subject exhibits great emotionality over the allegation during the pretest interview and produces deceptive charts;
3. When the subject is exhibiting equal responses to relevant and control questions.

Other possible advantages to administering a guilt complex test include as a procedure to validate the control questions on a deceptive subject for court purposes. By administering a guilt complex test the examiner can demonstrate that when the subject is asked a fictitious crime question, he or she is capable of responding to the control question. Second, when the examiner anticipated that a deceptive subject will refute the accuracy of the polygraph technique during interrogation, a guilt complex test can be used to support the accuracy of the technique. During interrogation the examiner tells the subject that the test clearly indicates that he or she is telling the truth about the one crime (the fictitious crime) but that the results are equally clear that he or she is not telling the truth about the other crime (the actual issue).

RATIONALE FOR TEST SEQUENCES

1. ST-CT-ST-MQT

This sequence is the most frequently used and is used when the subject's first two straight-through tests are clear in their indications of the subject's truthfulness or deception. This sequence also indicates that the subject is not engaging in any acts of purposeful noncooperation.

2. ST-ST-MQT

This test sequence (not regularly used), where the stimulation card test is not conducted, indicates that the subject has truthful factual and behavioral analysis, as well as a clearly truthful first straight-through test. The reasons the stimulation test is not administered is because the examiner does not want to overstimulate a subject who is already properly conditioned.

3. ST-CT-ST-YT-MQT

This sequence is used when the subject has clearly engaged in acts of purposeful noncooperation on either the straight-through tests or the stimulation card test.

4. ST-CT-ST-SAT-MQT

This test sequence is used when the subject's straight-through tests are erratic or hyporesponsive. The SAT is also used in this position when the subject produces answer distortions on previous tests.

5. CT-pretest interview-ST-SAT-MQT

This is a typical reexamination sequence when the subject's first examination results were inconclusive. The card test is administered before the pretest interview, and the card that the subject selected from the deck is asked only once. The examiner explains that the subject's responses to the card are very clear today and proceeds with the pretest interview.

6. CT-pretest interview-ST-SAT-MQT-YT

This is a reexamination sequence where the subject either engaged in acts of purposeful noncooperation on the first examination or the examiner is suspicious that the subject engaged in acts of purposeful noncooperation on the reexamination.

CAUTIONS AND STIMULATION TECHNIQUES

During the course of chart recordings, the examiners may observe that the subject is not following test instructions properly and therefore must be so advised. Similarly, some subjects will evidence poor question discrimination or inconsistent responses between different tests or question types, in which case the examiner may employ certain stimulation techniques between tests.

CAUTIONS

There are two different places in which an examiner may give the subject a caution during the course of a test. The first of these is at the time a particular behavior occurs. If the subject engages in gross body movements during the course of a test, sneezes, coughs, scratches himself, answers a question narratively, or answers a question differently than what his answer was during the question review, the examiner would stop the test, explain to the subject why the test was stopped, and start the test over again. In the event that the subject answers yes to a control question, for example, the examiner may have to rewrite the question to exclude the subject's new admission.

A second place the examiner may caution the subject is following the first control question (6). In those situations when the subject's behavior only minimally distorts the tracings, the examiner may allow the test to continue to determine whether or not there is a pattern of distortions, such as deep breaths on cue to irrelevant questions and late answers to irrelevant questions. If a pattern is established, the test is not stopped, but the examiner would administer a yes test later in the sequence. Other types of behavior are sniffs, closed eyes, clearings of the throat, or loud answers. When there is no established pattern to the subject's behavior, the test is stopped, the subject in reinstructed, and the examiner starts the particular test over again.

An exception to the previous two rules is the subject who engages in any of these behaviors (except an incorrect answer) during the stimulation card test or yes test. For example, if the subject engages in gross body movements during the stimulation test on the card he or she selected or to relevant questions during the yes test, the test would continue and the examiner would say nothing. However, if the subject answers yes to the card he or she selected, the test is stopped and the examiner administers a known card test. Similarly, if during a yes test the subject answers no to a relevant question, the test is stopped and the subject is reinstructed.

The final place a caution could be given is in between tests. These cautions generally relate to the subject's respiratory rate but could address such things as sniffs, late answers, or slight movements of the arm or fingers. With respect to respiratory rate, if a subject is obviously slowing down their breathing during the course of a test and returning to normal respiratory rate between tests, the examiner would first address this prior to administering the second straight-through test. The first caution is general, such as, "Joe, are you doing anything today to try to help the test? Remember to just allow your body to respond normally. If you are telling the truth, I will be able to show that."

If the subject's respiration remains controlled during the second straight-through test, the examiner would administer a yes test without commenting further to the subject about his respiration. Prior to the mixed question test the examiner would give a more direct caution to the subject, such as, "Joe, throughout the test today you are slowing you breathing down. It is important that you breathe normally during the test today so I get accurate results."

During a Reid examination the examiner does not remove the charts following each test and also continues to record respiration between tests during the time the subject is given test instructions. This procedure allows the examiner to record the subject's normal respiratory rate throughout the course of the examination and also protects the examiner from allegations that certain tests were administered but not included in the file.

STIMULATION TECHNIQUES

The most important concept with respect to stimulation techniques is to not direct any statement or procedure specifically toward either the relevant or control questions. Similar to a mathematical equation where relevant equals control, what the examiner does to one side of the equation must also be dome to the other side. The deceptive subject should perceive the stimulation statement as relating to the relevant questions, whereas the truthful subject should perceive that same statement as relating to the control questions.

The stimulation test is the first place during the examination that the examiner may attempt to affect the subject's responsivity or question discrimination. This is accomplished by the manner in which the examiner provides feedback to the subject with respect to his or her response to the card selected. This has previously been discussed under test types.

If the stimulation test is unsuccessful in producing a more interpretable second straight-through test, the examiner administers a silent answer test. If the subject is hyporesponsive going into the SAT, the following statement is made in conjunction with the SAT instructions:

Joe, the reason I run a test like this [the SAT] is that, as I'm sure you are aware, it is fairly easy to lie to someone else verbally but it is impossible to lie to ourselves. Because you'll be answering these questions to yourself, if you are not telling the truth to any of them it will be very apparent.

Another place that a stimulation statement may be made is before the mixed question test. The following are descriptions of different types of mixed question stimulation statements.[13]

HYPORESPONSIVE CHARTS

The hyporesponsive subject fails to exhibit significant autonomic arousal to any question type during the course of the examination. If this is the result of medications or physical condition, the examiner can do little to affect the subject's responsivity. However, if the subject's lack of emotional responses is the result of low motivation or another psychological origin, the following stimulation technique is appropriate before administering the mixed question test:

Joe, you are showing responses to some of the questions today that I am asking. Before I start this next test, I want to go over each of these questions with you to find out what is bothering you.

The examiner then proceeds to read each relevant and control question and attempts to elicit some remark from the subject. The purpose of telling the subject that he or she is responding to some questions is to create a concern in the deceptive subject's mind that he or she is responding to the relevant questions or within the truthful subject's mind that he or she is responding to the control questions. Again, it is important to emphasize that the examiner is not influencing the direction of response discrimination whatsoever (toward truthful or deceptive results) but merely attempting to obtain conclusive test results.

ERRATIC RESPONSES

Erratic responses refer to unstable physiology. This is typically observed in the respiratory parameter where the subject's volume, rate, or base line fluctuates erratically throughout the test. This could be the result of the subject engaging in acts of purposeful noncooperation (especially forced mental activity), but the examiner must eliminate other causes as well. Some nondeceptive sources of erratic recordings are subjects who need to use the bathroom, are hungry, are suffering from menstrual cramps, or are preoccupied with some event in their lives. The procedure to address erratic responses is as follows:

Joe, in looking briefly over your records so far, you seem to be thinking about something other than these test questions. What are you thinking about when I ask you these questions?

The examiner does not specifically read each question, but rather asks the subject in general what is on his or her mind. If the subject makes no significant statement, the examiner may follow up the inquiry by suggesting possible explanations based on information elicited during the pretest interview such as a subject on diuretics who may need a bathroom break.

INCONSISTENT RESPONSES

When a subject is responding to some relevant questions on some tests and not others, or exhibiting similar responses to the relevant and the control questions, the examiner may make the following statement before administering the mixed question test:

Joe, before starting this next test I want to go over each of these questions with you one more time to find out whether or not there is anything you want to clarify in a question.

The examiner then reads the relevant and control questions and asks the subject if he or she wants to change or add anything to the way the question is worded. If the subject indicates that the subject wants to change a question, the examiner would rewrite the question. If the subject indicates that he or she is confident in answering all the questions, the examiner simply continues on with a mixed question test.

This procedure is similar to the hyporesponsive subject, but there is no direct comment to the subject that he or she is showing responses. Our experience has been that subjects who exhibit inconsistent responses throughout an examination may have committed an act similar to the one under investigation or may have guilty knowledge regarding the issue under investigation. A secondary relevant question addressing these concerns is therefore useful in making this determination.

CONCLUSIONS REGARDING TEST PROCEDURES

The Reid control question technique relies, to a great extent, on examiner judgment and interaction with the subject during the course of chart recordings. It should be made very clear that the role of the examiner is not to influence the direction of the subject's responses to a relevant or control question, such as could be done by specifically addressing one particular question between tests or strengthening or weakening a control question. Rather, the examiner's role is to influence the subject's autonomic responsivity and the clarity (not direction) of question discrimination. Through factual and behavioral assessment, the examiner generally knows, going into chart recording, whether or not a truthful or deceptive outcome will be consistent or inconsistent with prior evaluations. However, to maintain the integrity of global evaluation, each assessment (factual analysis, behavioral analysis, chart analysis) must be mutually exclusive and independent from the others. This objectivity requires an examiner of high ethical standards and one who adheres to scientific methods.

CHART INTERPRETATION

PURPOSEFUL NONCOOPERATION (PNC)

The first consideration in chart interpretation is whether or not the subject attempted to engage in countermeasures by purposefully distorting the chart recordings. In the event that the subject was not cooperative, the examiner will render either an opinion of inconclusive or a general deceptive opinion indicating that because the subject engaged in acts of purposeful noncooperation during the examination it is the examiner's opinion that the subject is not telling the truth to one or more of the relevant questions asked during the examination. Approximately twenty-five percent of verified deceptive subjects engage in acts of PNC.

There are two different categories of PNC. Some subjects engage in PNC throughout the examination, generally through decreasing respiratory rate, and others engage in PNC only on portions of their examination, typically during the card and yes test.[14]

DIAGNOSTIC CRITERIA

For subjects to be reported as PNC on portions of their examination the minimal criteria is that the subjects select a pattern of PNC on the yes test. Figures 9–1, 9–2, and 9–3 are from verified deceptive subjects who were reported PNC on portions of their examinations.

This subject was suspected of shooting his girlfriend. On the card test (figure 9–1), the subject selected card number 2, and his efforts to exaggerate the reaction to the card are quite apparent. The uppermost channel is the muscle movement recorder. The downward movement of the pen is the result of the subject leaning forward in the polygraph chair. On this subject's yes test (figure 9–2), the subject exaggerated his response to relevant questions 3, 5, and 8 by increasing his respiratory rate and volume and conversely decreasing his respiratory volume on irrelevant questions 4 and 7. This type of somatic behavior clearly supports an opinion of deception.

In figure 9–3 the subject of the examination is an attorney accused of lying about a statement he made about a negotiation agreement. The yes test indicates clear attempts to distort the relevant questions. This figure is included to illustrate

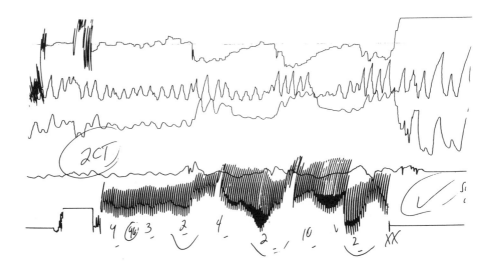

Figure 9–1. The Use of Countermeasures on a Card Test

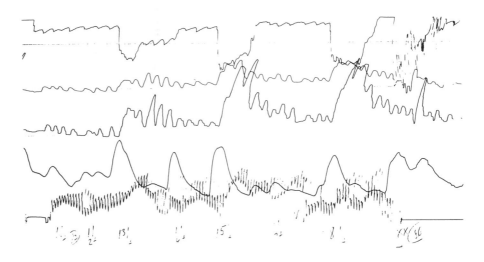

Figure 9–2. The Use of Countermeasures on the Yes Test in Respiration

that, from the intelligence or educational level of polygraph subject, the examiner should not assume that the individual is too smart to distort the yes test.

The subject in figure 9–4 was tested regarding the theft of $144 from her employer. Although there is no specific pattern of distortion on the relevant or irrelevant questions during the subject's yes test, the increase in respiratory fre-

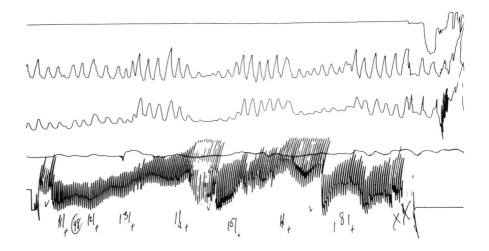

Figure 9–3. The Use of Countermeasures on the Yes Test by an Attorney

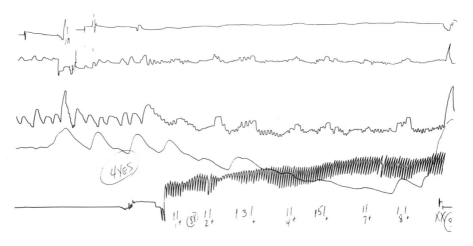

Figure 9–4. Countermeasures through Respiratory Changes

quency from a basal rate of fourteen breaths per minute to fifty breaths per minute during the yes test clearly supports the opinion of PNC.

To render an opinion that subjects engaged in PNC throughout their examination, the following criteria should be met:

1. The subject was given at least one caution.

2. There is documentation that the subject is capable of cooperating. This is generally accomplished through recording normal physiology at some point during the examination.

3. The subject's distortions continue during the yes test.

DIFFERENTIAL DIAGNOSIS

Before rendering the opinion that the subject engaged in acts of PNC on portions of his or her examination, the examiner must eliminate the possibility that the subject was merely trying to help the examination show his or her truthfulness. This subject will typically have truthful control question tests and greatly distorted physiology on relevant questions during the yes test. In addition, this subject is very open about his or her efforts to distort the yes test when questioned following the examination. Experience has demonstrated that a subject who openly admits engaging in acts of purposeful noncooperation should be reported as inconclusive rather than deceptive. When a subject engages in acts of PNC throughout the examination, the following truthful derivations must be evaluated:

1. **PSYCHOLOGICAL DISORDERS.** A subject with a history of anxiety disorders or depression may attempt to slow down breathing during tests to maintain emotional control. When these disorders surface with subjects who regulate their respiratory rates, the examiner should be cautious in reporting the subject deceptive.

2. **PULMONARY CONDITIONING/DISEASE.** Subjects who practice yoga, transcendental meditation, or other relaxation techniques may have affected respiratory patterns during the course of an examination, Similarly, opera singers, long-distance joggers or swimmers, and some musicians may develop naturally slower respiratory rates.

Some pulmonary diseases (such as emphysema and bronchitis) may cause affected respiration during the examination, as well as some asthma medications (bronchodilators). It is incumbent on the examiner to obtain pertinent medical information during the pretest interview to anticipate this cause of affected respiration. The differential diagnostic test to eliminate these causes of apparent PNC is to establish basal patterns of respiration between tests. If between-test respiration is the same as respiration during the test, a PNC opinion cannot be supported. In the case of pulmonary disease that affects respiration, the SAT will generally produce the most interpretable respiration.

3. **CONCERN OVER THE CONTROL QUESTIONS.** A subject who is very bothered about his or her deception to the control questions may attempt to purposefully regulate respiration during the examination. Differential diagnosis for this subject involves cooperation on the yes test. Because the control questions are not asked on a yes test, cooperation on that test, accompanied by noncooperation on other tests, is an indication that the subject is concerned about the control questions. In addition, this subject may very well exhibit truthful behavior during the pretest interview.

CHART INTERPRETATION FOR COOPERATIVE SUBJECTS

Chart interpretation of the cooperative subject involves a quantitative analysis of response duration occurring on relevant questions compared to the duration of arousal to a control question. Because a quantitative approach to chart interpretation is somewhat different than other techniques, a brief rationale will be provided.

In 1983 Reid college conducted a study in which several different measurements were made within each parameter on sixty sets of verified polygraph charts. These measurements were made with a ruler, and a percentage difference between the relevant and control questions was calculated. Through this procedure it was determined at what percentage difference an optimal accuracy was achieved within each measurement. The purpose for the study was to identify the best response criteria within each parameter and to evaluate the validity of using a multiple scoring method (seven-point scale) for numerical evaluation. To give the reader an idea of what the final graphs looked like, figure 9–5 plots the data for the measurement of duration of respiratory responses.

This graph is representative of seven of the eight measurements made of autonomic arousal in that once a maximum percentage difference was reached between the relevant and control questions, the accuracy did not significantly increase beyond that point. For example, from figure 9–4, the duration of respiratory response reached a maximum accuracy at approximately 12 percent difference between relevant and control questions and did not significantly change whether the percentage difference was thirty percent , sixty percent, or 100 percent. This finding casts great suspicion on a numerical scoring system that would give increasing numerical values for apparently more significant responses. In other words, if the multiple scoring system was valid, one would predict that a 60 percent difference between relevant and control question responses would be three times the accuracy as a 20 percent difference. This hypothesis was not supported for any of the measures evaluated.

This data therefore supports the use of a three-point numerical score $(-1, 0, +1)$ as opposed to the subjective seven-point scale. In addition, a particular measurement for each parameter that yielded maximum accuracies was identified as a required percentage difference between relevant and control questions before the response could be considered statistically significant.

RESPIRATION

Figure 9–6 indicates the reference points that are used in measuring a respiratory response, where point A indicates the onset of reaction and point B indicates, in most cases, the onset of recovery. A numerical score of -1 is given to the

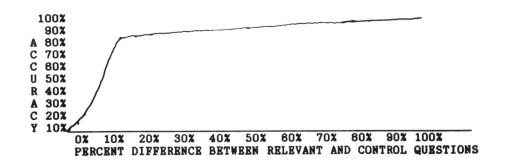

Figure 9–5. Percentage Differences between Relevant and Control Questions

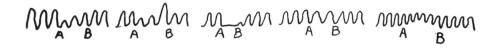

Figure 9–6. Reference Points for Measuring Respiration

relevant question is 10 percent greater than the response duration to the control question. A numerical score of $+1$ is given to the relevant question if the response duration to the control question is 10 percent greater than the relevant question. The relevant question is scored a zero if the difference in response duration between the relevant and control question is less than 10 percent.

The following rules are applied to determine whether or not the respiratory response is too early or too late for evaluation. Point S1 is the first stimulus mark indicating at what point the examiner began to read the test question, and S2 is the second stimulus mark, indicating that the examiner completed reading the test question. Therefore if any of the following conditions exist, the response is considered insignificant. This is shown in figure 9–7.

IDENTIFICATION OF RESPIRATORY RESPONSES

Determining whether or not a particular response is possibly considered as an index of deception depends on whether or not the physiological change is consistent with autonomic arousal. Of course, with respect to respiration, reflex somatic responses within the diaphragm can also be associated with emotional responses. With this in mind, the following responses are considered as possible criteria within the respiratory parameter.

1. **Suppressions** (two or more breaths with a volume of less than tidal volume);

2. **Staircase suppressions** (the first affected breath must be fifty percent less than tidal volume and the recover breath must enter inspiratory reserve volume);

3. **rate decrease** (two of more breaths with a rate less than prestimulus rate);

4. **Baseline rises** (two or more breaths in which the expiratory stroke does not return to prestimulus base lines);

5. **Apnea** (the period of diaphragm inhibition must be greater than the duration of one normal respiratory cycle).

The respiratory responses seen in figure 9–8 are generally not considered deceptive criteria within the Reid technique but may be indicative of purposeful distortions or a peak of tension response.

ELECTRODERMAL

Figure 9–9 indicates the reference points that are used to measure the electrodermal responses. Point A indicates the initial rise of the pen on cue to a stimulus, two to four seconds from recognition of the question. Point B is the highest peak within the response, and point C is the postresponse baseline. The actual measurement taken involves drawing an imaginary line connecting points A and C and measuring the height of a perpendicular line intersecting that line with point B.

An electrodermal response is considered significant for evaluation if there is at least a fifty percent difference between the relevant and control questions. No extra weight is given to the "saddle" response or to an electrodermal pattern that dives on cue to a question. Although it is tempting to consider this latter pattern as relief to the previous stimulus, atrichial sweat glands are not innervated by parasympathetic nerves.

CARDIOVASCULAR

Figure 9–10 indicates the reference points for cardiovascular responses. Point A indicates the first heartbeat reflecting sympathetic arousal. Point B is the first heartbeat indicating parasympathetic recovery, and point C is the heartbeat in

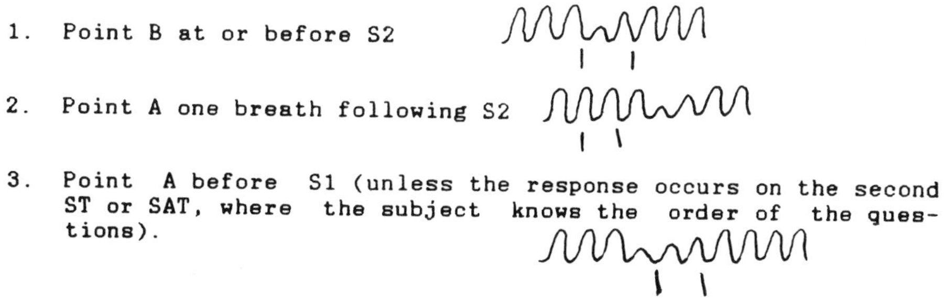

1. Point B at or before S2

2. Point A one breath following S2

3. Point A before S1 (unless the response occurs on the second ST or SAT, where the subject knows the order of the questions).

Figure 9–7. Insufficient Respiratory Responses

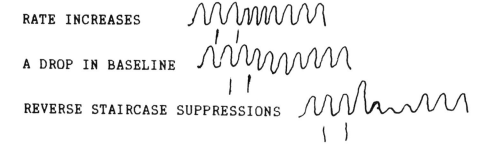

RATE INCREASES

A DROP IN BASELINE

REVERSE STAIRCASE SUPPRESSIONS

Figure 9–8. Respiratory Response That May Be Indicative of Purposeful Distortions

Figure 9–9. The Evaluation of Electrodermal Response

which the cardiovascular pattern establishes a poststimulus base line. Notice that in a double bounce response, point B is placed at that point where parasympathetic arousal overcomes the effects of adrenaline on the pattern.

The following timing rules are used to evaluate whether or not a cardiovascular response is considered on cue to a stimulus:

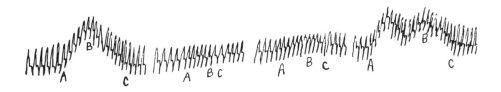

Figure 9–10. The Evaluation of a Cardiovascular Response

1. If point A occurs before S1, the pattern is typically not evaluated, unless it represents a peak of tension response.

2. If point B occurs at or before S2, the response is not evaluated.

3. If point A occurs later than approximately four heartbeats from S2, the pattern is typically not evaluated.

RESPONSE CRITERIA

For a cardiovascular response to be considered significant for evaluation, the duration of the pattern (measurement from point A to C) must exceed twenty-five percent difference between the relevant and control question. If there is less than a twenty-five percent difference in duration, a fifty percent difference in the height of the patterns can be used as a secondary criterion. The following patterns are considered significant:

1. Increases in peripheral resistance (blood pressure rises);

2. Increase in heart rate;

3. Increase in dicrotic notch position;

4. Decrease in peripheral resistance on cue to a question (indicates relief to the previous question).

FORMULATING AN OPINION

The previously mentioned numerical scoring system is generally used in the following manner: On the straight-through tests as well as the SAT, responses to relevant questions 3 and 5 are compared to the response to control question 6. Responses to relevant questions 8 and 9 are compared to the response to control question 11. On a mixed-question test, the relevant question is compared to the control question immediately following it. The yes test is not evaluated for autonomic arousal, only for somatic changes and therefore only to diagnose PNC.

The numerical scoring system used in the Reid technique is different in using only three-point scale and also in that no automatic cut-off points indicate truthfulness or deception. The reason for not relying on cut-off limits follows.

1. Some truthful subjects will focus more so to one control question that the other. For example, if control question 11 is more threatening than control question 6, the numerical scores might look as shown in table 9–2.

Although the total numerical score for this subject is +3, which would normally be considered inconclusive, it is apparent that control question 11 is the focus of this subject's psychological attention and a truthful opinion to all four relevant questions (provided that all questions investigate the same issue) is the most appropriate opinion. Oftentimes in such situations it is advisable to rescore the charts using control question 11 for comparison to all relevant questions.

2. An accumulative numerical scoring system does not take into consideration the possibility of a spot responder, as is shown in table 9–3.

This subject's total score is −1, yet if the spot responses were not considered, the score would be +8 (question 8 is asked in the first position on the mixed-question test). In a case like this, the examiner should report the subject as telling the truth to all relevant questions, provided that the questions all address the same issue.

3. The stimulation test not infrequently produces dramatic changes in the subject's response discrimination, as is shown in table 9–4.

On the above case the subject's accumulative score in −2, which would generally be considered inconclusive. However, there clearly is a deceptive response

Table 9–2. Numerical Scoring When One Control Is Stronger Than Another

		ST	ST	SAT	MQT	Total
	R	0	0	−1	0	−1
3	G	−1	−1	0	0	−2
	C	0	0	0	−1	−1
	R	0	+1	−1	+1	+1
5	G	−1	0	0	0	−0
	C	+1	0	−1	0	0
	R	+1	+1	+1	0	+3
8	G	0	0	0	+1	+1
	C	−1	+1	+1	0	+1
	R	+1	+1	−1	0	+1
9	G	0	0	+1	0	+1
	C	−1	+1	0	0	0

Table 9–3. Numerical Scoring with a Spot Responder

		ST	ST	SAT	MQT	Total
3	R	−1	−1	−1	+1	−2
	G	−1	−1	−1	0	−3
	C	0	−1	−1	0	−2
5	R	+1	0	0	+1	+2
	G	0	0	−1	0	−1
	C	+1	+1	0	0	+2
8	R	0	+1	0	−1	0
	G	+1	0	+1	−1	+1
	C	0	+1	+1	0	+2

Table 9–4. The Effect of a Stim Test on Reactivity

		ST	ST	SAT	MQT	Total
3	R	+1	−1	0	−1	+1
	G	0	0	+1	0	+1
	C	+1	−1	0	−1	−1
5	R	+1	−1	+1	−1	0
	G	+1	0	−1	0	0
	C	0	0	−1	−1	−2
8	R	+1	−1	−1	0	−1
	G	+1	0	−1	−1	−1
	C	0	−1	+1	+1	+1

trend following the stimulation card test, and if the first straight-through test is not counted, the total numerical score is −10, indicating deception. It should be noted that the opposite effect is observed as well, where a truthful subject may produce a deceptive first straight-through test but establish a truthful trend following the stimulation card test.

4. The secondary relevant question is used as a control. In this examination, question 3, 5, and 8 addressed principal involvement in a specific theft, whereas question 9 is worded, "in the last twelve months did you steal any money from [company]?"

This subject's accumulative score in −6 and the subject may incorrectly be diagnosed as deceptive to all questions. However, it is very clear that this subject's emotional focus is directed at the secondary relevant question much more than to the principal involvement questions that support the opinion of truthfulness to questions 3, 5, and 8. This is shown in table 9–5.

Table 9–5. The Use of a Secondary Relevant Question as a Control

		ST	ST	SAT	MQT	Total
	R	−1	0	+1	+1	+1
3	G	0	0	0	0	0
	C	−1	+1	0	−1	−1
	R	0	−1	+1	+1	+1
5	G	0	0	0	+1	+1
	C	−1	+1	−1	0	−1
	R	−1	0	+1	0	0
8	G	0	0	−1	0	−1
	C	+1	0	−1	+1	+1
	R	−1	−1	−1	0	−3
9	G	0	−1	+1	−1	−1
	C	−1	−1	−1	0	−3

There are other examples that also could be specifically cited that demonstrate the problems with simply adding up numerical scores and adhering to preestablished cutoff levels in determining truth or deception. In the Reid technique, numerical scoring provides a means of visualizing response discrimination within each question, each parameter, and each test. In formulating a final diagnosis of truth or deception, therefore, the examiner takes into consideration that the subject is potentially under different levels of motivation between different tests, that relevant and control questions differ in the degree of emotional weight the subject may apply to them, and that there are parameter distinctions that must be taken into consideration for different subjects. The following are some guidelines used during chart interpretation:

1. A subject who is truthful on the first two straight-through tests but becomes progressively more responsive to the relevant questions on the SAT to the point that he appears deceptive on the MQT is probably telling the truth.

2. A truthful subject may respond significantly to relevant questions during the SAT. This is especially true if the issue under investigation is emotional or the subject has previously been interrogated. In this case, little weight should be placed on the deceptive responses occurring on the SAT if the other tests indicate truthfulness.

3. The stimulation test, in some cases, can cause a subject to become hyporesponsive on subsequent tests. In these situations an opinion can be based on responses occurring on the first straight-through test, if the responses are very clear (this phenomenon is generally associated with truthful subjects).

4. A subject who exhibits consistent responses to a control question throughout the examination and inconsistently responds to different relevant questions on different tests is probably telling the truth to the issue under investigation.

5. Hyporesponsive subjects who are physically and psychologically capable of responding should be considered more truthful. Obviously the examiner wants to eliminate such factors as fatigue, depression, and certain medication and drug use.

6. Subjects who respond inconsistently to different relevant questions on different tests are frequently not telling the truth to a matter related to the investigation as opposed to the principal issue.

7. If the mixed-question test is inconsistent with the other tests (either truthful or deceptive), less weight should be placed on the mixed-question test.

THE RELEVANT-IRRELEVANT TECHNIQUE

10

Paul K. Minor

There is no such thing as a "lie detector." There are no instruments recording bodily changes . . . that deserve the name of "lie detector" any more than a stethoscope, a clinical thermometer, or a blood count apparatus with a microscope can be called an "appendicitis detector."

—Leonarde Keeler

The relevant-irrelevant (R-I) technique is the polygraph examination testing sequence from which the other most common techniques originated. The R-I technique is a highly versatile, high-utility test. It is comparable in accuracy to the other techniques in general use and may actually exceed them in some specific issue situations. It is also the technique of choice by a majority of examiners in preemployment and employee screening situations.

One of the few studies that directly compared the R-I and a standard control question test dealt with the administering of counterintelligence screening examinations.[1] This study concluded that the R-I technique and the reviewed control question test, MGQT format, produce similar results. They were similarly successful in developing information and were equally easy to interpret. The few significant differences that did occur suggest that the R-I technique testing approach may be preferable in counterintelligence suitability screening cases because time is required and fewer polygraph charts are necessary to reach a conclusion.

Haney concluded that in specific issue criminal testing situations there was no appreciable difference between the R-I and control question techniques—the R-I being successful seventy times and the control question technique being successful sixty-eight times in the total where both techniques were used in tandem.[2]

The R-I technique was developed by Leonarde Keeler and others. It is also known as the I-R technique, the general question technique (GQT), the Keeler technique, and the modified relevant-irrelevant (MR-I) technique.

The contemporary R-I technique is not simply a listing of relevant questions interspersed with irrelevant questions as it was in the late 1940s and early 1950s. As used today, it is a structured, complex testing sequence that is individually tailored to each examination scenario.

THEORY

Like all other polygraph testing techniques, the R-I is based on the belief that, with proper pretest interviewing, test question structure, and sequencing, an involuntary psychophysiological reaction will occur when an examinee is asked a specific question about an issue that is important to his or her well-being and to which that person is deceptive. This psychophysiological reaction will be distinguishable from the examinee's norm, taking into consideration the excitement level of the situational setting. The R-I technique employs relevant questions, control questions, irrelevant questions. The following principles apply to all specific issue R-I testing situations:

1. Truthful examinees know they are telling the truth to all aspects of the matter at issue.

2. Deceptive examinees know the matter that is at issue and prior to testing have made a conscious decision to deceive in all or certain portions of the story that they will put forth.

3. Truthful examinees have a mental set around their truthfulness—that they had nothing to do with the crime and are deliberately harboring no guilty

knowledge that they have not previously divulged. Their points of concern will be the overall situation in which they now find themselves, the fact that they are *connected* to the event at issue, the circumstances that connects them to this event, any guilt feelings or feelings of responsibility that they may have toward the event in question.

4. Truthful examinees have the expectation that they will be found to be truthful. They have concern for the relevant area but do not feel threatened by it. The more active threat will come from questions that deal with opportunity and their situational link to the crime or issue. Therefore, the mental set will deal with this overall situation and ties or situational links to the issue.

5. The deceptive examinee comes into the examination with the conscious goal of being reported as truthful. The areas of deception have been carefully thought out, and decisions have been made as to the position that will be taken to these issues based on known facts, other considerations, and so on. The story to be put forward will be material worked out and made to conform as much as possible with known facts and anticipated evidence. The mental set will be on the areas in which the examinee has decided to be deceptive. If the person is faced with a new situation or unanticipated evidence during the pretest interview phase, these decisions will be made as the situation arises.

Occasionally, examinees will attune to only one area or one question and react only to that area, although they are deceptive to other areas in the question sequence. Backster called this the anticlimax dampening concept.[3] This concept is valid in R-I and control testing situations.

CONTROL QUESTIONS (R-I)

Control questions, in the broad sense, are questions in a series that have comparative value against the question at issue. All known polygraph testing techniques use some type of control questions.

Legitimate control questions may be known truth, known lie, probable lie, questions with deliberate ambiguity, questions with measured relevance, questions with broad relevance, and so forth. The type of control question used is dictated by the type of examination technique the examiner chooses to use, the general issue scenario, examinee peculiarities, and so on.

Control questions generally used with the R-I are of measured relevance to the issue to be determined. These control questions are carefully designed to pertain to the situational setting of the individual's involvement in the crime or issue to be resolved. These questions will generally, but not necessarily, have a yes answer and when possible will progress from a situational link to the incident, to an opportunity to commit the crime. The question sequence may then progress in relevancy to the direct relevant question.

When a technique is used that uses control questions that are outside the relevant issue, the control question may be too strong because inadvertently incorporated behavior may overshadow that of the relevant issue. This is a problem that naive or inexperienced examiners may experience with the ZCT or MGQT.

Control questions were used by Keeler but were called cover questions.[4] These control questions were of the inclusive (relevant) type, not unlike those used in the Reid test. These cover questions, however, were used for more than their comparative value. The examiner also had a genuine interest in whether the examinee ever had committed a similar crime. John Reid introduced the idea of using these questions strictly as probably lie control questions. Interrogation was not normally conducted regarding control question reactions to verify the lie and possibly solve crimes other than the one in question. Keeler also used irrelevant questions, the intent question (sacrifice relevant), and nonlie relevant questions that linked the examinee to the event as comparative points against which the relevant questions were compared.

By introducing non–issue-related control questions, the examiner artificially causes conflict in the truthful examinee's decision-making process by presenting the examinee with a paradox. The truthful examinee is sure that he or she is not deliberately misrepresenting the facts pertaining to the matter. By the introduction of known or probable lie control questions, the truthful examinee is skillfully placed into a situation where he or she cannot be completely truthful for fear of casting serious doubt on his or her credibility to the relevant issue. The examinee is placed in a dilemma that was not anticipated and for which he or she is unprepared.

Control questions of the R-I technique should not be contrived to cause reaction but should capitalize on their linking of the examinee to the event. They should serve as a vehicle to introduce the examinee to the issue in a logical interrogatory form and allow possible guilt feelings, anger, frustration, and so forth to be vented in areas other than at the direct relevant questions. These questions allow the truthful examinee to react to the reasons he is tied to or associated to the issue in question. They provide a base line of comparison that includes the excitement level of the issue itself.

Example A: Assume that Jake is suspected of killing Bill, a friend of forty years. Jake admits visiting Bill shortly before the estimated time of death. Further, assume that Jake may be innocent but feel extreme loss, frustration, and some guilt in that he may have somehow let his friend down in a time of need. A possible R-I question sequence for example A follows:

Yellow	A. Is your first name Jake?	Yes
Yellow	B. Are you a citizen of the United States?	Yes

Yellow/red	1. Is it your intent to lie to me about anything here today?	No
Yellow/green	2. Are you aware that Bill Jones was killed on or about July 2?	Yes
Yellow	C. Are you a resident of the state of Virginia?	Yes
Green/red	3. Were you acquainted with Bill Jones?	Yes
Red/green	3. Were you in Bill's house on July 2?	Yes
Yellow	D. Are you now in the city of Richmond?	Yes
Red	5. Do you know who shot Bill Jones?	No
Red	6. Did you shoot Bill Jones?	No
Yellow	E. Is your full name Jake Elmore Smith?	Yes
Green/yellow	7. Are you afraid you might fail this test?	(Yes/No)

Example B: The body of Little Running Elk was found about four miles from the home of Buffalo Tail Wags. The cause of death was determined to be a .22 caliber gunshot wound. When questioned by reservation police, Buffalo Tail Wags stated that Little Running Elk had been at his house the previous evening in a drunken state but had departed on foot leaving his pickup truck at the home of Buffalo Tail. A search of the truck revealed traces of what was believed to be blood and a .22 rifle.

As a result of further questioning, Buffalo Tail Wags stated that on the night in question he had been drinking with Little Running Elk, Big Bear Jump, and Jacob Holds Close. He stated that all had been drinking heavily but maintained that Running Elk had left his house on foot and that he had no idea as to what happened to him after his departure. A possible question sequence for example B follows:

Yellow	A. Are you more than twenty-five years old?	Yes
Yellow	B. Are you called Buffalo Tail Wags?	Yes
Yellow/red	1. Do you intend to try to mislead me here today?	No
Yellow/green	2. Are you aware that this test concerns the death of Little Running Elk?	Yes
Yellow	C. Are you now in Flagstaff, Arizona?	Yes
Green/red	3. Was Running Elk at your house on the evening of September 23?	Yes
Green/red	4. Are you aware that Running Elk was shot sometime during the night of September 23?	Yes
Yellow	D. Do you live on the Blue Lake Reservation?	Yes

Red	5. Are you lying to me in any way about what happened to Running Elk?	No
Red	6. Do you know who shot Running Elk?	No
Yellow	7. Did you shoot Running Elk?	No
Yellow	E. Is today Tuesday?	Yes
Green/yellow	8. Are you now in the state of Montana?	No

Note: Questions such as 8 above are not surprise questions, but as stated elsewhere all question matter and questions are discussed thoroughly with the examinee to eliminate any surprise factor.

Example C: On July 23, 1984, $5,000 was reported missing from a teller cage of the First National Bank of Moline. The teller stated that she missed the money when she balanced her receipts at the end of the day. She further stated that she had reviewed her daily transactions and could not see where she could possibly have made a $5,000 error. A possible question sequence for example C follows:

Irrelevant	A. Is your first name Karen?	Yes
Irrelevant	B. Are you employed at the First National Bank of Moline?	Yes
Sacrifice relevant	1. Do you intend to try to mislead me about anything during this examination?	No
Irrelevant	2. Are you now in the state of Illinois?	Yes
Situational control	3. Were you working at the bank on July 23?	Yes
Irrelevant	C. Is today Tuesday?	Yes
Situational control	4. Did you report $5,000 missing from your bank on July 23?	Yes
Irrelevant	D. Do you live in county of Moline?	Yes
Red	5. Do you know for sure what happened to that missing money?	No
Red	6. Did you steal the money?	No
Irrelevant	E. Are you now in the state of Illinois?	Yes
Situational control	7. Did you prepare in any way for this test?	No

Note: Reports such as this frequently are true to the point of money missing;

however, not in the way the report implies. In many cases, the money is missing due to shortages accumulated over a period of time. These shortages may be due to smaller thefts or legitimate errors. The teller must be pretested on question 5 to cover these possibilities.

Example D: Suspect teller in example C was diagnosed truthful. Another teller who had access may be examined as follows:

A . Irrelevant

B . Irrelevant

1. Do you intend to lie to me about anything?

2. Were you working at the bank on July 23?

C. Irrelevant

3. Are you aware that $5,000 was reported missing from station 22?

4. Do you suspect anyone in particular of stealing that money?

F. Irrelevant

7. Have you tried in any way to ensure that you will pass this test?

PRETEST PROCEDURE

When using the ZCT or MGQT, it is necessary to review the test questions verbatim. These questions are specifically identified for the examinee as being the questions that are to be asked during the testing phase of the examination to the exclusion of any others. This is to cause psychological turmoil in the mind of the person who is truthful to the relevant area and to allow the psychological set to flow to one or the other area of control or relevant questions. These questions are normally reviewed more than once for reinforcement.

This is not necessary or normally desirable when using the R-I. When the R-I technique is used, as with the other techniques, the examiner is to discuss the overall issue in detail with the examinee during the pretest interview phase. During the discussion, the examiner is to ensure that all the questions to be asked during the examination are asked and pursued to the extent that a clear unequivocal answer is received. Prior to testing, the examiner should ensure that all questions to be used have been asked and discussed. The examinee should be told that, in addition to the questions already discussed, there will be questions dealing with present domicile, employment, location, and so forth. The irrelevant questions then should be specifically reviewed. The examiner never should use surprise questions.

QUESTION CONSTRUCTION

Irrelevant questions should not call for an answer that is disputable in any way, refer to the relevant issue, or be likely to cause controversy. Irrelevant questions usually are designed to require a yes answer. A no answer is permissible if the question is not disputable, argumentative, or controversial. Irrelevant questions required to complete the series should be reviewed. No pool of extra questions ever should be reviewed or used. In the event that an irrelevant question needs to be used out of sequence due to movement, an irrelevant from the normal listing may be repeated. Examples follow:

Are you now in Virginia?	Yes
Are you now in the state of Maryland?	No
Do you live in Petersburg?	Yes
Is today Tuesday?	Yes

Control questions should relate to the general situation in which the examinee now find himself or herself. Control questions asked in the sequence prior to the "Did you . . ." questions should generally pertain to the examinee's relevant situational setting or environment prior to the event, lead into the present situation, and then allow the presentation to the relevant questions in a logical fashion. Questions pertaining to unrelated events, which require a major refocusing of one's attention or concentration, common in other techniques, should be avoided. A standard progression would be

1. Identify the target;
2. Establish the examinee's linkage to the event;
3. State suspicions;
4. Explore knowledge/secondary involvement;
5. Explore direct involvement.

Relevant questions are short, concise, and direct. Normal rules apply. No more than three per series is most desirable. As additional questions are added, however, validity of reactions may diminish due to such things as dissipation of reaction potential, confusion, or the probing of ambiguous areas. Figure 10–1 provides an example of the four R-I charts presented in this chapter.

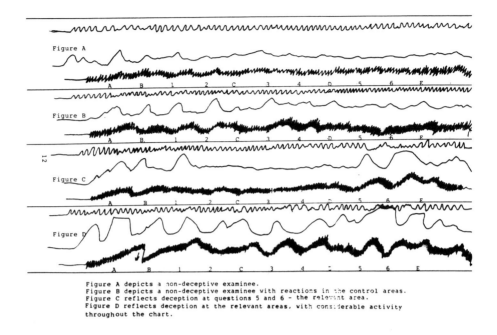

Figure A depicts a non-deceptive examinee.
Figure B depicts a non-deceptive examinee with reactions in the control areas.
Figure C reflects deception at questions 5 and 6 - the relevant area.
Figure D reflects deception at the relevant areas, with considerable activity throughout the chart.

Figure 10–1. R-I Series

PRECLUSIONS TO POLYGRAPH TESTING

11

It's not the people in prison who worry me; it is the people who aren't.

—Earl of Arvon

Polygraph testing is literally a voluntary procedure. Although it is true that individuals can be indirectly or directly coerced into participating, if they choose, an examination simply cannot be administered. Constant muscle movements, controlled breathing, or noncompliance with the instructions are more than sufficient to preclude testing. Excluding situations of this nature, anyone can be examined, but some subjects, because of certain physical or psychiatric conditions, cannot be evaluated accurately. There are others, however, whom it would not be wise to examine.

An individual never should be tested if there is any possibility that examination might worsen an already existing condition. For example, convulsions could be induced in an epileptic and an infarction might be brought about in a person with a significant coronary problem because of the stress associated with the procedure. It is conceivable that paranoid symptoms might be exacerbated if the examination is incorporated into the delusional state. Whenever any question exists about the effect of the procedure on the well-being of the subject, an evaluation should not be initiated without the written approval of the subject's treating physician.

Other conditions exist in which there is little likelihood of damage being caused to the examinees; the risk instead is to the polygraphist. The evaluation of a pregnant woman is a case in point. Testing can be accurately conducted, and there is little or no danger to either the woman or the fetus through the test procedures or the associated stress. However, if a problem such as a miscarriage ever were to occur at some later time, blame could be placed on the examination. In the litigious society in which we live, professionals are forced to practice defensively by avoiding evaluations of this type.

Polygraphists should be aware of certain psychiatric disorders because of questions about suitability for testing. Of the functional (nonorganic) disorders, the three major classifications discussed here are the psychosis, neurosis, and character disorders.[1]

PSYCHOSIS

This category includes those individuals with major personality disturbances who are characterized by a marked distortion and loss of contact with reality, severe personality decompensation, and an inability to function in a job situation or to relate to others. Although major tranquilizers such as Stelazine and Thorazine have allowed these individuals to remain out of a hospital situation, they often can live only marginal existences. Many live on skid row, others in halfway houses, and others are supported by families. Their behavior may range from bizarre to eccentric, based on the types of psychotic state, the level of chronicity, and the severity of their disorder. In legal terms, they are labeled insane or as having a mental disease that may result in their not being legally responsible for their actions.

The most common of the psychotic states is schizophrenia. Although it sometimes is called a split personality, it refers to the disintegration of the personality and should not be confused with the multiple personality that was described so graphically in the book *Three Faces of Eve*.[2]

Although there is considerable variety in symptomatology, certain characteristics are typical of this disorder. One of the major symptoms is the presence of a thought disorder. Logic is missing, and individuals simply may not make sense or sound coherent. They may experience hallucinations (perceiving stimuli that do not exist), delusions (false ideas such as the belief that one is God), echolalia (the meaningless repetition of words), condensation (a fusion of concepts into one such as describing something as a beetle bird), and disorientation (confusion as to time, place, or person). There is also a flattening or inappropriate affect (emotion). The person seems emotionally unaffected by situations that would cause others to be hurt, fearful, saddened, or angry. Schizophrenics have great difficulty in relating to others, and as their condition deteriorates, they begin to restrict their contact with others, becoming more seclusive and withdrawn into themselves.

An acute phase of the disorder should be readily recognized by the polygraphist because the bizarre symptoms are obvious. The schizophrenic listens to voices and claims that the neighbors are using ray guns against him because he is the president, which are easily recognizable signs of the disease process. However, with time, schizophrenics tend to burn out and become dull, emotionless loners who are uncommunicative. Eking out an existence, they are like empty cardboard figures and may appear retarded. It would seem unlikely that any polygraphist would consider administering an examination to anyone in this state. There are some schizophrenics whose condition is not severe and who would not be recognized as being psychotic, and some borderline cases swing in and out of this state so that at times they are viewed by others as only being odd.

It is logical to assume that the more severe the decompensation, the less likely that polygraph testing can achieve accurate results. Heckel et al. evaluated five normal, five neurotic, and five psychotic subjects.[3] Four polygraphists correctly diagnosed truth or deception in all of the normals, but they were accurate in only 75 percent of the neurotics and 45 percent of the psychotics. No inconclusive findings were reported for the normal group, but 20 percent of the neurotics and 38 percent of the psychotics fell into that category. Excluding the inconclusives the polygraphists were accurate on 87 percent of the neurotics and 69 percent of the psychotics. Although complete agreement existed among the four polygraphists for the normals, consistency (reliability) decreased with the intensity of this disorder. In another study of the testability of schizophrenics, Abrams examined twenty hospitalized schizophrenics using three peak of tension tests each administered twice.[4] Most of the twenty subjects were found to be inconclusive, and if their charts were excluded, there would not have been a large enough sample to evaluate the effectiveness of the polygraph with this population. Forcing a decision of truth or deception, three examiners obtained an average accuracy of 67 percent and a mean level of agreement of 71 percent. Although these are the only two reported experiments with a psychotic population, the results indicate that a high proportion of psychotics would provide inconclusive results and that the accuracy level on those remaining would be less than found in a normal population. These findings argue against the administration of polygraph tests to individuals in this psychiatric category. When psychotics are inadvertently tested because their symptoms are not recognized, a natural safeguard exists in that many of the findings will be seen as inconclusive.

A second psychotic diagnostic category is made up of the affective disorders. The word "affect" means emotion, and an affective disorder is a disturbance of mood generally involving depression or elation. At a psychotic level this disturbance involves profound depression, manic symptomatology, or a combination of the two in which the patient cycles back and forth between them and periods of normalcy. The predominant mood in the manic state is one of expansiveness, during which time the patients demonstrate hyperactivity, inflated self-esteem, and a reduced need for sleep. In this euphoric state they enthusiastically become involved in planning all manner of things but do not have the ability to complete what they start. They may invest money unwisely using poor judgment that is obvious to everyone but them. Like the rest of their lives, their speech is quite pressured in that they are quite verbose demonstrating a flight of ideas as they flit from one subject to another. They do not display the disorganized confused speech patterns of the schizophrenic, for what they say makes sense, it is only that they cannot stay on one subject for any length of time.

In a heightened manic state these individuals would be completely untestable because of their hyperactivity, distractibility, and generalized pressure to respond. In a less extreme state it would be possible to test them, but again problems would occur due to their difficulties in concentration. There has been no research on the validity of the polygraph with the manic patient; it can be assumed that like the schizophrenic, many would respond inconclusively and that validity would be lowered. Therefore, testing these individuals is not recommended. It should be recognized, however, that their mood swings will include periods in which they function at a normal level so it would be wise for the examiner to delay any testing until that time.

At the other end of the affective disorders is depression. When it is profound, it can reach psychotic proportions. Unlike the normal experience of sadness that everyone experiences, severely depressed patients can be mute and unresponsive to the extent that the saliva may putrify in their mouths. When their condition is that extreme, it can easily be mistaken for the withdrawal of the schizophrenic. Polygraphists will not be seeing examinees who are that disturbed, but those with lesser states are so involved with their depression that they may not have sufficient concern about the test to react appropriately to the questions. Their depression tends to blunt the fear, anger, or conflict that causes sympathetic arousal and that allows for the detection of truth or deception.

The symptoms typically seen in a depressed person are tied in with an overall retardation that is part of their movement, speech, and thinking. This does not imply intellectual dullness, but a general slowing of responses. They are apathetic and difficult to arouse emotionally, usually having a sleep and appetite disturbance. Physical symptoms are common, as is suicidal ideation. Depression is generally precipitated by a loss of some nature, such as a relationship or a job. The examiner also should be aware that a defendant facing the stress of a possible conviction that might result in the loss of many things could be thrown into a despondant or a decompensated state. It is conceivable that the criminal act was not committed during a state of emotional disturbance but that the deterioration occurred after he was apprehended. This is important from a psychiatric standpoint because one of the questions asked by a court relates to the individual's mental state during the commission of the crime. The fact that the defendant is depressed or psychotic after apprehension does not at all mean that he or she was in this state when the criminal act was committed.

Once again, there is no research available on the testing of individuals with deep depression. It is assumed that there would be a blunting of affect so that the fear of detection of a lie on both the control and relevant questions could be reduced, creating a greater likelihood of an inconclusive reaction rather than an inaccurate finding.

The final psychotic state to be discussed is the paranoid, which deals with a condition that is likely to come in conflict with the law. The principal feature of this condition is a persecutory delusion. It is often so well organized as to be quite believable to the extent that one must check the environment to determine if it is real or imagined. If the original premise is accepted, all that follows appears to be logical. A case in point was a man who was privy to considerable top secret data and believed that Russian agents were trying to kidnap him. If one accepted this first assumption as accurate, then everything else made sense. He saw people watching him and following him, and he interpreted such occurrences as the position of a neighbor's window blinds and how his newspaper was placed as signals to the Russian agents. Perceiving danger all around and enemies coming at him from all directions makes the paranoid prone to fight back, and it is at this time that they can be dangerous.

There is also a paranoid disorder in the schizophrenic category that is not logical and is easy to recognize as growing out of a mental condition. There may be bizarre hallucinations, and the delusions may be filled with ray guns and aliens from outer space.

If the delusions in any manner touch on the issue to be studied then clearly the emotional disorder will impact on the test results. Polygraph literature frequently indicates that if an examinee believes that he did not commit a specific act even if he did, he will pass the test. Although this is a logical assumption, the research argues against this. The writer has examined delusional psychotics and tested them on the truthfulness of their delusional belief. Although they were completely convinced of their belief they failed the test. In other instances, subjects claiming amnesia were examined for psychological purposes rather than for legal reasons. In these cases the person had absolutely nothing to lose if deception were found; instead, the results would serve to assist in the treatment process. Once again, it was found that deception had occurred even though the subject had complete amnesia for the act that they had unquestionably committed. It is the opinion of this writer that the polygraph tests unconscious processes as well as conscious recall, which has been corroborated by research in this area.

Bitterman and Marcuse had subjects select one word from a series of words and then hypnotized them, instructing them that they would have no recall of having chosen that word.[5] When they were taken out of the hypnotic state they, in fact, had no memory of that specific word. Employing a peak of tension test, they found that every subject responded to their chosen stimulus despite having no conscious awareness of it. In a somewhat related investigation, Weinstein et al. had half of their subjects commit a mock crime by stealing money from a desk.[6] Those who stole the money (a $1, $5, or $10 bill) were hypnotized and told that they had not taken the money and would have no recall of having committed the act. An equal number of subjects who had not taken the money were hypnotized and told that they had taken the money and then were told which denomination of bill that they had taken. When the polygraphist tested the guilty subjects, his findings in each case were inconclusive. Of interest, every subject who did not participate in the mock crime but was told that he had under hypnosis was found deceptive. Moreover, the examiner accurately detected which bill they had purportedly taken. In research by Germann similar results were obtained with lying subjects who had been hypnotized[7] Although he found that hypnosis blunted the emotions associated with lying, thereby reducing sympathetic arousal, there was enough leakage of unconscious material to result in inconclusive rather than truthful findings. Had the hypnosis been completely effective, the subjects would have been found to have been truthful, but it was partially successful in that it resulted in inconclusive findings. It should be recognized, however, that these are laboratory studies in which the subjects have nothing to lose if their deception is detected. Therefore, it is felt strongly that in a real situation hypnosis would not be an effective countermeasure. In fact, these were the findings in a number of cases in which the writer has been involved in instances of this sort, and those who used hypnosis were quite easily detected when they lied.

The research findings do suggest that unconscious material can be detected through the polygraph procedure, but current research is not sufficiently convincing to rely on in a discussion of truthfulness or deception. As an aid in criminal investigation it should certainly be considered.

The testing of the paranoid is not recommended for a number of reasons. Although it is likely that the examiner could successfully differentiate delusion from real data through the test procedure, evidence for its accuracy is not sufficiently strong. Moreover, the very nature of the polygraph instrument with its electrical connections and tubing could be interpreted by these subjects as a device to control or injure them in some manner, which would evoke enough emotional disturbance to distort the tracings. If hallucinations were present, they would be a distraction that could not be controlled because the polygraphist would have no idea when the voices were being heard.

NEUROSIS OR ANXIETY DISORDERS

The predominant symptom in this category is anxiety and includes such diagnostic groups as anxiety neurosis, phobic conditions, and the obsessive compulsion disorder. In a somewhat related area are hypochondriacs, hysterics, and the disassociative reactions. In addition to tension and anxiety, these individuals are also troubled with self-doubt, dissatisfaction, physical symptoms such as head and back pain, difficulty in interpersonal relationships, hypersensitivity, and general inefficiency. They are not generally hospitalized and do not engage in violent behavior or experience extreme symptoms like hallucinations, delusions, or thought disturbances. Instead, they are generally ineffectual. They have difficulties in work, in social situations, and in life in general. Therefore, they are unhappy, fearful of doing poorly, of not being accepted by others, and worry about these things, which only adds to their difficulties.

With the exception of their excessive anxiety they do not constitute much of a problem to examine. Their anxious state may make it more difficult to interpret their tracings, but if this were to be severe, it would lead only to an inconclusive chart rather than an invalid finding.

The dissociative reaction is where one separates the awareness of an act from the actual act itself. It occurs in a process, such as in somnambulism (sleep walking), where the individual performs certain acts without awareness of or recall of these actions. Although this reaction has been included in this category, it does not quite fit among the neurotic disorders. The dissociative states are patients suffering from amnesia, fugue, and multiple personality. Amnesia due to psychological factors rather than physical trauma is typically associated with an urge to be out of a situation that is unacceptable. Therefore, patients simply forget everything.

The fugue state (which means "flight") is similar to amnesia and is evidenced when someone suddenly "wakes up" to find he has assumed a new identity and a new life after having left his previously unacceptable life some time back.

But the multiple personality is of most significance for the polygraphist because of the role that the examiner might play with this individual. This person experiences one or more separate and distinct personalities in addition to his or her primary personality. The vast majority of people have conflicting aspects of their personality such as love and hate feelings or ethical or immoral ideas, but these are dealt with by integrating them into the personality as a whole. In contrast to this, the multiple personality finds certain aspects of his or her personality so unacceptable that they are split off and become almost separate entities. In many instances, the primary personality is unrealistic and inhibited, denying unacceptable feelings such as hostility and sexuality. In the secondary personality, therefore, those denied facets come to life as a separate being who can be quite antisocial. It is this personality that may end up in conflict with the law. Most often the primary personality is unaware of the others and experiences only unexplained blackouts and strange phenomena such as excessive mileage on the odometer, clothing soiled that had not been worn, and having complete strangers greet them as if they knew them well. Abrams described a case in which a combination of hypnosis and polygraphy were used to determine involvement in a case of embezzlement.[8] The subject was polygraphed and found deceptive in denying the embezzlement, but she was seen as truthful when she denied faking the existence of the other personality. It was felt that even though the patient had no awareness of having embezzled the funds, she failed that portion of the test because this awareness did exist at an unconscious level.

It should be recognized that defendants frequently attempt to reduce their responsibility for a particular crime through a plea of diminished responsibility or emphasizing the existence of some other mitigating circumstances. This writer feels that many claims of blackouts, as well as occasional multiple personality defenses, fall into this category.[9] An effective interrogation will often bring out feigning of these conditions. The easiest manner of accomplishing this is to know something about the particular disorder itself and point out the difference in their enactment of the disease and the disease itself. In the well-known Hillside strangler case, Orne pointed out to Bianchi that individuals with a multiple personality have more than two separate personalities.[10] Shortly thereafter, Bianchi developed a third personality. In a somewhat similar situation, a suspect claiming amnesia involving a homicide of his parents was told that people with amnesia typically recall bits and pieces of a particular experience rather than having no memory for the event at all. He then remembered some aspects of the killing, and from there it was easy to manipulate him into recalling more until he was ready to reveal the whole story.

It is felt that the polygraph can be a significant addition to the investigation of any case where a multiple personality is allegedly involved. If the other personality can be coaxed out through hypnosis, the crime situation can be clarified. In addition, it is believed that the polygraphist could be helpful in determining the identity of an amnesiac through the use of a searching peak of tension procedure. By asking questions related to age, place of birth, and residence, the examiner can narrow the search. Although this writer has never had the opportunity to test this notion, some degree of success has been achieved in a search for lost objects.

PERSONALITY OR CHARACTER DISORDERS

These disturbances differ from those already discussed in that they are the result of deviant development rather than from a decompensation under stress. Where the psychotic disintegrates in a tension-provoking situation and a neurotic responds with an increase in symptoms, an individual suffering from a personality disorder has simply developed a maladaptive personality. Just as all people form particular sets of personality traits, whether passive, outgoing, submissive, or shy, these long held patterns of behavior and attitudes are part of the individual and basically resistant to change. Although there are a number of different kinds of personality disorders, it is the psychopath who is of real significance to the polygraphist.

The psychopath or sociopath, as the individual with this disorder also is called, makes up about a third of the prison population and assumedly will comprise a large percentage of the individuals each examiner tests. They are not psychotic, and no matter how bizarre their behavior, they are largely responsible for their actions. Psychopaths manifest a lack of moral development and do not follow or accept usual codes of behavior. Typically, they are bright, spontaneous, and often quite charming. They appear to relate well and develop friendships easily, but they are superficial and interested only in gratifying their own needs. Psychopaths lack the ability to empathize with others so that they feel no sympathy for anyone and have a callous disregard for the feelings of others. There is little or no conscience, and therefore no remorse is felt for even the most heinous acts that they commit. They are impulsive, need excitement, and are prone to deviant and unconventional behavior. They lack the ability to put off immediate pleasure for some future gain as they self-centeredly operate only to gratify their immediate needs. They experience considerable difficulty with authorities and tend to be negativistic, often becoming involved in criminal activities. They do not profit from treatment, rehabilitation, or punishment, and only the aging process reduces their acting-out behavior. Their major defenses are projection and rationalization. They are most apt to project the blame for their difficulties onto others: "The store should have had an alarm system," or "If the prison system had better treatment facilities, I would not be in the fix I'm in now." Rationalization means to give an acceptable reason for a real one, and sociopaths will say things like, "It's all right to steal from that store because it cheats people all of the time, and it's my way of getting even with them."

The psychopath can be involved in all manner of antisocial activity, from very minor acts to the most serious, some of which will be discussed under the sexual psychopath in chapter 12.

In the past, it was felt that because the psychopath had no sense of guilt and did not experience anxiety to any great extent, he was not amenable to polygraph testing. Even recently, Lykken discussed them in terms of ice water running through their veins, indicating that valid testing on them cannot be conducted.[11] However, Barland and Raskin studied seventy-seven criminal suspects in which portions of the MMPI were administered.[12] A comparison of the polygraph charts of those fifteen who had the highest score on the psychopathy scale was made with those fifteen with the lowest score. No difference in detectability was found, with the mean accuracy being 85 percent. A second investigation by Raskin, in which polygraph tests were administered to forty-eight inmates in a prison facility demonstrated that in a mock crime situation, excluding inconclusives, 96 percent accuracy was achieved with the psychopathic population.[13] These findings indicate that the psychopath can be as readily detected in truth or deception as the nonpsychopathic subject. One should be very wary of their ability to charm, and the examiner should not be influenced by this. In direct contrast to the anxious neurotic, psychopaths will appear self-assured, free of anxiety, open and friendly. They will look directly into the examiner's eyes, creating the appearance of candor and honesty.

Although neither trained nor experienced in diagnosing emotional disorders, the polygraphist should be sufficiently observant to detect blatant symptoms. In all likelihood the polygraphist will be much more able to recognize the "con job" of the psychopath than most mental health specialists but will experience difficulty with the more subtle signs of the other diagnostic categories. Obtaining a good history can be helpful in accomplishing this. Particular emphasis should be placed on past treatment and diagnostic procedures as well as symptomatology. If problems existed in the past, remnants, at least, of these will persist. Learning which medications examinees presently are taking and those used in the past will provide some insight into their condition. Employing a *Physicians' Desk Reference* (PDR) (which should be part of every polygraphist's library), the examiner can ascertain the subject's medical or psychiatric condition based on the drugs prescribed. Lithium, for example, is the treatment of choice for some manic depressive conditions, Valium for anxiety, and Elavil for depression.

The following is a suggested list of questions:

1. Have you ever been hospitalized? For what problems and at what age?
2. Have you ever seen a psychiatrist or psychologist?
   a. When was your treatment and for how long?

b. Did you take medications?

c. Have you ever been treated in a psychiatric setting?

d. How many times, when, and how long?

e. What were the treatment approaches?

f. Were any of the psychiatric hospitalizations involuntary?

g. What were you diagnosed?

h. What symptoms did you experience? Did you ever hear voices?

3. Have you ever had a serious head injury?

4. Have you ever experienced convulsions or had blackouts?

5. Have you had any major illnesses?

6. Have you been in the service? How long? What type of discharge?

7. How much school have you completed?

a. Have you ever been in special classes?

b. Have you ever had academic or behavioral problems?

c. Do you know your intelligence level?

8. Have you had a drinking or drug problem?

Certain organic conditions are particularly relevant to polygraph testing. Intelligence is an important factor, especially at the lower levels. Like most things in life, intelligence falls into a bell-shaped curve, with the average group making up the largest proportion—50 percent of the population falls between IQ 90 and 109. Dull normal IQ is between 80 to 89, while above average is between 110 and 119. These two groups each comprise 32 percent of the population, with half the remaining 18 percent being superior in intelligence (IQ 120 and above) and half retarded (80 IQ and lower). Figure 11–1 shows the bell-shaped curve.

Although it is difficult to estimate intelligence in any exact manner, it can be approximated by responses that indicate how much information the subject has accumulated, vocabulary, mathematical ability, memory, and common sense

Figure 11–1. Distribution of Intelligence
(percentage)

Retarded	Borderline retarded	Dull normal	Average	Above average	Superior	Very superior
<69	70–79	80–89	90–109 50% 82% 95% 100%	110–119	120–129	130>

knowledge. In conversing with the individual approximations can be made by comparing his or her ability with your own or that of acquaintances. If there is some concern about retardation, inability to answer some of the following questions might confirm the examiner's suspicions:

1. What is the capital of England?
2. How many days are there in a year?
3. In what continent is Argentina?
4. What is the population of the United States?
5. Name four men who have been president since 1900.
6. What does this saying mean?
   a. A stitch in time saves nine.
   b. A bird in the hand is worth two in the bush.
   c. An early bird catches the worm.
   d. One hand washes the other.
   e. A penny saved is a penny earned.
7. How much is $6 and $7?
8. How many oranges can you buy for 36¢ if one orange costs 6¢?
9. If you buy 8¢ worth of candy, how much change would you get back from a quarter?
10. How many inches are there in one-and-a-half feet?
11. A man with $18 spends $7.50; how much does he have left?
12. Define the following words:
    a. Winter
    b. Conceal
    c. Regulate
    d. Commence
    e. Cavern
13. How are the following the same? (The answer should be abstract, with animals, for a and directions for b.)
    a. Dog and cat
    b. North and west
    c. Table and chair
    d. Axe and saw
    e. Eye and ear

There is only one study that examines the effectiveness of the polygraph approach with retardates. Abrams evaluated sixteen subjects, nine of whom had IQs of less than 64.[14] They were found to be completely untestable. The remaining seven ranged in IQ from 65 to 80 and were evaluated by two polygraphists. Although they were in complete agreement in their findings, demonstrating high reliability, the average accuracy was only 71 percent. Finding that retarded adults with a mental age below twelve could not be accurately tested, the experimenters hypothesized that testing of normal children below this age would be less than accurate. To test this, Abrams[15] employed three separate peak of tension tests, each administered twice to children between the ages of nine and thirteen. The accuracy noted for detecting deception in the ten-year-old was only 57 percent but for the eleven-, twelve-, and thirteen-year-olds, validity was found to be 83 percent, 96 percent, and 94 percent, respectively. These results would suggest that polygraph testing of at least average intelligence children could be accurately conducted on individuals who are eleven and older. As with the psychotic populations, testing retardates, even those at the borderline level, is not recommended because of the possibility of low validity being obtained.

There are a wide variety of other organic brain dysfunctions that result in symptomatology ranging from intellectual deficit to mental confusion. These might be of a transient or permanent nature and vary with the extent of the damage, the age that it occurred, the area of the central nervous system involved, the progression of the disorder, and the mode of occurrence. The factor responsible for the disorder may be a primary disease of the brain, a systemic disorder that secondarily affects the brain, a toxic agent, or head trauma. Whatever the causation, many different emotional and behavioral abnormalities may be associated with organic mental disorders. The symptoms observed may be the result of the brain damage itself or the psychological reactions that are a direct response to the psychic trauma of the brain changes. Depression, anxiety, and even antisocial behavior may result.

Whether these individuals can be accurately examined is dependent on the degree that their functioning is impaired. Therefore, it falls on the polygraphist to judge the degree of distractibility, inability to comprehend, loss of logical thinking, impairment of memory, and inappropriate affect, and base a decision to test on those factors. If there is the least doubt, the situation should be discussed with the subject's physician, or a consultant should be called in to evaluate the examinee.

The polygraphist should decide whether to make this determination without outside help based on a response to a question that the examiner should ask anytime a significant testing decision needs to be made: How will the opposing attorney argue if the case is heard in court? Will the attorney be able to present a legitimate argument supported by experts in the field that the information available and the experience and training of the examiner were not adequate to make a decision of this nature or that the approach used was not appropriate or sufficient? Each test administered and each decision made should be done as if this case were going to be admitted into evidence and other polygraphists for the opposing side will be reviewing the entire procedure, questions, and charts. Practicing in this defensive manner will inevitably reduce the number of errors made and avoid that one time in court when the polygraphist wishes that the problem had been approached differently.

In contrast to evaluating individuals with psychiatric problems, those with a straightforward medical diagnoses are much less difficult. Although there might be some interference with the responsivity to one of the sensors, it is likely that sufficient data will be available through the other measures to allow the examiner to make a decision. Medication more than the disease is apt to interfere with the examination. The effect of various drugs will be discussed later under countermeasures.

There is, however, one area of interference that can grow out of medical problems, and that is pain. Because it causes changes in autonomic response, it can be expected that it will affect the subject's physiologic responses and therefore his or her tracings. In consideration of this, the extent and type of pain that is present should be evaluated prior to the examination. If the response of pain is rare or minimal in intensity, there is no reason why the subject should not be tested. The examinee should be questioned throughout the evaluation as to how he or she feels so that the issue of pain will not be raised in an attempt to invalidate the findings. It would be wise to note when the subject was asked the questions and the responses. If there is evidence of sharp and frequent pain, the examination should be delayed until this pain does not present a problem.

THE POLYGRAPH AND SEXUAL DEVIANTS

12

It is as difficult to modify the orientation of those who are sexually deviant as it would be to make those of us who are normal, abnormal.

—Stan Abrams

At the present time, the most frequently administered polygraph test involves the alleged child molester. Statistics show that 6 to 62 percent of girls under age ten and 3 to 31 percent of boys in that age category have been sexually abused.[1] Almost all of those acts are carried out by males, and on the occasions when women are involved, it usually is in association with a male.[2] It has generally been assumed that child molesting has always occurred but today is reported more often. However, there have been dramatic increases in two other sexual aberrations as well—rape and serial murders. The increase in rape figures may be partially explained by a greater tendency to report these crimes, and serial murder may show an increase because this crime was in the past not recognizable. There is also a good likelihood that sexual deviancy in general has grown.[3]

The sexual revolution not only has produced a significant change in values and therefore behavior but also has been responsible for an almost constant display of explicit sex in the media. Movie viewers and magazine readers are bombarded by constant images of sex that affect the erotic urges of the normal and deviant alike. Added to this is the violence often associated with sexual activity. Research has demonstrated that this has made violence to women more acceptable, and one investigation reported that 60 percent of normal males would force sex on a woman if they felt that they could get away with it.[4]

Added to these changes in sexual mores is the effect of the women's liberation movement. As women gain economic and social strengths, they interact with men less passively and ingratiatingly. Males who are now angry at women also feel threatened by them. As women have become more aggressive, more men have become impotent.

Figure 12–1. Drawing by a Serial Murderer

Some sexually dysfunctional men find sexual gratification through nonthreatening activities such as fetishism (sexual stimulation attached to a nonsexual object such as shoes or women's undergarments) or pedophilia (sexual attraction to children). Others gratify their sexual needs violently by raping or committing serial murders. The three drawings in figures 12–1, 12–2, and 12–3 done by serial murderers reveal their view of themselves as weak, helpless, and emasculated as compared to their perception of women. Two sets of drawings were done of nudes, and although the females have all of their appropriate body parts, the males have no genitals. In the third drawings, the male is puny as compared to the large and threatening female.

THE SERIAL MURDERER

Although this is still a relatively rare crime pattern, when it occurs it is given a great deal of media attention. In nineteenth-century London Jack the Ripper killed and mutilated six prostitutes, but there are few other reports of this manner of murder until the twentieth century. The lust or recreational murderers, as they are also called, seem to occur more frequently.

For some reason, the sadistic and sexual needs of the serial murderer have been fused together so that violence greatly enhances the sexual experience or even

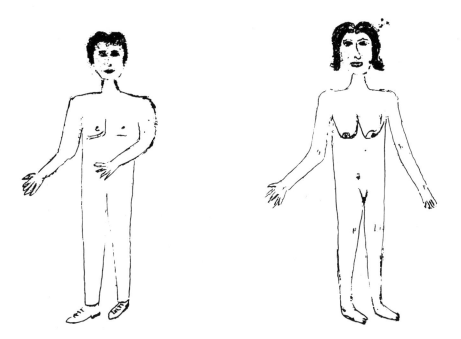

Figure 12–2. Drawing by a Serial Murderer

Figure 12–3. Drawing by a Serial Murderer

makes it possible. A great deal of fantasy occurs prior to the act, causing a buildup of tension that makes the act that follows almost compulsive. During this fantasy period every action is planned and enacted over and over again in the killer's mind. He only has to find a victim, and this is, generally, accidental, in that he may drive until he finally finds someone who is vulnerable. Mutilation of the sexual parts of the body may precede the killing or might be done afterwards. Intercourse also may take place before or after death, and in some instances, the murderer may only masturbate in the area of the body. Torture is something akin to foreplay, and the killing, which is of a contact nature, may stimulate a spontaneous ejaculation. It is as if the thrust of the knife is a symbolic penetration. One serial murderer indicated that before he started killing he had burglarized houses for women's underclothing. He would automatically ejaculate everytime he entered a house through a window. With repetition, some of the excitement was reduced, and at times he would have to go through the window a number of times before this reaction occurred.

Frequently, the killer will leave his trademark in the manner in which the mutilation is carried out, by the removal of certain body parts or clothing, or even the positioning of the body. The Boston Strangler left his victims facing the door with their legs spread apart so that this would be the first thing seen by whoever entered.[5] It was as if it were an attempt to debase the victim even further. When body parts are taken it may be to help the killer relive the murder and be restimulated by it at some later time, and cannibalism is not unusual. One serial murderer in Oregon was found to have a number of vaginas neatly packaged in his freezer for later use.

These individuals are sexual psychopaths with personalities like the psychopaths described in chapter 11. They are unable to empathize with others and so they are capable of inflicting great pain on their victims. Cortez kidnapped two eleven-year-old girls and tortured one of them for twenty-four hours before finally killing her. They feel no remorse for their actions, and therefore there are no limits to their brutality. One killer sent the foot of his victim to her parents to add further to their pain and suffering. They are generally clever and can develop all manner of convincing arguments to help themselves. The Hillside Strangler was quite capable of manipulating some psychologists and psychiatrists into believing he had a multiple personality and should not be held responsible for his acts.[6] Another of these individuals so convinced his minister that he found Jesus that the congregation picketed the prison with placards demanding his release.

As evidenced by the Williams case in Alabama and the Green River murders in Seattle, serial murderers are difficult to apprehend. Primarily, these are stranger murders with accidental victims so that good leads are not available.[7] Often the victims are prostitutes, in part because they are easily accessible victims. These murderers do not attack anyone on their home ground, but instead they are sufficiently mobile to go some distance in their search for a victim. To complicate matters further, they are bright and personable and often play helpful roles in the community, so that they do not appear to be capable of committing heinous acts. When sensationalism is involved, copycat killers can complicate the picture even further. Serial murderers generally follow the same modus operandi, however, which allows law enforcement to trace their path, even through different states.

In crimes of this nature, the polygraphist can play an extremely important role. Typically, many suspects exist and can be effectively screened through the polygraph procedure. Ideally, law enforcement authorities should withhold significant details of the homicides so that peak of tension testing can be utilized. Each murder should be dealt with in a separate test, which allows for a firm basis of comparison between the subject's responses to the various killings. Some cases in which he could not have been involved should be included in the testing.

Although the guilt complex approach has fallen into disuse, this is one situation where it can be an effective addition to the test battery.[8]

When using the control question technique, it must be recognized that the efficiency of this approach may be reduced because the subject may be equally concerned about murders that he has committed in the past. Large physiological reactions may occur in response to the control questions even though he is guilty of the murder in question. Therefore, more emphasis should be placed on guilty knowledge tests but with the recognition that more false negatives (calling a deceptive person truthful) can occur in this procedure.[9]

Although it occurs infrequently, there are instances of the psychotic serial murderer, who is much more difficult to accurately examine.[10] Unlike the killings committed by the sexual psychopath, these murders are unplanned impulsive acts committed with any weapon at hand close to the area where they live. The mutilations are more extensive and gory. Psychotic serial murderers may return to the scene to further mutilate their victims or satisfy their sexual needs. Needless to say, those individuals are much more easily apprehended then sexual psychopaths.

In contrast to the serial murderer, the mass murderer kills a number of people at the same time.[11] Here the motivation may be revenge or to eliminate witnesses. Because sex is not involved, there are no mutilations and the weapon is generally a gun.

THE RAPIST

Like the serial murderer, the rapist may require a sense of power or have a need to inflict pain in order to enhance or even complete the sexual act. This has been amply demonstrated through the use of the penile plethysmograph.[12] This instrument measures the amount of blood flow to the penis, and the greater amount of blood to the genitals the larger the erection. It is employed in the evaluation and treatment of sexual deviants. By displaying a variety of sexual stimuli, a therapist can determine if the subject is more responsive to children, homosexual acts, or normal adult heterosexual experiences. It has been found that many rapists react sexually to pictures of women being brutalized even without the presence of sexual stimuli.

The penile plethysmograph also provides a measure of progress of treatment. Aversive conditioning is a commonly used treatment approach. Pedophiles (child molesters), for example, will be shown sexual stimuli of children while noxious stimuli (electric shocks or the smell of ammonia) are presented. They also are given the opportunity to achieve positive stimulation through masturbation while observing normal sexual stimuli. Preliminary studies have shown that with time and repetition, the patient becomes more responsive to normal sexual interactions and less excited by children. Of particular interest to polygraphists is the fact that this approach is sometimes used in conjunction with the polygraph to determine if a man who has been accused of child molesting is sexually stimulated by children. His response to pictures of nude children is compared to nude women, and if he responds more to the latter, it is assumed that he has not molested the child. There is a very real weakness in employing the penile plethysmograph in this manner because there is good evidence that there are a number of ways for a guilty subject to cause a false negative response to occur. These findings then might well conflict with the polygraph results because of the ease of using countermeasures with the plethysmograph.

Polygraphists must be aware that rapists may be misleading in another manner. Because they may be more responsive to the sadistic aspect of their act than to the sexual, this response might have some impact on the polygraph findings. Asking a suspected rapist of a child if he touched the child in the vaginal area for sexual reasons might not be effective because his motivation was primarily sadistic. Groth has classified rapists into three categories of rape that can be of assistance in formulating questions; knowing motivation also can be helpful in enhancing the impact of the interrogation, which can be directed toward the suspect's area of vulnerability.[13] In the anger rape, more force is used than required and the victim is traumatized throughout her body. The assault itself is relatively short, with the motivation being to get revenge on women for real or imagined injustices. In contrast to this, in the power rape the victim is not usually physically abused, but instead the motivation is to be able to control the victim. Therefore, the woman may be kept in this situation for an extended period of time. The dynamics involved in this type of need relate to the rapist's strong sense of inadequacy, particularly as a male. In the final group, the sadistic rape, the anger has been eroticized resulting in a long assault with trauma to the sexual parts of the body. Bondage, torture, and mutilation may become part of this act.

There is a new variable that is being added to the rape experience that will have a profound effect on our society. It has been reported that one out of every four women will either be raped or have to fight off a rapist. Obviously these men are self-centered, angry, and uncaring of any hurt that they create, and in fact, inflicting pain on others is an important part of rape. The rapist with AIDS will be even more angry with the world about him, and instead of attempting to protect those around him from contracting this disease, he may take pleasure in the new power that it provides him. Whether it is an assault in the streets or the prisons, to an adult or a child, he can condemn his victim to a slow and painful death and yet will be immune from punishment for the murders that he commits.

THE CHILD MOLESTER

Child molesting has become a complicated phenomenon. Examiners have been flooded with tests that were almost totally indicative of deception, only later to find that some accusations made by teenagers were made for revenge or manipulative purposes. Accusations also have been made by mothers to aid in custody battles. From this chaos, new groups of specialists have evolved: those who evaluate the child victim with anatomically correct dolls to determine their truthfulness; professionals who do psychological and psychiatric evaluations of the accused to ascertain if his personality is like that of the child molester; those who operate the penile plethysmograph; those who treat the victims; and those who treat the abusers. Court orders mandating years of treatment have made child molesting a big business. In some instances, particularly when incest is involved, it is likely that there has been only one victim. However, when the molester is a friendly neighbor, A Boy Scout leader, or a nursery school worker, the examiner must consider the possibility of multiple victims. The Oregon State Hospital reported that fifty-three offenders had admitted to being responsible for 23,000 sexual acts with charges being brought in only eighty-eight of these cases.[14]

As in the case of the serial murderer, the examiner must formulate control questions recognizing that the suspect probably has had a series of victims. More than that, the polygraphist is to determine whether the accused has molested the particular child in question but also other children as well. The questions should not be limited by using the word "girl" because there is ample evidence that boys are abused as well. Queries related to whether the suspect has been involved in the making or sale of pornography, in prostitution, or even in the kidnapping and sale of children should be considered. Child pornography has become big business that sometimes includes brutalizing or even killing children specifically for the purpose of a film. Pictures of child victims are circulated throughout the country for the purpose of sale or trade, so this area also is pertinent for questioning. When the children reach an age in which they are less desirable to pedophiles, they are discarded and left to their own resources, which often means walking the streets as teenage prostitutes. To complete the circle of abuse, as the abused grow older, they often become the abusers. Therefore, it is quite pertinent during the pretest phase of the examination to ask the subject questions about any unusual sexual experiences that he has had. This is helpful in the development of control questions, but an admission to having been molested as a child should serve as a warning signal to the examiner. Moreover, if the subject is found to be deceptive, his having been abused as a child serves as a handy rationalization to present to him to open the door for an admission.

As is always the case, the key questions are more easily developed than the control questions. Recognizing that there is some tendency to obtain more false positives (finding the truthful person deceptive) with the control question technique, care must be employed in developing effective controls. Queries related to sexual fantasies about children are pertinent for the abusers and nonabusers alike. Sixteen- and seventeen-year-old girls can be quite mature and catch the eye of any normal adult male; therefore, the denial of any sexual impulses toward children would very likely be a lie for both pedophiles and normals. The following control questions operate well because the innocent person will feel that if his lie is detected, it will certainly imply to the examiner that he is a pedophile, whereas for the guilty, the questions related to having committed the act are still more a threat than the fantasies of such an act:

Have you ever had any sexual fantasies of any kind about a child?

Have you ever seen a child whom you would have liked to have touched in a sexual area?

Have you ever seen a child whom you would have liked to have seen nude?

Have you ever seen a child whom you would have liked to have done something to sexually?

These questions are appropriate to use when testing a parent or stepparent:

Have you ever had any sexual thoughts about Betsy?

Have you ever had any sexual fantasies about Betsy?

Have you ever been tempted to touch Betsy in a sexual area?

Have you ever thought of ever having Betsy in a sexual situation?

Have you ever had sexual thoughts about any of Betsy's friends?

When testing a parent, difficulties can occur when the only accusation has been in regard to inappropriate touching. As a father the accused has undoubtedly washed the child, helped clean her after using the toilet, or applied medication. If the parent denies having had any of this contact in the recent past, then it is easy enough to avoid difficulties in developing relevant questions by using age brackets. The examiner also must be certain to eliminate any accidental contact that might disturb the innocent that might have occurred during wrestling or other activities.

In the last five years, have you ever touched Betsy in the vaginal area?

Other than when cleaning Betsy, did you ever touch her in the vaginal area?

If the child is still young and there is an overlap in the time period in which the father cleaned the child and when he was supposed to have molested her, then more care must be taken in formulating the key questions. Qualifying the above question with the phrase "for sexual reasons" changes it into an intent question with all of the weaknesses inherent in this. It is this writer's strong opinion that an individual who has molested a child cannot rationalize this act into convincing himself that he was merely cleaning her. On the other hand, if a father were washing his daughter and had a fleeting thought relating to how child abusers obtain gratification fondling a child, the concern about this thought could create a reaction to a question related to touching. The latter notion, however, is not accepted by polygraphists in general. A survey of twenty law enforcement and twenty private examiners who had attained some degree of renown generally indicated that the intent question should be avoided if possible.[15] If there were no option, it was believed that it could be employed accurately with either the guilty or the innocent. No significant difference in opinion was found between police and private polygraphists.

POLYGRAPH SURVEILLANCE

Prisons throughout the country are full, and individuals who have committed lesser crimes or nonviolent crimes are either released early or are not sentenced to prison at all. Placed on probation or parole, their supervision is minimal because the parole officers lack the time to maintain close contact with all of their charges. Because the recidivism rate is in the area of 80 percent, inevitably many probationers and parolees reoffend.[16]

Polygraphy can provide a means of reducing the prison population, protecting society, and acting to deter further reoffending. Just as periodic testing in the business realm deters theft, periodic polygraph testing of parolees and probationers can function in the same manner. This is of particular importance in the case of pedophiles on probation who are receiving aversive conditioning therapy. For this treatment to be effective, the patient should not be involved in any deviant sexual behavior. Polygraph supervision can determine if this behavior is, in fact, taking place, but more important, it serves to deter that behavior. Abrams and Ogard reported that this approach was found to be a highly effective deterrent to reoffending, and Teuscher emphasized the value of this technique in the recovery of stolen property and money.[17]

This is a new area of polygraph testing, and like periodic testing in the employment realm, no well-controlled validity studies have been carried out. In the Abrams and Ogard study some evidence for accuracy was obtained when interrogation after deceptive test findings resulted in an admission. For those who were found to be truthful, there is no guarantee that they had not reoffended other than the fact that they had not been apprehended. Whether repeated testing weakens polygraph validity is still a question that remains unanswered. It is not felt that periodic testing negatively affects the relevant question but that instead, if there is any detrimental effect, it is with the controls that are used. Assuming that the probationer passes the test, it also implies to him that he has been found truthful on the control questions, which he has almost definitely responded to deceptively. Because that will create the impression that he has beaten the test, he may feel that he can accomplish the same thing with the real issues. This placebo effect—the sense of assurance that he can mislead the examiner—conceivably could reduce his anxiety enough that it might result in a false negative finding. To combat this, after a probationer passes a test, some emphasis must be placed on the control questions to indicate that the examiner feels that there was deception present. The polygraphist might settle for a minor admission or indicate that this area will be checked more thoroughly the next time. In no case should the subject be allowed to leave believing that he has beaten the test.

If probation testing is to serve its purpose as a deterrent, rather than simply apprehend the subject at breaking the conditions of his probation, a rigid and formal testing procedure must be developed. At sentencing, the court must make it very clear that these tests will be administered every three months (the time should vary with the individual case) at a cost to the probationer. Should he fail to appear for the examination or fail the test, he automatically will be subject to a revocation hearing. If this procedure is not followed, the deterrent effect will be reduced.

Relevant questions will be based on the conditions of probation. For pedophiles conditions typically will deal with never being alone with a minor child without other adults present and having no sexual contact with a minor. Control questions should follow the same form as the critical items:

> Since your last polygraph test in May, have you had any sexual fantasies about a child?

Formulated in this manner the control questions appear as meaningful in the test as the relevant questions. If the therapy requires that the child abuser have deviant fantasies during the aversive conditioning, the questions should be preceded with "other than your therapy." The test questions can be developed so as to deal with any condition of probation, whether the probationer has been found guilty of burglary, drug abuse, or molestation of children.

If this approach is as successful as the early research indicates in deterring the criminal from further reoffending, it will play a major role in corrections. It may even aid in keeping an individual from getting involved in criminal activity long enough to be successful in work, family life, and the community.

There is, however, another use for polygraphy within the realm of the pedophile that has received little research attention. Polygraphy can be employed as a deterrent to reoffending, but in many treatment centers for the sexual abuser in the Northwest it also has become part of the treatment process. Denial of the particular act of which the individual was accused, however, precludes treatment because an individual who claims he did not molest cannot be treated. In addition, therapy related to one specific act is meaningless if the pedophile is guilty of many assaults as well as a wide variety of acts. Polygraphy therefore is being used to determine how many acts were committed, the ages and sex of the victims, and the degree of violence used. It has been found that even the announcement of testing has resulted in massive admissions preceding, during, and following the examination.

POLYGRAPH VALIDITY AND RELIABILITY

13

Research is the process of going up alleys to see if they are blind.

—Marston Bates

Determining the effectiveness of the polygraph technique would seem to be a simple matter of evaluating the research, but it is a complex procedure in which many different variables interact. Generalizations from the experimentation that has been conducted must be made with caution and only if the procedures, presentation, and even the cases under study are similar. In interpreting research findings it must be recognized that differences exist between laboratory and field testing, among schools of thought and their approaches, between techniques such as the guilty knowledge procedures and the control question approaches, among types of subjects and crimes, and even in the expertise and training of the examiners. As pointed out by the Office of Technology Assessment, these factors make polygraphy a complex and difficult field to study.[1] It is, however, no more complicated than other aspects of the psychological sciences. Certainly an evaluation of interviewing techniques or projective testing is no less complicated, and yet major conclusions are regularly made based on these findings. Moreover, the decisions developed through these procedures are routinely admitted into evidence despite questions related to the validity of these approaches.

Polygraph research findings have been complicated further by the divergence of opinions that emerge when reviews of the literature are conducted. These discrepancies occur because a determination of validity is greatly influenced by which studies are included or excluded as part of the evaluation of the research. When investigations are excluded on the basis of their being poorly conducted, a selective procedure is allowed to operate that opens the door to inadvertent bias. As will be seen, this is of particular significance in the emotion-laden field of polygraphy.

Two of the major divisions of polygraphy are specific and commercial testing. The former deals with such cases as rape, homicide, and burglary in which the issue is clear and relatively narrow. Commercial testing, on the other hand, con-sists of the screening of large numbers of individuals and by its very nature is complicated. Job applicants are examined in order to eliminate those who would be undesirable to the employer because of such background factors as accident proneness, drug use, or employee theft. Large-scale testing of employees can be conducted to determine who is responsible for security leaks, while periodic testing not only allows for the detection of individuals involved in misconduct in the employment situation but serves as a deterrent to those who might act out in this manner. Knowing that they will be tested every six months inhibits employee theft.

Any study of the value of commercial testing is complicated by emotional and political issues. Civil libertarians strongly object to the use of these procedures on the basis that the rights of the employees are threatened. Unions also have taken a strong stand against examinations of this nature in order to provide protection for their membership. Because they control large voting blocs, unions wield considerable influence with legislators, which, in turn, has resulted in the increase of antipolygraph legislation. A third group that has examined commer-cial testing is composed of scientists who generally are not in themselves poly-graphists. Their role has been to review the literature, usually at the request of the legislators. The pathway to this scientific review of the literature starts with the unions, which want polygraphy out of the working place. Unions approach the legislators, who want the votes that the unions control. In turn, the legisla-tors refer this request to a group of scientists, who undoubtedly understand what research outcome is desired. Therefore, these scientists must be cautious and objective, particularly when they review the literature, and select only those investigations that they feel are properly conducted. Not being a polygraphist severely weakens the ability of an individual to evaluate the research. According to Orne, "With a few notable exceptions, statements by scientists have tended to be based on very limited experience with the technique as well as strong prejudice against it."[2] The various negative statements made against commercial polygraph testing have been sensationalized by the news media. Inevitably, some of these reactions have rubbed off onto specific testing and influenced the courts, attorneys and even polygraph subjects.

Specific polygraph testing includes two basic types types of experimentation—field and laboratory. The former deals with studies of real-life situations, and the latter involves research in a laboratory setting employing volunteer subjects. Each has advantages and disadvantages.[3] The most significant negative feature associated with experimentation of the laboratory type is that the subject has little or nothing to lose if a lie is detected. In a real situation, the examinee risks possible imprisonment, financial loss, and personal embarrassment if a deception is discovered.[4] Even in analog studies that attempt to simulate actual testing conditions through the use of mock crimes, the emotions associated with deception are simply not the same and not of the same degree. Because of this, the examinee does not experience the same degree of sympathetic arousal that stimulates the physiological reactions that allow for the detection of lies. It is logical to assume that polygraph validity cannot be as high in a laboratory setting as in a field situation.

Research of this nature is also weakened by the fact that many experiments do not employ trained experienced polygraphists using field techniques. Moreover, the typical college student volunteer is quite different from those individuals who make up the criminal population. One must also question how effectively the control question technique can be studied in the laboratory. The relevant question would relate to a mock crime that has relatively little meaning for the subject, whereas the control question, which deals with real personal issues, would be a threat to the individual's privacy. It would seem, therefore, that the control question could become more relevant than the relevant item. Even enhancing the power of the relevant questions by providing money rewards if the subjects pass or electric shocks if they fail cannot duplicate the emotional reactions of a criminal suspect being polygraphed. This has led Kugelmass and Lieblich, Barland and Raskin, and Berrien to point out that laboratory findings have only limited generalizability to field procedures.[5]

The distinct advantage that laboratory investigation has over field research is that ground truth is known so that an exact determination of accuracy can be made. This is clearly not the case in the field, where only about 60 percent verification is obtained.[6] Confession is the best criterion for the confirmation of polygraph results, but some scientists even question this since occasional false admissions occur. One such case should be noted.[7] A bank employee failed a periodic polygraph examination related to embezzlement and subsequently failed two additional tests. Following this he not only admitted to embezzling bank funds but indicated how the embezzlement was carried out. An audit, however, showed that no money was missing and that the method of embezzlement that he described was not possible. Later investigation demonstrated that the employe did not take the money but did feel guilt related to some financial dealings with his wife and mother-in-law, who were customers of the bank. Although false confessions are a possibility, they are rare.

Another positive aspect of laboratory research is that a design can be developed to study whatever the experimenter wishes, such as the effect that variables such as age, emotional condition, intellectual ability, or motivational state could have on validity. The effect of countermeasures such as hypnosis, drugs, movement, or pain can be studied, as well as the value of various sensors. Laboratory research clearly serves a role in expanding the polygraphist's knowledge and understanding of polygraphy.

LABORATORY RESEARCH

Research in polygraphy has indicated that certain types of individuals cannot be accurately examined. Floch stated that psychopaths, psychopathic liars, and those with circumscribed amnesia are not testable.[8] Highleyman added psychotics, neurotics, and children to this list,[9] and Eliasberg reported that hardened criminals tend to be immune to the polygraph approach.[10] More recently, Lykken indicated that psychopaths cannot be validly examined because their lack of anxiety associated with the test probably will lead to their being misdiagnosed.[11] The research has not been in agreement with all of these hypotheses. In a study by Waid et al. a comparison was made of the subject's score on the Socialization Scale of the California Psychological Inventory.[12] It was found that deceptive subjects who were not detected scored lower in socialization and that the truthful who were misdiagnosed had higher socialization scores. Although these findings would suggest that those with low moral values who were lying might be able to pass the test and and that false positives would be apt to occur among the truthful who possessed a strong conscience, other research has not corroborated these findings.

In a laboratory study of psychopaths, Raskin and Hare used a sample of fifty-four prison inmates who volunteered to be subjects for the experiment on the basis of the possibility of earning $20 for a successful performance on the task assigned them.[13] Employing a mock crime situation, the subjects were divided into psychopathic and nonpsychopathic groups of twenty-four each. They were randomly distributed into the guilty, who were instructed to take a $20 bill from a desk and conceal it in their pockets, and the innocent, who were aware of but did not take the money. Both groups were informed that if they could pass the test they would be given the $20. A control question technique was administered to each subject. Of the total sample, 88 percent were correctly diagnosed and 4 percent were incorrectly categorized. The remaining 8 percent were rated as inconclusive. Both of the errors made were false positives; one occurred in each of the two groups. Of the psychopathic group, twenty-three of the decisions were correct as compared to nineteen of the nonpsychopathic group. The findings indicated that the psychopaths were more accurately tested than the non-psychopaths, but that validity was high for both groups.

Hammond studied psychopaths, and he too reported that they were as easily detected, if not more so than the normals.[14] Using a GKT procedure, Balloun and Holmes found no difference in detectability of those who scored high on the Psychopathic Scale of the Minnesota Multiphasic Personality Inventory (MMPI) and those who were low in this trait.[15] In a field study of the testability of psychopaths, Barland and Raskin withdrew from a sample of seventy-seven criminal suspects those fifteen with the highest score on psychopathy and those fifteen with the lowest score based on their MMPI findings.[16] No differences in polygraph detectability were found to exist between the two groups. All of these investigations rather strongly demonstrate that the psychopath is as readily detected in a lie as nonpsychopaths.

"Circumscribed amnesia" is a term that assumes that an act that an individual has committed is so unacceptable that it is repressed into the unconscious. Although this writer has had years of experience in the psychiatric realm, this type of response has been seen only rarely. Many criminal suspects have claimed amnesia, but excluding those with head injuries or drug-induced states, not one has had true memory loss. Of the studies that were reported in chapter 11, Bitterman and Marcuse, Weinstein et al., and Germann all demonstrated that polygraphy was able to evaluate unconscious material.[17] Even if the subject had no conscious awareness of having committed an act, when he or she denied committing it, physiological changes occurred that were typical of deception. It can be assumed that if an amnesia of a psychological nature exists, it probably will not negatively affect the value of the polygraph approach.

In this writer's study of psychotics, the charts on almost every subject would have been judged to be inconclusive.[18] These tracings were so erratic and disturbed that a determination of truth or deception could not be made. When a decision was forced by completely deleting the inconclusive category, the findings indicated that individuals in this diagnostic category could not be accurately tested. In the study of Heckel et al. testing of psychotics was found to be much less accurate than neurotics and normals, and the inconclusive rate of 38 percent was quite high.[19] Accuracy in neurotics fell between normals and psychotics but reached the 75 percent level. Both of these studies are reported in more detail in chapter 11.

In regard to children, the findings of a study conducted by the author demonstrated that accuracy is lessened with younger children.[20] Accuracy at age eleven was found to be 83 percent, twelve-year olds were at the 96 percent level, the thirteen-year-olds 94 percent. This would suggest some risk in testing children who are ten years of age or younger. Somewhat related to this is the testing of retardates. Because intelligence can be classified in terms of both IQ and mental age, a comparison could be made between the testing results of children and of adults with the same mental age. In a study by Abrams and Weinstein individuals below IQ 65 were simply not testable, whereas those from IQ 65 to 75 ranged in accuracy from 66 to 75 percent.[21] It is of interest to note that an adult with an IQ of 75 would have a mental age of about eleven years and three months.

A question frequently asked relates to the effectiveness of polygraphy as compared to other procedures. In a very clever study by Widacki and Horvath, eighty volunteer college students were divided into twenty groups of four subjects each.[22] One in each group was randomly chosen as the perpetrator and assigned the task of picking up a parcel from one of two doorkeepers of a building. Each of these twenty individuals brought an information sheet and envelope and left it with the doorman. The subjects then signed a form in order to receive the package. The doormen knew in advance that participants would be coming and were able to make a conscious effort to recall them. All eighty subjects were fingerprinted, and examples of their handwriting were provided. The doormen were each shown a set of four pictures and had to select the person from each group who had picked up the package. A handwriting expert compared the exemplars of each group of four with the writing of the perpetrator's written statement and signature. The fingerprint expert attempted to lift the prints of the individual from the envelope and forms that were left with the doormen. A polygraphist examined each set of four subjects and made a decision as to who the guilty person was in the group. Table 13–1 shows the results of this study.

From the results, it can be seen that eyewitness testimony, as has been well documented, is quite poor. Although fingerprint findings were completely accurate, a decision could be made in only 20 percent of the cases. In contrast to this, the handwriting expert did quite well, but polygraph examination was 95 percent accurate and only 5 percent inaccurate.

Table 13–1. A Comparison of Investigative Approaches in the Widacki and Horvath Research[22]

	Accurate	Inaccurate	Inconclusive
Polygraphy	18	1	1
Handwriting	17	1	2
Eyewitness	7	4	9
Fingerprints	4	0	16

Other laboratory studies have been important because they have demonstrated that certain factors enhance validity. Gustafson and Orne have shown that the more motivated a subject was, the more readily the deception was detected.[23] Davidson, on the other hand, employing a guilty knowledge test and rewards ranging from $1 to $50, did not find that differences in motivation affected detectability.[24] In a simulated murder experiment, 92 percent of the guilty and 100 percent of the innocent were correctly classified. Studies by Ruckmick and Marston have shown that some individuals have a greater aptitude for interpreting polygraph tracings.[25]

COUNTERMEASURES

Although Lykken has indicated that people can be successfully trained to defeat the polygraph approach,[26] he did not find the same results in his investigation into the guilty knowledge technique. Employing only GSR in a simulated crime study, he obtained 94 percent accuracy,[27] but when he trained and provided practice in the use of countermeasures, correct judgments increased to 100 percent.[28] Dawson studied cognitive countermeasures and did not find them effective.[29] Employing actors trained in the Stanislavsky method, his result were 88 percent accurate, 8 percent inaccurate, and 4 percent inconclusive. In Kubis's experimentation, relaxation and dissociation were not effective as countermeasures, but accuracy was reduced from 75 percent to 25 percent when exciting imagery was used.[30] Moore also found reduced validity with this approach, but accuracy was diminished only from 95 percent to 80 percent.[31]

Research on the effect of hypnosis on polygraphy has demonstrated that distortions can be induced. In the study by Weinstein et al., subjects who were innocent of having committed a mock crime were given posthypnotic suggestions that they were guilty and were readily seen as deceptive when they denied having committed the crime.[32] There was also some evidence that hypnosis could reduce the detectability of the guilty to the extent that they were seen as inconclusive. Germann attained similar findings with guilty subjects.[33] In contrast, Corcoron et al. reported that both biofeedback and hypnosis were effective in reducing detectability.[34]

The most effective countermeasures were those that used movement. Rovner et al. used seventy-two subjects in a control question technique and attempted to determine whether validity could be reduced by providing information related to polygraphy, training in specific countermeasures, and practicing these methods.[35] The groups that were given information and the one that was not demonstrated the same results. Accuracy was 88 percent, inaccuracy was 4 percent, and inconclusive was 8 percent. The success rate on the group that was allowed to practice countermeasures was reduced to correct judgments of 63 percent, inaccuracy of 25 percent, and inconclusive of 12 percent. Of note is the fact that validity was equally reduced in the innocent and guilty subjects. Honts and Hodes, employing a mock crime paradigm, provided fifteen minutes of training in the theory of the CQT and taught tongue biting and toe pressing techniques during control questions.[36] The subjects were instructed to relax during the relevant items. It was not possible for the examiners to detect the use of countermeasures, and the accuracy in the guilty was reduced from 67 percent ot 58 percent. False negatives went from 0 to 6 percent and inconclusives rose from 33 percent to 37 percent. In a second investigation, Honts and Hodes had their examinees press down with their toes and bite their tongues simultaneously during the control questions.[37] In addition, there was a thirty-minute training period and a practice session. Once again, the examiners could not detect the successful use of countermeasures, and accuracy on the guilty dropped from 84 percent to 34 percent, inaccuracy rose from 1 to 26 percent, and inconclusive increased from 16 percent to 37 percent.

In a study by Stephenson and Barry, it was reported that movement countermeasures not only were able to create changes in the tracings that resembled deceptive responses but that these movements could not be detected by a polygraphist who was specifically watching for these movements.[38] Employing an activity sensor placed beneath two of the legs of the polygraph chair, they found that these same movements were readily detected. Abrams obtained similar results in replicating this study, demonstrating that undetectable physical movements can reduce polygraph accuracy but that the activity monitor can successfully detect these movements.[39]

In an investigation by Waid et al., meprobamate, a mild tranquilizer, significantly affected the accuracy of the polygraph procedure to the extent that only 27 percent of the deceptive were detected as compared to 77 percent of those on placebo or no drugs and 100 percent of those who were truthful.[40] In direct contrast to these findings, Iacono and Baisvenu, studying the effect of Valium, methylphenidate, and a placebo, reported that the drugs did not affect the outcome of the examination.[41] An overall accuracy of 94 percent was achieved using a guilty knowledge test procedure. In a similar investigation, Iacono et al. employed Valium and meprobamate, both mild tranquilizers; propanolol, a beta blocker; and a placebo.[42] None of the drugs lowered the detection rate, and overall accuracy was 90 percent. The authors concluded that these medications cannot be used to defeat the guilty knowledge test. Gatchel et al. also reported that no significant drug effects from propanolol were found. These findings would rather strongly indicate that drug use is not an effective countermeasure.[43]

NUMBER OF TESTS ADMINISTERED

Van Buskirk and Marcuse obtained an accuracy of 72 percent when two charts were administered and 84 percent with four charts.[44] Eliminating inconclusive charts, 92 percent accuracy was reached. Elson et al. also found accuracy increased with the number of charts.[45] They reported 50 percent success after the first test, 62 percent following the second, and 79 percent accuracy after the third administration of the test. Raskin and Hare compared the accuracy for those who received three administrations of the test with those who were given more than three tests.[46] They found that additional charts reduced the number of inconclusive findings. This would explain Kleinmintz and Szucko's low accuracy rate of 75 percent for the guilty and 63 percent for the innocent in their field study. Their findings were based on only one administration of the examination.[47]

SENSORS

Comparing the effectiveness of the various sensors, Waid et al. found the greatest degree of success was with the electrodermal response (EDR).[48] Bradley and Janesse, employing electrodermal activity, heart rate, and pupil size, also reported greatest accuracy with the EDR.[49] Comparing electrodermal responses with respiration, Ohnishi et al. found 72 percent and 46 percent accuracy, respectively.[50] Skin resistance was also reported to be superior in Barland and Raskin's study,[51] and Hammond found no significant differences among the physiologic measures.[52] Raskin and Hare reported that all measures successfully differentiated the guilty from the innocent,[53] but in Podlesney and Raskin only EDR and the plethysmograph achieved significant differences.[54] Dawson found EDR and cardiovascular measures differentiated between the guilty and the innocent but not respiration.[55]

In a field investigation of the evaluation of the heart rate monitor and its effectiveness compared to the usual sensors employed, Abrams reported that electrodermal activity was most effective, followed by cardiograph, heart rate monitor, and finally respiration.[56] A rather consistent finding in the laboratory research is that EDR is generally found the most effective sensor and respiration the least.

DIRECTION OF ERROR

The various laboratory studies employing the control question technique (CQT) have demonstrated a greater tendency for errors to be in the direction of false positives. False positives occur when the innocent are inaccurately diagnosed as deceptive, whereas false negatives occur when the guilty are incorrectly considered to be truthful. Barland and Raskin reported 4 percent false negatives and 8 percent false positives.[57] In a study by Ginton et al. no false negatives were obtained, but there was a 15 percent false positive rate.[58] In contrast to this, Podlesney and Raskin reported 8 percent false negatives and 2 percent false positives.[59] Widacki and Horvath obtained 5 percent false negatives and no false positives.[60] In Kircher's study false positives and negatives were equal at 3 percent each.[61] Raskin and Hare in their study of psychopaths had no false negatives but reported 4 percent false positives.[62] In Dawson's study employing actors, no false negatives were found,but 25 percent false positives were reported.[63] Honts and Hodes had no false negatives, but there were 17 percent false positives in their first study[64] and no false negative, but 16 percent false positives in their second experiment.[65] In the Hammond investigation 3 percent false negatives and 20 percent false positives were obtained.[66] Of these ten laboratory studies, eight of them showed higher levels of false positives and only two had false negatives that were greater. The false negatives averaged 5 percent, and the false positives came to an average of 15 percent.

VALIDITY OF THE CONTROL QUESTION TECHNIQUE IN THE LABORATORY

Overall validity for laboratory research was reported to be 81 percent in this author's first book.[67] This included all of the studies, good and bad, in order to present some picture of the effectiveness of the polygraph approach. It was believed to be a lower figure than what could be obtained in the field because of the reduced emotional involvement of the subjects, but considering that subjects felt little or no fear of detection it was viewed as an impressive figure. That review was conducted about fifteen years ago. The following studies are more current.

Barland and Raskin employed a mock crime design with seventy-two students who were randomly divided into three groups—those who were told how effective the approach was, those who were informed that the instrument was not operating properly, and those who received no information.[68] Of the total group, 53 percent accuracy was reached, 12 percent inaccuracy, and 35 percent inconclusive. Excluding inconclusives, total accuracy was 81 percent. Using the entire sample generally would not result in a reasonable evaluation of the technique because the latter two conditions would not occur in an actual testing situation, but no meaningful differences occurred with the various feedback conditions. In the research of Podlesny and Raskin, three different types of control questions were employed—a guilt complex, exclusive controls, and nonexclusive controls.[69] Exclusive or bracketed controls are the Backster type, which, for example, excludes the date of the crime: "Prior to the age of forty did you ever . . . ?" The nonexclusive controls are the Reid controls, which are more apt to read "Did you ever . . . ?" Greater accuracy was obtained with the bracketed controls (Backster), 85 percent correct judgment, 5 percent incorrect, and 10 percent inconclusive. In the nonexclusive control (Reid), 75 percent accuracy, 15 percent errors, and 10 percent inconclusive was obtained. The combined results were 80 percent correct, 10 percent incorrect, and 10 percent inconclusive. Employing the guilt complex as a control method was not as effective.

Although the Raskin and Hare study used a very special population in which psychopaths made up half of their population of forty-eight, high levels of validity were still achieved.[70] Their overall accuracy was 88 percent, 4 percent were incorrect, and 8 percent were inconclusive. In the Rovner et al. study one group of subjects received information on polygraphy and the use of countermeasures, another received the same data but was given the opportunity to practice defeating the test; and the third group did not receive either of these treatments.[71] Because only the control group was in a situation that was comparable to an actual field situation, only these results will be considered. A total of 88 percent correct judgments were made, 4 percent were incorrect, and 8 percent were inconclusive. Kirchner used 100 subjects, and an independent rater obtained an accuracy of 87 percent, an inaccurate in 6 percent, and inconclusive in 7 percent.[72] Widacki and Horvath in their comparison research of fingerprints, handwriting, eyewitnesses, and polygraphy obtained an accurate diagnosis in 90 percent. They misdiagnosed in 5 percent and were inconclusive in 5 percent.[73] In the two Honts and Hodes studies, like Rovner, the effectiveness of countermeasures was being evaluated.[74,75] In their first investigation accuracy in the noncountermeasure group was 48 percent, inaccuracy 9 percent, and inconclusive 43 percent. In their second evaluation of the noncountermeasure group, correct diagnosis was made in 58 percent; they were inaccurate in 10 percent and inconclusive in 34 percent. In Hammond's study alcoholics and psychopaths were employed along with normals, but this group will be included in the total validity sample because neither of these two diagnostic categories demonstrate the disruptiveness and confusion that might be expected in a more disturbed population—psychotics, for example.[76] Correct judgments were made in 57 percent, incorrect judgments in 11 percent, and 32 percent were inconclusive.

In research by Barland comparing different test procedures, he reported 66 percent accuracy, 18 percent inaccuracy, and 16 percent inconclusive for a ZOC technique.[77] When he employed a method in which the relevant questions were compared to the control that showed the greatest reaction, accuracy with the guilty was reduced but accuracy for the innocent remained at essentially the same level. Total accuracy was 64 percent, inaccuracy 20 percent, and 16 percent were inconclusive. Despite the use of a beta blocker as a countermeasure, Gatchel et al. achieved an accuracy of 64 percent, inaccuracy of 4 percent, and inconclusive at 32 percent.[78] These findings for laboratory analog CQT research are shown in table 13–2. Although the total average accuracy of 72 percent does not seem impressive, when one considers the 20 percent inconclusive rate and the 9 percent inaccuracy level, it is a much higher figure, certainly indicative of a high level of validity. Considering that greater validity would be obtained in the field, this is an even more impressive figure.

Table 13–2. Analog CQT Research
(percentage)

Author	Accurate	Inaccurate	False +	False −	Inconclusive
Barland and Raskin[68]	53%	12%	17%	8.0%	35%
Podlesney and Raskin[69]					
(Backster)	85	5	0	5	10
(Reid)	75	15	5	10	10
Raskin and Hare[70]	88	4	4	0	8
Raviner et al.[35]	88	4	14	8	8
Kircher[72]	87	6	2	4	7
Honts and Hodes[74]	48	9	17	0	
Honts and Hodes[75]	58	10	16	0	34
Widacki and Horvath[73]	90	5	0	5	5
Hammond[66]	57	11	20	3	32
Barland[77]	66	18	24	19	16
Greatest control	64	20	17	32	16
Gatchel et al.[78]	64	4	0	12	32
Average	71.0%	9.5%	10%	8%	19.7%

Table 13–3. Reliability Studies of Analog CQT Research

Author		Percentage of agreement
Barland and Raskin[68]	Original examiner plus five evaluators	82
Podlesney and Raskin[69]	Original examiner and independent rater	100
Hammond[76]	Student examiners with polygraph rater	79
Honts and Hodes[75]	Original examiner plus rater	100
Average reliability		90

RELIABILITY OF THE CQT IN LABORATORY STUDIES

In legal literature, the word "reliability" is often used to indicate accuracy, but in statistical terms, "reliability" reflects consistency and "validity" is indicative of accuracy. Reliability in polygraphy is the degree that a test can be repeated with similar results being obtained or the amount of agreement among examiners on the same test. In a review of laboratory literature from about fifteen years ago, reliability was found to be at 85 percent.[79] Table 13–3 shows the reliability findings for some of the research just discussed.

The findings for the CQT in the laboratory, for all of its weaknesses, indicate both high validity and reliability. Although the 71 percent accuracy appears to be low, this figure is distorted by the 20 percent inconclusives obtained. Excluding the inconclusives, accuracy would be in the range of 87 percent. False positives exceeded false negatives. Reliability was at the 90 percent level. Considering the fact that the autonomic arousal in a real-life situation is greater than in a laboratory, one would anticipate a higher degree of validity and reliability in the field.

VALIDITY OF THE GUILTY KNOWLEDGE TEST
IN LABORATORY STUDIES

Analog studies of the guilty knowledge procedure are more readily accomplished because of the ease of developing research of this nature. Despite this, relatively few investigations of this type have been conducted. Some differences exist in this approach, mainly associated with the Lykken style of administration and scoring as compared to the peak of tension procedure developed by Keeler. There are also differences based on whether a false key was used.

Lykken randomly assigned forty-nine students to one of four roles: committing a mock theft, a mock murder, both, or neither.[80] Two GKT's were conducted on each subject, one for each crime. The key item was randomly varied in its position among five alternate items with each administration of the test. Only an electrodermal response was used. Accuracy was reported to be 94 percent. In a second study, Lykken provided a fifteen-minute lecture on the GNT, lie detection, and electrodermal activity.[81] In addition to this, the twenty subjects were given the opportunity to practice producing false responses. In spite of this, complete accuracy was obtained.

Podlesny and Raskin used cardio, pneumo, electrodermal, response, and the photoplethysmograph.[82] They achieved 90 percent accuracy, and the 10 percent that were incorrect were false negatives. In an investigation in which individuals with high levels of anxiety were tested to determine if that would confound the results, Giesen and Rollison used forty female undergraduates as subjects.[83] Employing only EDR they achieved an accuracy of 97.5 percent, missing only one of the guilty. Although the anxiety level had no effect on the EDR, those individuals with greater anxiety who were guilty demonstrated greater EDR than the anxious subjects. Davidson's study of forty-five students in which the mock crime was murder, achieved 98 percent accuracy using only EDR.[84] The only error was in the false negatives. In an investigation in which the accuracy was far lower, Bradley and Janesse examined 192 subjects with EDR.[85] Only 74 percent accuracy was reached with a 20 percent false negative rate. Even less accuracy was obtained when heart rate changes were studied. Accuracy was 45 percent with 28 percent false negative.

It should be noted that a higher rate of false positives occur in the CQT, while false negatives are greater in the GKT. However, the average rate of accuracy in the GKT of 88 percent in a laboratory situation is again most impressive as shown in table 13–4.

Two studies have been conducted that lie between laboratory and field research. They carry the distinct advantage of having the positive aspects of both approaches. Ground truth is known, yet the subjects believe that the situation is real and that they have something to lose if their deception is discovered.

In a class for Israeli police officers, twenty-one were tested on the course curriculum.[86] Without their awareness, their answers to the test were recorded, but they were told that they were to grade their own papers. Later, however, they were informed that cheating was suspected and that they would be given the opportunity to take polygraph tests to prove their innocence. It was emphasized that their future in law enforcement could be affected by the polygraph results. Actually, seven of the twenty-one had changed their answers. Although all of them agreed to the examination, one of those who cheated did not appear for the test, three admitted that they cheated, and one of those who changed his answers and one who did not refused to be examined. The remaining two guilty and thirteen innocent were tested. The original polygraphist was completely accurate on the guilty and 85 percent correct on the innocent. The two errors were false positives using a CQT.

Employing a similar design Balloun and Holmes compared the reactions of eighteen college students with high psychopathic scores on the MMPI with sixteen who were low in this trait.[87] Each individual was tested on a bogus intelligence test and given the opportunity of cheating. Of the thirty-four subjects, eighteen in fact did cheat. Polygraph tests were administered to all the subjects who were informed that if they were found to have cheated on the test it could lead to dismissal from school. A GKT was administered with EDR, heart rate, and fin-

Table 13–4. Laboratory Studies of the Validity of the Guilty Knowledge Test (*percentage*)

	Accuracy	False +	False −	Inaccurate
Lykken[80]	94%	0	6%	6%
Lykken[81]	100	0	0	0
Podlesney and Raskin[82]	90	0	10	10
Giesen and Rollison[83]	97	0	3	3
Davidson[84]	98	0	2	2
Bradley and Janesse[85]	74	6%	20	26
Average	88%	2%	10%	12%

ger pulse volume being measured. Significant findings were attained only on the EDR. On the first administration of the test, 60 percent of the deceptive and 88 percent of the nondeceptive were correctly classified, and seventeen percent of the deceptive and 94 percent of the truthful were accurately judged on the second testing. Previous research has demonstrated that single test scores produce a lesser degree of accuracy.

To ascertain degree of validity in the field, the examiner must cope with the problem of incomplete verification of the polygraph findings. As will be seen, this has been accomplished in a variety of ways. There are a few reports where complete verification was obtained with large samples. The office of Technology of Assessment (OTA) has chosen to exclude these studies in their review based on the idea that investigations of single crimes with only one possible guilty person "raises the possibility of accurate detection . . . to a level too high for the study to provide valid information."[88] That is, with 100 suspects, one could diagnose all of them as innocent and be accurate in 99 percent of the cases. These studies were not done in this manner, however, and to exclude them discards the only investigations in which complete confirmation was obtained.

The first two studies of this nature were conducted by Larson prior to Reid's development of the control question technique.[89] In essence, these were relevant-irrelevant procedures. An attempt was made to determine who in a dormitory of 100 women was responsible for a series of thefts totalling $600. After examining thirty-five of the subjects, the tracings of one stood out as being indicative of deception. When confronted with the findings, she admitted to her involvement. In a similar case, Larson tested thirty-eight college women to ascertain who among them was shoplifting from a nearby store.[90] Once again, only one had a record that suggested deception. As in the previous instance, a confession was obtained. Prior to the examinations, Larson had no way of knowing how many of the women were involved, but in each case he accurately determined who the innocent and who the guilty were so that complete accuracy was achieved. In a similar investigation, Winter studied a series of thefts in a women's college dormitory.[91] After examining the twenty-five residents, the only one who indicated signs of deception was questioned and she admitted her guilt. As was the case with Larson, 100 percent accuracy was achieved in a non-control question procedure. The one study that was in line with the objections raised by the OTA was conducted by Bitterman and Marcuse.[92] In this case, $100 was stolen from the room of one of the eighty-one men living in a college dormitory. They reported that the majority of the examinees showed anxiety but only seven demonstrated charts that were indicative of deception. With re-examination, they concluded that none of these subjects were deceptive. This was later confirmed when someone outside of the dormitory was found to have been involved. This investigation, however, was conducted by two college professors who were not polygraphists.

There are a great many instances in which it has been reported that accuracy has been found in all of those cases that have been confirmed, but there is no way of knowing if the same success was achieved in the unverified cases. In fact, if errors were to occur, it would seem likely to be in those that were not verified. An individual called deceptive who was truthful certainly would not confess any more than a deceptive person diagnosed as truthful would admit his or her guilt.

Typical of reports of this nature was that of an early study by Marston.[93] At the Harvard Laboratories, he studied twenty criminal suspects, and his findings indicated that of the eleven verified charts, accuracy was attained on every one. Lyon randomly selected 100 juvenile cases in which R-I polygraph tests had been administered.[94] Of these, forty-eight had been verified, and every one of those was found to be accurate. More recently, Patrick and Iacono studied 402 cases in which 89 were confirmed.[95] These were drawn from the files of the Royal Canadian Mounted Police polygraph examiners. Their findings indicated that complete accuracy of the guilty and 90 percent correct judgments of the innocent were made. Elaad and Schahar evaluated all of the polygraphs administered by the Israeli police during 1973 and 1974.[96] Of the 184 cases confirmed by either conviction or confession, there were 91 percent accurate, 3 percent inaccurate, and the remaining 6 percent inconclusive. It should be recognized, of course, that conviction is not an ideal criterion for ground truth. In a somewhat similar study in which conviction was employed as the criterion for ground truth, Peters reported 98 percent accuracy with the guilty and 88 percent accuracy with the innocent.[97] It should be noted, however, that in 11 of the 163 cases studied, polygraph testimony was given that would certainly have influenced the jury or the court. From this, one can see a pattern beginning in 1921 with Marston's work using a simple measure of systolic blood pressure to the findings of Lyon in 1936 in which an R-I test was employed. Finally, Patrick and Iacono's evaluation of the CQT in 1987 continues to demonstrate the high validity of the polygraph approach.

Another manner of coping with the problems associated with the lack of complete verification was developed by the Reid school. Verified charts were reevaluated by polygraphists who were aware of only basic case facts and of which questions were controls and which were relevant. They had the distinct disadvantage of having no information about the test, not administering or even observing the testing procedure, and not knowing how the subject responded physically or verbally except for his answer to the questions. Those polygraphists scoring the test blindly were handicapped to a degree that leads one to expect a lesser level of accuracy.

Horvath and Reid selected polygraph charts from twenty verified guilty and twenty verified innocent subjects involved in a variety of criminal cases.[98] These charts were not selected randomly, but those that were too obviously truthful or deceptive were excluded. Of the ten examiners who blindly scored the charts, seven had over a year's experience and three had only four to six months of experience and were still involved in their internship. All were Reid trained. The more experienced polygraphists were found to be accurate in 91 percent of the cases, whereas the inexperienced examiners achieved a success rate of 79 percent. For the total group an average accuracy of 88 percent was attained. The evaluators were pressured into avoiding a diagnosis of inconclusive, which further reduces accuracy. The error rate was 10 percent for the innocent and 15 percent for the guilty, demonstrating a greater percentage of false negatives.

In the Hunter and Ash study, ten verified guilty and ten verified innocent charts were used.[99] The seven examiners trained in the Reid technique blindly analyzed the charts on two occasions with at least a three-month period in between the evaluations without knowing that they were the same charts. Of the seven polygraphists, one was an intern with four and a half months of experience and the remaining six had over one year of experience. The examiners accurately scored 86 percent, 13 percent were inaccurate, and 1 percent was considered inconclusive. The overall error rate was 14 percent for the innocent and 11 percent for the guilty. The individual with the least experience had the lowest level of success.

Slowick and Buckly randomly selected fifteen verified guilty charts and fifteen verified innocent charts dealing with a variety of cases.[100] Seven examiners with an average of 3.8 years of experience blindly scored the charts with no data available except the control and relevant items. The overall accuracy was 87 percent. Comparing the three measures employed, greatest accuracy was found for respiration at 81 percent, EDR was next at 80 percent, and cardiograph was least effective with 77 percent. Of the innocent, 90 percent were accurately detected, 7 percent were inaccurate, and 3 percent were inconclusive. Among the deceptive, 84 percent were correctly judged, 15 percent inaccurate, and 1 percent inconclusive.

In a similar investigation by Wicklander and Hunter, six evaluators scored the charts of ten verified guilty and ten verified innocent individuals.[101] The overall accuracy was 90 percent, inaccuracy 6 percent, and inconclusive 4 percent. The error rate for the guilty was 5 percent and for the innocent 7 percent. In this instance, the false positives were slightly higher.

Davidson randomly selected ten confirmed guilty and eleven confirmed innocent charts.[102] Seven evaluators attained 89 percent accuracy with an error rate of 3 percent and inclusives at 8 percent. In comparing the various sensors utilized, he reported that the cardio activity monitor (CAM) was 90 percent accurate as compared to 87 percent for total polygraph decisions with the guilty. With the innocent, 86 percent of the decision made using the CAM alone were correct in contrast to 84 percent for the total polygraph approach.

The studies just discussed were all conducted in the same manner and the accuracy ranged from 86 percent to 90 percent. Little significant difference occurred between false positive and false negatives. In a study by Kleinmuntz and Szucko six examiners evaluated fifty verified guilty and fifty verified innocent charts.[103] Only 75 percent accuracy was reported on the guilty and 63 percent on the innocent. However, two major weaknesses existed in this research that destroyed any value it might have had. The polygraphists who evaluated the charts were interns, but more significant was the fact that only one test was scored. This unquestionably reduces the degree of accuracy that could be attained and serves little purpose because one cannot generalize to actual testing situations. A single test polygraph is never used because of the risk of reactions that might be caused by an artifact of some nature. For example, an excess of generalized anxiety or even a random thought on the first test might distort the results. The repetition of the test will allow for responses of this kind to be balanced out.

Of more concern are the findings of Horvath, who used ten examiners to evaluate twenty-eight verified guilty and twenty-eight verified innocent charts.[104] Only 77 percent accuracy was achieved on the guilty and a remarkable 50 percent on the innocent. Unlike the experiments described, these charts were drawn from police files. Attempts have been made to determine why accuracy was at such a low level. Barland hypothesized that it was due to the presence of an excessive number of charts of witnesses and victims. Horvath, on the other hand, believed that the original charts were flawed and that effective evaluators would continue to make errors in interpreting them. Because the original examiners had been accurate in their findings, they must have employed data in addition to the charts to make their determinations of truth or deception. This discrepancy points up the weakness in blind interpretation of the charts rather than the lack of accuracy of polygraphy. All of the studies out of the Reid school were also completely accurate, but less than total accuracy was attained in the blind evaluations of the charts. More recently, Patrick and Iacono compared the results reached by the original examiner with those of evaluators who blindly rated the charts.[105] As previously indicated, the original examiners achieved 100 percent accuracy for the guilty and 90 percent accuracy for the innocent. However, the blind evaluations resulted in 98 percent correct judgments for the guilty but only 55 percent for the innocent.

Holmes examining this issue drew 100 verified charts from police files and randomly selected 25 for study.[106] These were evaluated by six police polygraphists who knew only the numbers of the control and relevant questions. An average accuracy of 75 percent was reached. Each examiner was then provided with additional data including police reports, statements of witnesses, and a description of the behavior and demeanor during the testing. With this additional information, accuracy increased to 83 percent. Wicklander and Hunter compared the results of the blind interpretation of twenty verified charts when the only information presented to the evaluators was the type of case involved with a second evaluation when they were informed of the subjects' verbal and nonverbal behavior, information on the subject himself, and a brief description of the case.[107] Employing the first approach, correct judgments were made on 87 percent of the truthful and 90 percent of the deceptive. With the additional data accuracy was reported on 87 percent of the truthful and 98 percent of the deceptive. These studies argue that validity can be increased by the incorporation of information outside of the polygraph findings into the decision-making process.

Another research design was developed to deal with the problem of incomplete verification. Bersh compared polygraph results with the opinion of a panel of four army judge advocate general attorneys.[108] Each lawyer made a determination of guilt or innocence based on a study of the case files excluding polygraph data. A total of 157 individuals involved in criminal investigations who had been administered polygraph examinations were randomly chosen from the files. When the majority of the panel was in agreement, there was 75 percent concordance with the polygraphist. In those cases where the panel's decision was unanimous, the agreement with the examiner was 92 percent. Combining the findings of the modified general question test and the relevant-irrelevant test, the examiner classified 97 percent of those deceptive who the panel judged to be guilty and 90 percent truthful deemed innocent by the panel. In the group in which zone of comparison was employed, 90 percent agreement with the panel on the deceptive and 94 percent on the innocent was achieved. A weakness of this investigation was that the polygraphist had access to a limited amount of case information that was the same information available to the panel. This could have increased the degree of agreement between the panel and the examiner.

In a similar study by Barland and Raskin, 102 criminal suspects were examined using the federal modification of the ZOC in all but one of the cases in which a Reid test was employed.[109] It was noted that thirty-four examiners were tested on an instrument that was in poor condition. Each case was reviewed by a panel consisting of two prosecutors, two criminal defense attorneys, and one judge. None of the panel had access to the polygraph findings or judicial outcome. They were instructed to disregard legal technicalities and make their decision only on the facts that were made available to them. Excluding inconclusives, when there was concordance among a majority of the panel, agreement between the panel and the polygraphist's findings were at the 87 percent level. When compared to judicial outcome in those forty-one instances in which the jury was not aware that a polygraph examination had been administered, 91 percent agreement was reached and 9 percent were inconclusive. Of the eight innocent subjects, only one was in agreement, one was inconclusive, and the percentage of disagreement was 75 percent. However, when a comparison was made between those judged guilty and innocent by the panel, there was 92 percent agreement between the polygraphists and the panel on the guilty but only 29 percent with the innocent. There was also an 18 percent inconclusive rate with the innocent as compared to 8 percent with the guilty subjects. Raskin reevaluated sixteen of these cases employing twenty-five evaluators.[110] When a numerical scoring system was used, 92 percent correct judgments and 8 percent inconclusives were obtained with the guilty, and with the innocent there was 75 percent accuracy and 25 percent inconclusive. Using a nonnumerical approach reduced the accuracy among the guilty to 83 percent, inaccuracy to 8 percent, and the inclusives to 9 percent. More dramatically, among the innocent, only 25 percent were accurately diagnosed, 50 percent were inaccurate, and the remaining 25 percent were inconclusive.

The overall accuracy for these varied approaches is 88 percent. However, excluding the four R-I studies, omitting the Kleinmuntz and Szucko and the Balloun and Holmes studies because both deal with only one test administration, and excluding Raskin because it deals with the same charts employed in the Barland and Raskin research, the level of successful diagnosis is 85 percent. False positives are 18 percent and false negatives 10 percent. These findings are shown in table 13–5.

Table 13–5. Validity Research of Field Studies
(percentage)

Researcher	Number of subjects	Accuracy	Inaccuracy	False +	False −	Inconclusive
Larson[89]	35	100%	0			0
Larson[90]	38	100	0			0
Bitterman and Marcuse[92]	81	100	0			0
Winter[91]	25	100	0			0
	G / I					
Horvath and Reid[98]	20 / 20	88	15%	10%	15%	—
Hunter and Ash[99]	10 / 10	86	13	14	11	1%
Slowick and Buckley[100]	15 / 15	87	11	7	5	2
Wicklander and Hunter[101]	10 / 10	90	6	7	5	4
Davidson[102]	10 / 11	90	5	—	10	5
Horvath[104]	20 / 20	63	36	19	23	0
Kleinmuntz and Szucko[103]	50 / 50	69	31			0
Bersh[108]	32 / 36	92	8	9	7	0
Barland and Raskin[109]	47 / 17	100	14	53	0	8
Ginton et al.[86]	2 / 13	87	13	13	—	0
Patrick and Iocono[105]	89	95	5			
Balloun and Holms[111]	34	73	27			0
Average		88%	12%			1%

It is important to be aware that many of these results are based on verified charts in which the original examiner achieved complete accuracy. These percentages reflect the accuracy level of the blind evaluation of charts and not the accuracy of the polygraph approach. It is clear from these findings that additional data is obtained during the examination and that this enhances the accuracy of this procedure. Although this takes away from the objectivity of the test because such factors relate to the demeanor of the subject and cannot be scored, they are part of the art of the testing process, just as a psychologist obtains clues to a patient's emotional state from vocal inflection, body movements, and other unscorable data. The 85 percent accuracy obtained is a significant underestimate of the validity of this approach. There is strong evidence that the tracings readily point out the guilty and that it is largely the innocent who present nontracing information that leads to their accurately being diagnosed as nondeceptive. It would seem that the difference between false positives and negatives is not as great when other data are included when making a diagnosis. These findings strongly suggest that the examiner must be aware of this other information until such time as the control question can be strengthened. It is abundantly clear that the emotional effect of the control question on the innocent is not as powerful as the effect of the relevant question is on the guilty. Until a method is developed to make them equivalent, false positives will exceed false negatives in CQT testing. This can be partly dealt with by Backster's method of requiring a lesser score to pass a test than to fail one.

FIELD GKT RESEARCH

Only one study of the GKT has been reported in a real testing situation and that is the research of Balloun and Holmes.[111] As indicated earlier, this was a laboratory investigation in which the subjects were made to believe that the situation was real. The purpose was to compare those with high and low psychopathic scores in the MMPI and to determine if greater reactions occurred on the first testing as compared to the second. Because the study does not provide a determination of accuracy through the use of both tests, it does not present a great deal of information as to the overall validity of the approach. Balloun and Holmes reported that in the first testing correct judgments were made in 61 percent of the deceptive and in 88 percent of the truthful, whereas in the second administration of the test 17 percent of the deceptive and 94 percent of the truthful were accurately detected. As in the laboratory research, a greater tendency toward false negatives was noted.

RELIABILITY IN FIELD RESEARCH

The writer's prior evaluation of polygraph reliability some fifteen years ago found 85 percent consistency when the literature was reviewed. The findings at this time are essentially the same. There is still a lack of reliability studies, which is surprising considering how easily this research can be conducted.

Barland and Raskin studied 102 cases from referrals made by police, prosecutors, and defense attorneys. They were evaluated with a numerical scoring procedure and then blindly rated by another polygraphist.[112] When both examiners made a decision, they were in agreement in every case. When inconclusives were included, 84 percent agreement was reached. In a second evaluation of reliability, comparisons were made between law enforcement and private examiners and the ratings of the researchers. Compared to police agencies including inconclusives 64 percent agreement was found, and 92 percent concordance was found without inconclusives. Interestingly enough, the degree of agreement was less with private organizations—52 percent including inconclusives and 80 percent without them. In the Hunter and Ash research, twenty verified truthful and untruthful charts were scored blindly.[113] On two occasions seven examiners reevaluated the charts with a three-month gap between the evaluations. An average agreement of 81 percent was attained.

Barland administered seventy-seven polygraph examinations to criminal suspects, and then, six months later, rescored them.[114] There was an increased number of inconclusive decisions on the second evaluation, but in no case was a decision reversed. Therefore, 100 percent agreement occurred when inconclusives were excluded and 84 percent when they were included. Horvath had ten examiners evaluate the polygraph charts of 112 criminal suspects drawn from law enforcement files.[115] Half of the findings had been truthful and the other half deceptive; likewise, the charts were equally divided into verified and unverified cases. Substantial agreement among the ten examiners was found with little difference between the verified and unverified charts. The average degree

Table 13–6. Field Research of Reliability
(percentage)

Research	Number of cases	Agreement
Barland and Raskin[112]	102	100%
		92
		80
Hunter and Ash[113]	40	81
Barland[114]	77	100
Horvath[115]	112	76
Davidson[116]	21	89
Edel and Jacoby[117]	40	96
Kleinmintz and Szucko[118]	100	28
Average		82%

of agreement was at the 76 percent level. In Davidson's investigation, which included the CAM among the other polygraph measures, agreement was at the 89 percent level for the polygraph including the CAM and 86 percent for the polygraph without the CAM.[116] Edel and Jacoby randomly selected forty cases from preemployment screening tests that used relevant, irrelevant, and control questions.[117] The examiner chose those responses in which a significant physiologic reaction occurred. A blind rater was found to be in agreement with his decision in 96 percent of the cases. In contrast to the findings presented, Kleinmuntz and Szucko reported much lower reliability figures.[118] This, however, was research in which interns were used, and an inconclusive decision was not allowed. They did report that when the evaluators were permitted to use all of the charts, they still achieved an average reliability of only about 28 percent. Although this figure reduced average reliability, when all of the research was considered the findings still indicated a consistency of 82 percent. Table 13–6 shows the reliability findings for the field research.

For more complete data on these studies dealing with validity and reliability, the reader is referred to Ansley and Garwood's *The Accuracy and Utility of Polygraph Testing* and the OTA's review of the literature on validity.[119]

THE LEGAL STATUS OF THE POLYGRAPH

14

It is better that many guilty persons should escape unpunished than one innocent person should suffer.

—John Adams

On August 22, 1921, James Alphonso Frye confessed to the murder of one Dr. Robert Brown.[1] Later he rescinded his admission and was subsequently examined by William Marston, who employed the systolic blood pressure test of deception. This early precursor to the polygraph indicated that Frye was truthful when he denied the commission of the homicide. These findings, however, were not admitted into evidence, and Frye was found guilty of second-degree murder. This decision was appealed, in part because of the rejection of the lie detector findings. In 1923 the United States Court of Appeals for the District of Columbia affirmed the conviction, stating,

Just when a scientific principle or discovery crosses the line between the experimental and demonstrable stages is difficult to define. Somewhere in this twilight zone the individual force of the principle must be recognized, and while the courts will go a long way in admitting expert testimony deduced from a well-recognized scientific principle or discovery, the thing from which the deduction is made must be sufficiently established to have gained general acceptance in the particular field in which it belongs.[2]

Frye v. United States not only set the precedent for the courts to reject lie detector evidence of any kind but developed a standard for the admissibility of new scientific procedures. The majority of courts have accepted this landmark decision as the standard for omitting and rejecting a wide range of scientific testimony. More recently, however, courts have been deluged with new scientific approaches and have begun to question the principle behind the *Frye* decision. Moreover, the Federal Rules of Evidence, which were adopted in 1975, do not address this test of general acceptance, leaving the courts to determine for themselves the status of the *Frye* test.[3]

Grannelli argued that the court's use of this standard has been inconsistent and selective and that many scientific procedures are not being held to the *Frye* standard.[4] Facts having probative value are often accepted into evidence if they aid in establishing some issue unless it biases, misleads. or preempts the fact-finding province of the jury. Polygraphy also has been accepted into evidence in many states where the courts routinely accept into evidence stipulated examinations but not those offered over objection.

Another important point made by Grannelli is that the concept of scientific community is vague. This is particularly the case in the polygraph field because all but a handful of scientists have divorced themselves from this area of interest. Therefore, psychologists, psychiatrists, physiologists, and physicians rarely administer such tests, nor are they much involved in experimentation in this area or do they keep up with the literature. They therefore are not an appropriate group to either accept or reject polygraphy. The only group in the position to provide general acceptance would be polygraphists.

Recently, judicial recognition was given to another area of expertise based on its acceptance by those within the field who were actively involved with the approach, despite the fact that the overall group was basically uninformed about it.[5] When judicial notice is given, it is not necessary to establish a foundation because the court recognizes that a technique is sufficiently valid to dispense with requiring proof. There must be evidence of the validity of the approach and of the underlying theory. Despite continuing arguments involving the accuracy of the polygraph technique, there is ample evidence of its accuracy. Moreover, the theory underlying the method is sound and accepted by the scientific community. When a technique has become firmly established and validity in both of these areas exists, the courts should take judicial notice and should be concerned with the qualification of the expert, whether proper procedures were employed, and the condition of the instrumentation used. If these require-ments are met, this testimony should be as readily admitted into evidence as other scientific data are.

At the present time, a publication by Norman Ansley on polygraph admissibility indicates that on the federal level, the approach has been admitted into evidence in ten of the eleven circuits.[6] Only the Third Circuit has rejected it. Of these, it has been admitted over objection in five of the circuits, and in three of the circuits admissibility has been granted in civil cases. The military and the District of Columbia both have admitted polygraph testimony over objection. In the civil realm, it has been admitted over objection in a total of eight states, and in two of these it has also been accepted on a stipulated basis. However, in the area of criminal cases, it has been accepted into evidence on stipulation in thirty-eight states, and in eighteen states it has been admitted over objection. Ansley also reported that polygraph licensing laws exist in thirty-three states and that there is antipolygraph legislation in twenty-seven states.

In some states, polygraphy has taken a backward course. In Oregon expert po-lygraph testimony was routinely admitted on a stipulated basis. In *State v. Brown* the Oregon Supreme Court determined that a decision on polygraphy's validity could not be established from the scientific evidence and therefore ruled it in-admissible in cases in which there was an objection.[7] That court went a step further in *State v. Lyon*, indicating that a stipulation does not alter the validity of the procedure.[8] Now polygraphy is not admitted into Oregon courts on either a stipulated or unstipulated basis. Another reason for the decision was based on the undue delay in administering justice resulting from challenges to the accu-racy of the test, the introduction of opposing test results, and challenges to the qualifications of the examiner. There was also concern about how the test would affect the jury.

In 1974 the Supreme Court of Wisconsin employed the *Valdez* criteria for the admission of stipulated polygraph testimony in *State v. Stanislawski*.[9] Seven years later the court in *State v. Dean* overruled the *Stanislawski* decision and found that polygraph evidence submitted pursuant to stipulation was inadmissible.[10] This was followed by *State v. Greer* in North Carolina, which ruled that the prior acceptance of admissibility under stipulation does not enhance polygraph relia-bililty.[11] There was also concern that the jury might be unduly persuaded by the polygraph testimony. This decision overruled *State v. Melano*.[12] Other states, however, continue to admit polygraph testimony on a stipulated basis.[13]

Probably the first case in which lie detection results were admitted into evidence was *People v. Kenny* in 1938.[14] Reverend Walter Summers, who chaired the grad-uate psychology department at Fordham University, used electrodermal re-sponses to determine whether a man accused of robbery was responding truth-fully in his denial of this act. The testimony was admitted over objection, and

Kenny was acquitted. This lower court decision to accept this evidence was not appealed to a higher court. However, in *People v. Forte*, a homicide case, the evidence was ruled inadmissible, which was later affirmed by the New York Court of Appeals.[15] A long string of rejections by the courts followed for a variety of reasons. In 1948 in *People v. Houser*, polygraph testimony was ruled admissible into evidence at an appellate level for the first time.[16] A stipulation had been made prior to the examination, but when deceptive findings were obtained and the defendant found guilty, the decision was appealed. The California District Court of Appeals affirmed the trial court's decision. In a similar situation in *State v. McNamara*, a stipulation had been entered, but the defendant objected to the admission of this testimony after he was found to be lying.[17] The stipulation was upheld by the Iowa Supreme Court in 1960. the Arizona Supreme Court also upheld the admission of polygraph testimony in a stipulated agreement in *People v. Valdez*.[18] Similar decisions were reached in *State v. Chavez* in New Mexico[19] and *State v. McDavett* in New Jersey.[20] Polygraph testimony is frequently accepted at the trial level, but these cases are not appealed and therefore are not reported.

To assist in developing a procedure for the admission of polygraph findings under stipulation, the Arizona Supreme Court developed the following set of procedures:[21]

1. The county attorney, defendant, and defendant's counsel sign a written stipulation providing for defendant's submission to the test and for the subsequent admission at trial of the graphs and the examiner's opinion thereon on behalf of either defendant or the state.

2. Notwithstanding the stipulation, the admissibility of the test results is subject to the discretion of the trial judge. If the trial judge is not convinced that the examiner is qualified or that the test was conducted under proper conditions, he or she may refuse to accept such evidence.

3. If the graphs and examiner's opinion are offered in evidence, the opposing party shall have a right to cross-examine with the examiner respecting (a) the examiner's qualifications and training; (b) the conditions under which the test was administered; (c) the limitations of and possibilities for error in the technique of polygrahic interrogation; and (d) at the discretion of the trial judge, any other matter deemed pertinent to the inquiry.

4. If such evidence is admitted, the trial judge should instruct the jury that the examiner's testimony does not tend to prove or disprove any element of the crime with which a defendant is charged but at most tends only to indicate that at the time of the examination the defendant was not telling the truth. Further, the jury members should be instructed that it is for them to determine what corroborative weight and effect such testimony should be given.

Two states have opened the door to admission of polygraph evidence without stipulation. In 1974 in *Commonwealth v. A Juvenile* the Massachusetts Supreme Court held that under certain circumstances and at the prerogative of the trial judge, the results of polygraph testing could be admitted into evidence.[22] In *State v. Lecaro* in New Mexico a series of five rules were developed for admitting polygraph testimony:[23]

1. Both parties stipulate to the test and its admission as evidence.
2. No objection to its admission is offered at trial.
3. The court hears evidence of the qualifications of the examiner to establish his or her expertise.
4. Testimony to establish the reliability of the testing procedure is heard to determine whether the procedure is approved by authorities in the field.
5. Validity of the tests is established.

In 1975, however, in *New Mexico v. Dorsey* the court found that the first two rules were too restrictive, which served to allow polygraph testimony into evidence over objection.[24]

There have been a wide variety of reasons for rejecting polygraph testimony. One of the most common relates to what the courts have called "reliability." In statistical terms this refers to validity or accuracy. Although there is solid evidence for the high level of validity that exists, the court's dilemma is to sort through the data. There are actually few critics of polygraphy, but they have managed to make themselves heard, and objections will continue to be based on the assumption that the polygraph approach lacks adequate validity. The facts are that it is not infallible; there are errors made. There is also a tendency to err in the direction of false positives when control question techniques are employed. Still, it remains one of the most accurate—if not *the* most accurate—psychological test in existence.

The courts have presented a number of other reasons for excluding polygraph testimony. A frequent concern has been that it will usurp the role of the jury. Unlike other evidence, it reportedly gets to the heart of the matter under consideration. As is discussed in chapter 15 this writer strongly feels that the effectiveness of the expert witness who presents this information to the jury, not the data conveyed, determines its effect. Expert testimony presented by the opposing side will balance out any undue influence of polygraph testimony on the jury. It should also be noted that despite concerns about the jury's being overly influenced by polygraph testimony, there are many instances where jury decisions have been inconsistent with polygraph testimony.

Some attempts have been made to determine how much effect polygraph testimony has on a jury. In *People v. Kenny* Forkosch polled the jurors to determine the effect that Reverend Summers's testimony on the effectiveness of the galvanometer that he employed had on their decision.[25] None of the jurors made a determination on the basis of this test alone, but five of the ten indicated that they accepted the testimony without question. It is suspected, however, that the jury might be more likely to accept any evidence presented by a priest. More recently, Barnett interviewed the jurors in *United States v. Grasso,* in which polygraph testimony was admitted.[26] The five jurors who could be reached indicated that they were impressed with the foundation testimony and that they were convinced that the procedure would differentiate between truth and deception. However, they considered the other evidence first and found that it was sufficient for them to reach a decision without using the polygraph findings. If, however, a determination could not have been made on the data that they had available to them, the polygraph findings would have influenced their decision. The court questioned the jury as to the helpfulness of polygraph testimony in *Wisconsin v. Loniell & Grignano.*[27] The jurors indicated that it was of assistance in determining the credibility of the witnesses and defendants.

In a research situation, Koffler had law students determine guilt or innocence in three hypothetical cases.[28] In the first case there was slight evidence of guilt but no polygraph test had been administered, and in the other two instances there was also marginal evidence of guilt but polygraph findings were indicative of deception. The findings were that defendants could be convicted on minor evidence if deceptive polygraph results were reported and the less chance of polygraph error reported, the greater the jury's decision was influenced by the test findings.

The effect of polygraph testimony on a jury also can be greatly affected by the judicial instructions that are given. Too strong a warning can negate its probative value, while little or no instructions might increase its impact on the jury. The instructions to the jury in *United States v. Valdez* are felt to be sufficiently adequate to not overly influence the jury in either direction:[29] "The examiner's testimony does not tend to prove or disprove any element of the crime . . . at most [it] tends only to indicate that at the time of the examination the defendant was not telling the truth . . . it is for them to determine what corroborative weight and affect such testimony should be given."

A lack of acceptance by the scientific community is still being presented as a reason to reject polygraph testimony. In the *Frye* case it was appropriately noted that general acceptance did not exist for the systolic blood pressure deception test. This issue was studied by McCormich in 1927.[30] He polled eighty-eight members of the American Psychological Association who were likely to be interested in this particular field. They were asked if this particular device furnished results of sufficient accuracy to be used in court to determine the credibility of witnesses. Only thirty-nine replied, but of those, eighteen indicated that it was accurate, and thirteen felt that it was not. From these findings, McCormich indicated that although the respondents viewed this approach as resting on sound theory, there should be greater acceptance before admitting this testimony into evidence. In 1953 Cureton sent questionnaires to all individuals who were known to be competent on polygraph procedures.[31] Out of a total of 1,682, 711 responded. When asked whether polygraphy was a highly valid measure for recording physiologic responses, 83 percent of the examiners, 63 percent of the psychologists, and 63 percent of the psychologist-polygraphists answered in the affirmative. For those respective groups, 47 percent, 63 percent, and 60 percent recommended that the approach be admitted into evidence. Concerning its use in business and industry, 83 percent of the examiners, 28 percent of the psychologists, and 51 percent of those who were both recommended this. Twenty years later, in 1973, Ash surveyed behavioral scientists and attorneys.[32] He reported that 69 percent of psychologists, 60 percent of sociologists, 82 percent of prosecutors, and 72 percent of defense attorneys favored admission on stipulation. As to whether it should be admitted into evidence over objection in exceptional cases, the same groups respectively agreed that it should be 38 percent, 23 percent, 42 percent, and 30 percent. Lower figures were obtained when respondents were questioned as to whether it should be generally admissible even over objection. Only 28 percent of the psychologists, 13 percent of the sociologists, 32 percent of the prosecutors, and 11 percent of the defense lawyers agreed with this. There was high agreement on its use in criminal investigations, with 76 percent, 59 percent, 96 percent, and 75 percent, respectively, favoring it. It can be seen that both admissibility on a stipulated basis and its use in criminal investigation was viewed rather positively by all four groups. Most recently, in December 1982, a sample of the Society for Psychophysiological Research was polled by the Gallup organization.[33] A group of 155 of approximately 900 members was randomly selected. As would be expected in a group of psychologists and physiologists, only 11 percent had ever used a polygraph to determine truthfulness or deception, but despite this, 33 percent considered themselves very informed and 57 percent saw themselves as somewhat informed about the state of the art. When asked if the approach were sufficiently reliable to be the sole determinant of truthfulness, only 1 percent agreed that it was, but 62 percent believed it to be a useful diagnostic tool when considered with other available data.

The question of scientific acceptance would seem to be answered. From the Ash study an approximate average of 67 percent indicated that polygraphy should be admitted on a stipulated basis, and 63 percent of the members of the Society for Psychological Research viewed it as a useful diagnostic tool to measure truth and deception. If the *Frye* standard is to be employed, these findings should argue in favor of polygraph admissibility.

Other objections to polygraph admissibility include questions as to the validity of the underlying theory.[34] Smith argued that polygraphy was not a scientific truth method because its underlying theory was not developed through research and it has not been refined through continued experimentation.[35] In contrast to this, polygraph research has grown over the years, particularly with the increase in interest now being expressed by psychologists. This is true not only in the United States, but experimentation is being conducted in Canada, Poland, Japan, and Israel as well. The validity studies have demonstrated not only the accuracy of the technique but the foundation on which it rests as well. Although there is not a high correlation among autonomic responses, the combination used effectively serve their purpose. They differentiate between truth and deception. It should also be recognized that polygraphy, like other sciences, has national and local societies that accredit the schools, monitor its members and provide education in the form of seminars at both the local and national levels. Continuing research is published in polygraph journals and in other law, psychology, and physiology journals. A move initiated by Backster to standardize the approach has unquestionably had an effect on the field. Question formulation, pretest interview procedures, chart interpretations, and numerical scoring have all moved in this direction of standardization. Polygraphy has reached the stage where it can be considered a science—not a hard science like biology, but one within the realm of the social sciences that it still partially art and partly science.

Lykken has indicated that polygraph instrumentation is far behind that employed in laboratory situations.[36] Unfortunately, laboratory equipment is not economically feasible nor is it portable. Moreover, there is no clear evidence that laboratory instrumentation results in findings that are more valid than those made with portable equipment. Moreover, significant improvements are being made as new sensors are developed and modifications are made on portable equipment that is already in use.

Criticisms have been raised that examiners are not adequately trained and that polygraphy would have been routinely admitted into evidence years ago if tests were being administered by psychologists or psychiatrists.[37] Attempts have been made to require a minimum of a bachelor's degree for admission into polygraph schools and into the American Polygraph Association, with exceptions to this rule based on years of investigative experience. Other changes in requirements include a six-month internship and an extended training period. One facet of polygraphy has been ignored, however. Psychologists and psychiatrists have had little contact with the criminal population and can be rather gullible. Although they are trained and practiced in interviewing procedures, they lack knowledge of interrogation. Considering this lack of experience, they are ineffective in coping with the manipulation, denial, projection, rationalization, and blatant lying that law enforcement officers experience every day. In many ways, an individual with investigative background is more able to accomplish his or her purpose than a rather naive professional who is accustomed to accepting what a patient says.

There have been claims made that many examiners are unethical. Raskin has made strong statements to this effect, questioning both the competence and ethics of polygraphists.[38] He stated that there is "poor training and levels of competence on the part of polygraph examiners; and unfortunately often low levels of ethics and integrity . . . there are many polygraph examiners whose integrity is so low that I think it borders on criminality." Polygraphy, like any other field, has practitioners who are unethical and incompetent. There is no reason to assume that this occurs any more frequently in this field than in others.

Another concern that persists is that the courts could be overburdened with complex testimony and the battles of experts that would follow admission of polygraphy results.[39] Each science has its own theories, research, and methods to present, and as long as there are trial lawyers, the opposing attorney will always find an expert witness to present a contrary opinion. These conflicting opinions could be avoided if only court-appointed experts were permitted to testify, but it is argued that this would unduly influence the jury and would dispense with the usual checks and balances that are integral to the judicial system.

A philosophical argument has been brought out in the courts and in some countries that precludes the use of polygraphy. This objection was recently raised by the Oregon Supreme Court in *State v. Lyon,* where it was indicated that "the polygraph seeks to turn the human body against the personality that inhabits it in a way that other tests do not" and "The polygraph turns the subject into an object."[40] Germany has operated under the concept that because physiologic measures were used the individual was responding involuntarily if he or she were lying to avoid the discovery of guilt. Because the subject cannot deny culpability, the test is an involuntary act. France also precludes polygraph testing on the grounds that it operates against the free will of the individual. Silving emphasized the loss of human dignity that is the right of both the good and the evil, the innocent and guilty.[41] According to Falick, penetrating the inner being violates both the right to privacy and human dignity.[42] Perhaps, however, with increasing crime rates, high degrees of recidivism, and overcrowded prisons we must consider the victims as well. For too long society has lived under the threat of robbery, burglary, or being victimized in more sophisticated crimes. Rape, murder, and child abuse have risen to unprecedented levels, that require a little less dignity and more protection for society.

In 1953 Inbau and Reid indicated that polygraphy was not yet ready for judicial acceptance, but in 1966 they stated that examinations that had been competently conducted should be admitted into evidence.[43] The examiner should meet certain requirements, including a college degree, completion of a six-month internship, and five years of experience, and testimony should be based on charts that are presented before the court for cross-examination. It was also recommended that the court instruct the jury that polygraph results are not conclusive but should be considered along with the other evidence. Tarlow has indicated that if polygraph evidence is accurate enough to be admitted on a stipulated basis, it should be admitted over objection as well.[44]

A variety of decisions made on different aspects of the polygraph procedures are pertinent to examiners. In regard to statements being made during the trial process referring to refusal or willingness to take a polygraph test, the courts are not in agreement. In some instances this has been viewed as harmless error, but in other cases it has been seen as improper because it invited prejudice. In *Commonwealth v. Saunders* the Supreme Court of Pennsylvania affirmed the trial court's decision to reject evidence that the defendant was willing to take a polygraph examination.[45] Often it has simply been considered to be harmless error.[46]

Generally, the courts have ruled that the defendant was not entitled to pretrial discovery of polygraph results because those results could not be used in evidence. This holds even in cases of those individuals who testified against them.[47] In contrast to this, in *Ballard v. Superior Court* it was decided that even though generally inadmissible, the defendant who was accused of rape had pretrial discovery of the polygraph results of the alleged victim.[48]

Admissions made associated with polygraph testing have generally been ruled admissible.[49] Those admissions were not perceived in terms of a confession being made with threats, force, or promise.

It would seem from the foregoing that courts will continue to disagree on this issue. Because judges generally tend to be conservative, however, and follow the majority opinion, it is difficult to decide against precedent and face the possible negative reaction of the appeals court. Because of these factors, there has been little significant change in the status of the polygraph in the last ten years. Advances have been made in some states, and losses have been experienced in others. The next ten years should produce some dramatic changes, including the almost inevitable elimination of commercial testing outside of the government realm. Much more research is being conducted, psychologists are becoming more involved in testing, and crime is increasing. The pendulum is expected to swing away from civil rights and in the direction of tougher laws and longer sentences. The costs of crime—not only in losses, victimization, and the housing of these people, but the costs of trials—are overburdening the public. It is believed that these factors will inevitably force the recognition of polygraphy.

THE POLYGRAPHIST AS AN EXPERT WITNESS

15

A jury is made up of a group of people who decide who has the better attorney.
—Unknown

Some courts are concerned that polygraph testimony will influence the jury to the degree that it will usurp the jury's role as fact finder. But jurors are influenced by many factors, including the demeanor of the defendant, the arguments of the attorneys, and the effectiveness of expert witnesses. Polygraph findings alone will not influence any juror, but the credibility of the polygraphist will certainly have an effect on this panel, and effectiveness in presenting testimony can influence the jury's final decision. Recognizing this, attorneys often prepare their witnesses and sometimes bring in specialists to train them to be more believable. Shadow juries are similar to the panel that will be selected in a pending trial, and various witnesses testify in a mock trial, being examined by attorneys as though under actual trial conditions. Members of the shadow jury are questioned as to how they were affected by both witnesses and lawyers. Verbal comments or behavioral acts that made witnesses appear credible to the jury are reinforced, and negative actions are eliminated. Even factors such as voice, inflection, posture, and clothing are considered because all of these variables influence the jury.

While juries purportedly are composed of our peers, this is not the case because many people are able to avoid jury duty. Juries may have a preponderance of persons holding low-paying jobs, unemployed persons, retirees, and housewives. Nevertheless, it is felt that the jury functions as a unit and its collective intelligence, memory, and overall aptitudes allow it to comprehend much of the technical data that is presented in court. It is true that sometimes jury members doze, read magazines, or day dream, but basically what one member misses, the others will hear and understand. Together the jury provides a unique set of checks and balances that reasonably effectively determines the facts of a case. As it has been said before, the jury may not be the best fact-finding system, but it is the best we have.

The testimony of the expert witness can have a large effect on jury members. Therefore expert witnesses are not chosen because they necessarily are the best in their fields but rather because they will most likely present their testimony in an understandable, believable, interesting, and personable manner. The better their credentials and the more knowledgeable they are, the greater their effect on the jury. Knowing this, the polygraphist must learn the principles of effective testimony.

For the person who has never testified, the courtroom can be a frightening experience. Having seen Perry Mason destroy people on the witness stand, the neophyte often anticipates the same treatment. Fortunately or unfortunately, there are few Perry Masons, and many lawyers are less than adequate. Moreover, lawyers are often unprepared, and some prosecutors actually may not have a case assigned to them until the day of the trial. Lawyers also cannot be experts in the field in which the expert is testifying. All too often they cram before the trial trying to learn as much about the area as they can or else they bring in a consultant to assist them in questioning the witness. Inevitably, their knowledge is superficial, and when they ask all of the questions that they have prepared, they generally can go no further. The polygraphist should recognize that he or she is the expert and knows the field far better than the attorney.

It is recommended that novices to the courtroom sit in on trials to get some feel for the arena. Observing where and how witnesses are sworn in, where the witness box is situated in relation to the jury, and how different lawyers deal with witnesses eliminates much anxiety.

The newcomer also should question the attorney who has brought him into the case about the style of the opposing counsel and about the questions the attorney will ask. Once again, the polygraphist is the expert and should inform the lawyer of the questions that should be asked. This writer prepares a list of questions that considerably simplifies the attorney's role. For establishing a foundation, the following questions have been found to be helpful:

1. **How frequently is polygraphy used today?** The answer deals with other countries that employ polygraphy, how government and law enforcement use it, its value in the business realm, and its admission into evidence.

2. **Would you provide a brief history of the field?** Here the emphasis is that polygraphy has been in use in criminal investigations for about a hundred years and that research has been conducted throughout this period.

3. **Is polygraphy accepted by the scientific community?** The various surveys of the scientific community should be presented, including the most recent poll of the Society for Psychophysiological Research.

4. **What is the psychophysiological basis for the effectiveness of this approach?** At this point the examiner should be able to discuss the effect of the emotional state on the autonomic nervous system when a subject lies during the examination.

5. **What does the polygraph measure?** The expert must be prepared to discuss each of the sensors employed, detailing how each operates and the typical signs of deception.

6. **How is a polygraph examination administered?** The entire test procedure from pretest to posttest is discussed, including an explanation of the control question technique and why it is effective, if this is the test that has been employed.

8. **What is the validity and reliability of this procedure?** The expert must differentiate between laboratory and field research and must be able to quote from memory the authors, methods, and results of a great many studies.

9. **Are countermeasures effective against this approach?** Once again the polygraphist must be able to cite studies demonstrating his or her position.

10. **What were your findings in the case of the defendant?** The numerical scores, their meaning, and the degree of confidence one has in the results should be presented.

The questions and the responses should be discussed with the attorney prior to the trial. Any weaknesses that exist must be presented as well because it might be better for these to be brought out under direct examination (questioning by the lawyer who engaged the expert) rather than during cross-examination (questioning by opposing counsel). Redirect examination is when the attorney who brought the expert into the case has another opportunity to question the witness after cross-examination by opposing counsel. An effective preparation before the trial is for the attorney to cross-examine the witness so that any areas of weakness in the test results can be detected prior to actual trial. It also provides the expert with the opportunity to learn how to cope with the expected questions and the attacks on his or her competence.

It is important to be prepared before the trial. Materials being brought into the court should be well ordered so that the examiner is in control and can locate data easily. Anything that is brought into the courtroom by the expert can be requested by opposing counsel. In one case the expert for the plaintiff inadvertently brought in a test that had been covertly administered by a different polygraphist, who found the results to be indicative of deception. Being forced to show these results, which were inconsistent with the examiner's own findings, severely injured the plaintiff's case. The witness must bring all of his or her tests and data, but not necessarily other information.

The examiner should know the case extremely well and should be able to explain various aspects of the test. Detailed notes should have been taken during testing to confirm what occurred, and the expert should be able to smoothly and coherently describe the entire procedure. The charts may have to be displayed while the polygraphist rescores the test for the jury. The jury members will always be impressed when an expert can show how and why a response is either truthful or deceptive and also why the literature demonstrates that this is the case.

The witness's attire is important. Research shows that dark blue and black present an air of authority, and a white shirt and conservative tie add to that image. It should be noted, however, that in some areas of the country informal dress might be appropriate; the attorney is best qualified to determine this.

One of the first questions to be asked when the expert finally is seated in the witness stand is what are his or her qualifications. These first questions are asked by the attorney who employed him or her. The attorney has already reviewed the examiner's resume and will know which areas to emphasize to impress the jury with the experience, training, and expertise of the witness. The opposing attorney may attempt to stipulate to the examiner's qualifications, but typically the expert's attorney will not permit this. Therefore, it is to the witness's advantage to have as expansive a resume as possible. You are your resume. The more degrees attained, seminars attended, talks presented, societies belonged to, offices held, papers published, and tests administered, the more credible the witness appears to the jury.

Although there is a tendency to look at the attorney when responding to a question he or she has asked, the witness should instead look at the jury. If there is no jury, remarks should be directed toward the judge. The expert's voice should be loud enough for the farthest juror to hear. In the art to presenting testimony, the witness does not talk over the heads of jury members, which results in their not understanding and becoming bored, and does not talk beneath them, which causes resentment. Perhaps the best middle ground is the analogy of a teacher explaining a new subject to a class. If the class looks tired or even starts to doze, which is not terribly unusual, something has to be done to make students more interested. More inflection, examples, hand movements—something to bring them back to attention. In court, the expert should lean toward the jury members, making eye contact, watching for nods to indicate that they understand. If they look puzzled, the statement should be repeated in a different manner to make it clearer.

The testimony should not be memorized, which makes it sound rehearsed, dull, and perhaps untruthful. There is also the possibility that a question posed by an attorney will cause the witness to lose his or her place, resulting in some confusion. At all times the expert must be in control, appear calm, and be able to deal with various questions. The opposing attorney cannot be allowed to take this control away by setting the pace of the answers, by creating confusion, or through the use of other techniques to diminish the witness's credibility.

Responses to the opposing attorney should be courteous, regardless of his or her attitude. The attorney cannot afford to be too nasty because the jury might then sympathize with the witness and the attorney would lose ground. For the same reason, hostile remarks by the expert should be avoided. Responses to questions should be slightly delayed to be certain that the answer is completely correct and also to give an opportunity for an objection to the question. The answer then should be presented in a fairly definite manner. Phrases such as "I think" or "I believe" should be replaced with those such as "It is my opinion that" or "The research demonstrates that."

If an error is made, it should be corrected, and by no means should there ever be an untruth or an exaggeration; if the opposing attorney can demonstrate that the witness is biased or lying, his or her credibility is destroyed.

A demeanor of infallibility or superiority not only affects the jury in a negative manner but places the opposing lawyer in a better position to make a fool of the polygraphist. Juries can readily forgive an error in a courteous forthright person, but not in one who is cocky. Then they almost enjoy seeing the witness taken down a notch or two; one who acts superior falls hard when he or she loses a point to the opposing attorney. Although an air of infallibility is inappropriate, so too is a humble or submissive style. The most appropriate approach is to adopt the attitude of being an authority in the field who maintains composure and becomes neither angry nor anxious. The expert should be polite and agreeable and attempt to respond to each query without evasiveness, distortion, or exaggeration. His or her role is to report information, and if opposing counsel makes a correct statement, the reply should be, "You are quite right." If the expert admits to those points that the lawyer is attempting to make, the jury will more readily accept those with which the expert disagrees. The expert witness should be seen as an objective, unbiased scientist.

In interactions with the opposing side, the expert must listen closely to the questions to determine where the attorney is trying to trick him or her. Usually, this is rather obvious. The witness must be wary of traps, and the more gentle the counsel appears to be during cross-examination, the more wary the witness should be. An expert tired by long, arduous hours of questioning is open to making errors. Continuous attacks can lead the witness to admit things that are not correct. Making the witness angry reduces his or her thinking capabilities, all of which cause the witness to look bad before the jury. Because the major role of the attorney in court is to destroy the credibility of the witness, the opposing attorney may sneer at the witness, make disparaging remarks, and imply that the witness has been bought to testify, but these tactics are part of the courtroom game. Just as opposing attorneys might bitterly attack one another in court and then have lunch together when the case is over, the examiner might be assailed by an opposing attorney in the witness box one morning and then receive a call from that attorney in the afternoon requesting his or her services as a witness.

How the questions should be answered is a matter of personal preference. In almost any case, the response should be simple and direct and respond only to the question asked. Additional information should not be volunteered because this might provide the lawyer with additional data to hurt the witness's testimony. If, however, the expert is extremely competent in the field, more information may strengthen a point.

In most instances the most obvious approach to presenting evidence is to provide testimony in an objective scientific manner and avoid showing any bias. The alternative, and the role that most attorneys prefer their witnesses to play, is to become part of the adversary system and speak as an advocate for the defendant. If the expert is very certain of his or her findings and not simply being seduced by the attorney, this advocacy is acceptable. The danger in this approach lies in the witness's appearing so biased that his or her testimony becomes suspect by the jury.

Lawyers will frequently ask and sometimes demand a simple yes or no answer. This can result in a misleading response, and the witness has the right to indicate that he or she cannot respond in this manner. Although most times the witness will be allowed to elaborate, in those instances when this is not permitted, his or her attorney will provide the witness the opportunity to answer the query more fully during redirect. When the expert is questioned as to whether he or she is aware of a particular study that he or she is not familiar with, the expert can reply that he is not but is knowledgeable about other research in this realm. The opposing lawyer probably will not allow this research to be presented, but this response cues the witness's attorney to ask about this research during redirect examination.

A favorite lawyer's trick is to refer back to a previous statement made by the polygraphist but in the paraphrasing distort the meaning to the lawyer's advantage. If this should occur, the expert witness should quickly point out that this statement was not made and reiterate what was actually stated. If there is any doubt, the court reporter can read back what was stated. If a question is asked that is not clear, the attorney should be asked to repeat or rephrase it. Lawyers frequently use long hypothetical questions that often lose their meaning as the verbiage increases. Requesting that the question be repeated often results in their giving up and asking another question. The polygraphist, on the other hand, should not hedge in answering; if he or she does not know the answer, the witness should simply say so. Any attempt at bluffing will be detected by a smart attorney, who can make the witness appear foolish and destroy the value of his or her entire testimony. Although an "I don't know" response is appropriate, the witness should avoid a series of them. Out of concern for appearing incompetent the expert might be tempted to answer questions out of his or her realm of expertise, but this most certainly will result in trouble for the witness. There is some tendency for one's own attorney to ask questions of this nature, but the expert must be wary of responding to these queries as well.

Probably the major advantage held by attorneys is that the game is being played in their ball park. They are accustomed to the courtroom and know how to manipulate witnesses. For polygraphists, the courtroom is an alien land, and they, as authorities, are not accustomed to having opinions doubted or to being treated rudely. It is important for the expert to maintain his or her composure and not take the attacks personally. The attorney's knowledge of the field may be minimal, but if he or she gets into difficulty with a witness, the attorney only has to ask questions in another realm. If the expert is in trouble, the opposing attorney will continue to hammer away. For the most part, the witness must protect himself and cannot rely on either an attorney or a judge to help him out of an awkward position. A lawyer may object to a particular line of questioning, but the judge may overrule it, which means the witness must respond. If objection is sustained, no answer is necessary.

Some rather typical trick questions asked include, "Are you being paid to testify in this case?" The simplest reply is, "I'm being reimbursed for my time away from the office." "How much are you being paid?" "My out-of-the-office consulting fee is _____." Another common question is, "Could you be biased in favor of the defendant?" The best response is, "Yes, and being aware of that I make an additional effort to guard against it."

One polygraphist witness was obviously concerned about responding "I don't know" a number of times in a row. Sensitive to this, the opposing lawyer began asking if the witness was familiar with specific books. In desperation, the witness stated that he knew those texts. At this, the attorney turned to the jury and said that there were no such books; he had simply made up the titles and authors. Once again, a good response is, "No, I'm not, but I am familiar with the major polygraph books, which are . . . "

Specific questions that develop a trap and discredit the witness and polygraph technique can be anticipated. Questions relating to how the examiner knew the subject was in the proper physical, medical, and psychological condition to be examined may well be followed with the expression of doubt of the examiner's ability to make this decision. Because the test itself involves psychology and physiology, the opposing counsel may go into a long argument, indicating that without a degree in psychology and physiology the polygraphist is not competent to administer the examination or interpret the results. In response to this, if he in fact is allowed to respond, the polygraphist must be able to present a concise and understandable explanation of the psychological and physiological bases for the polygraph. He or she should also indicate how the subject's behavior and polygraph tracings gave no indication that either a sufficient psychological or physiological problem existed to invalidate the findings. This should be justified through the polygraphist's training and knowledge, demonstrating through examples how some drug conditions, medical problems, or psychiatric disorders create obvious responses that would cause the examiner to label the findings as inconclusive. As is true throughout the testimony, the witness must present an air of control and confidence. The jury's acceptance of what the witness presents will, to a large extent, be based on an emotional response. Was the witness likeable, believable, confident, forthright, personable?

Although the preceding material might make the courtroom appear to be a battlefield, it rarely is one. Attorneys cannot afford to be too hard on a witness; they are poorly prepared, know little of polygraphy, and often simply are not very impressive. For example, an attorney can spend five minutes between questions, digging up the next question from an old law journal. In another instance, the examiner's attorney asked all the wrong questions, but the opposing attorney asked those that should have been asked so that the opposing attorney destroyed his own case.

At the conclusion of the testimony, the examiner should leave the witness stand, demonstrating an expression of confidence rather than relief, fatigue, or anger. The entire situation could be treated as an important competitive match in which each opponent plays his or her role as effectively as possible. The stakes are high, but as in any competition, the witness should remain calm and deliberate and plan moves in advance. Like a chess player, the witness also should be aware of the meaning of each of the opponent's moves and try to determine the opposing lawyer's strategy so that he or she will be prepared for it. The witness should be constantly aware of what is occurring and the direction the cross-examination is taking and especially look for the setting of any traps. If the polygraphist is prepared for traps, they can be avoided.

A deposition is quite different from a courtroom situation. It can take place in the polygraph examiner's office or at his or her attorney's suite. The purpose is the discovery of facts by the opposing counsel. Opposing counsel conducts the proceedings and attempts to determine what the witness is prepared to say in court, search for weaknesses, test the knowledge of the witness, and look for statements that might contradict statements made in the trial.

Because the environment is more relaxed at a deposition, there is a tendency to respond too casually and thereby provide the opposing side with too much information. As in a courtroom setting, the expert should be cautious and unquestionably respond only to the question in a minimal way. The more information that is provided, the more ammunition the opposing counsel has to use against the expert in court.

APPENDIXES

POLYGRAPH QUESTIONNAIRE

APPENDIX A

⬛

Name _____ Date _____

Address _____ Telephone _____

Age _____ Date of birth _____ Place of birth _____

Referred by _____ Address _____

Telephone _____

EXAMINEE'S HISTORY

Past medical problems _____

_____

Present medical problems _____

_____

Medications presently taking _____

_____

Medications taken since midnight _____

_____

History of psychiatric treatment _____

_____

Present psychiatric treatment _____

Education:

    Level completed _____ Degree attained _____ School _____

    Educational problems _____

Police record _____

_____

Service:

    Branch _____ Dates _____ Type of discharge _____

Vocation:

    Type of work _____ Employer _____

Marital status _____ Number of marriages _____

Number of children _____

Purpose of testing:

    Accusation _____ Time and place _____

Alleged victim _____

Examinee's description of events _____

_____

_____

_____

To the best of my knowledge, this information is true and complete.

Signature _____

EXAMINER'S COMMENTS

The following is to be completed by the examiner:

Police description of events _____

_____

_____

_____

_____

Place of testing _____ Subject's driver's license no. _____

Examinee's physical state _____ Prior polygraph _____

Examinee's medical state _____

Examinee's emotional state _____

Examinee's estimated intelligence _____

Interview time _____ Test time _____ Concluding time _____

Last instrument calibration date _____

Test results:

Comments _____

_____

_____

POLYGRAPH SCORE SHEET

APPENDIX B

Subject _____ Date _____ Examiner _____

Decision _____ Reviewed by _____ Date _____

Chart 1   *Comments*

Respiration					
Electrodermal					
Cardiovascular					

Chart 2

Respiration					
Electrodermal					
Cardiovascular					

Chart 3

Respiration					
Electrodermal					
Cardiovascular					

Chart 4

Respiration					
Electrodermal					
Cardiovascular					

Respiration _____

Electrodermal _____

Totals					

Cardiovascular _____

RIGHTS STATEMENT

APPENDIX C

Place _____

Date _____

Time _____

YOUR RIGHTS

Before we ask you any questions, you must understand your rights.

You have the right to remain silent.

Anything you say can be used against you in court.

You have the right to talk to a lawyer for advice before we ask you any questions and to have your lawyer with you during questioning.

If you cannot afford a lawyer, one will be appointed for you before any questioning, if you wish.

If you decide to answer questions now without a lawyer present, you will still have the right to stop answering at any time. You also have the right to stop answering at any time, until you talk to a lawyer.

WAIVER OF RIGHTS

I have read this statement of my rights and I understand what my rights are. I am willing to make a statement and answer questions. I do not want a lawyer at this time. I understand and know what I am doing. No promises or threats have been made to me, and no pressure or coercion of any kind has been used against me. I voluntarily and knowingly waive the above rights.

Signature _____

Witnesses:

_____

_____

Time: _____

PERMISSION TO TEST MINOR

APPENDIX D

I, _____ (parent/guardian), authorize

_____ to administer a polygraph to

_____ at the request of _____
(please print)

Juvenile Court. The results of the polygraph will be disclosed to the above

named court.

_____   _____
Witness signature   Parent/guardian signature

_____   _____
Date   Date

MEDICAL RELEASE BY PHYSICIAN FOR TESTING

APPENDIX E

I, Doctor _____ , physician of

_____ , find no reason why my patient should experi-

ence any negative effects, either physical or psychological, from the administra-

tion of a polygraph examination. Therefore, if she/he is willing to take this test,

I see no medical reason why she/he should not take part in this procedure.

Physician's signature _____

Date _____

Witness's signature _____

Date _____

MEDICAL RELEASE BY SUBJECT FOR TESTING

APPENDIX F

Place _____

Date _____

I, _____ , have requested a poly-

graph examination and recognize that I will be totally responsible for any neg-

ative effects of either a physical or psychological nature that occur to me. I rec-

ognize that my medical condition of _____

makes me prone to risk, but I am willing to absolve the examiner,

_____ , of all responsibility if any

negative results should occur.

Examinee's signature _____

Date _____

Witness's signature _____

Date _____

NOTES

PREFACE

1. Freud, S., "Psycho-analysis and the Ascertaining of Truth in Courts of Law," in E. Jones (ed.), *Sigmund Freud Collected Papers*, Vol. 2 (New York:Basic Books, 1959), pp. 13–24.
2. "Scientific Validity of Polygraph Testing: A Research Review and Evaluation—A Technical Memorandum" (Washington, D.C.: U.S. Congress, Office of Technology Assessment, OTA-TM-H-15, 1983).
3. Patrick, C.J., and Iacono, W.G., "Validity and Reliability of the Control Question Polygraph Test: A Scientific Investigation," *Psychophysiology* 24 (1987); 605–06 (abstract).
4. Ansley, N., and Garwood, M., "The Accuracy and Utility of Polygraph Testing" (Washington, D.C.: Department of Defense, 1984).

CHAPTER 1

1. Ekman, P., *Telling Lies* (New York: Norton, 1985).
2. Lombroso, C., *L'Homme Criminel*, 2d ed. (1895).

3. Larson, J.A., *Lying and Its Detection* (Montclair, N.J.: Patterson Smith, 1969); Trovillo, P.V., "A History of Lie Detection," *Am. J. Police Sci.* 29 (1939):848–81, 30 (1939):104–19.

4. Benussi, V., "Die Atmungssymptome der Lüge Arch Für," *Die Gesante Psycholgic* 31 (1941): 244–73.

5. Burtt, H.E., "The Inspiration-Expiration Ratio during Truth and Falsehood," *J. Exper. Psych.* 6 (1921):1–23.

6. Marston, W.M., "Systolic Blood Pressure Symptoms of Deception," *J. Exper. Psych.* 2 (1917): 117–63.

7. Marston, W.M., "Sex Characteristics of Systolic Blood Pressure Behavior," *J. Exper. Psych.* 6 (1923): 387–419.

8. *United States v. Frye*, 293 F. 1013 (D.C. Cir. 1923).

9. Abrams, S., *A Polygraph Handbook for Attorneys* (Lexington, Mass.: Heath, 1977); Matte, J.A., *The Art and Science of the Polygraph Technique* (Springfield, Ill.: Thomas, 1980).

10. Marston, W.M., *The Lie Detector Test* (New York: Smith, 1938).

11. Starrs, J.E., "'A Still-Life Watercolor': *Frye v. United States*," *J. Forensic Sci.* 27 (1982): 684–94.

12. Larson, J.A., "Manipulation of the Marston Deception Test," *J. Crim. L.* 12 (1921): 390–99.

13. Highleyman, S.L., "The Deceptive Certainty of the Lie Detector," *Hastings L.J.* 10 (1958): 47–64.

14. Larson, J.A., "The Cardio-Pneumo-Psychogram in Deception," *j. Exper. Psych.* 6 (1923): 420–54.

15. Larson, J.A., *Lying and Its Detection;* note 3.

16. Keeler, L. "A Method of Detecting Deception," *Am. J. Police Sci.* 1 (1930): 38–51.

17. Keeler, L., "Scientific Methods of Criminal Detection with the Polygraph," *Kansas Bar Assn.* 2 (1933): 22–31.

18. Wolfle, D., "The Lie Detector: Methods for the Detection of Deception," prepared for the Emergency Committee in Psychology of the National Research Council (October 8, 1941), appendix E.

19. Eliasberg, W., "Forensic Psychology," *S. Calif. L. Rev.* 19 (1946): 349–409.

20. Reid, J.E., "Simulated Blood Pressure Responses in Lie Detection Tests and a Method for Their Detection," *J. Crim. L.* 36 (1945): 201–14.

21. Reid, J.E., "A Revised Questioning Technique in Lie Detection Tests," *J. Crim. L. & Criminol. & Police Sci.* 37 (1947): 542–47.

22. Backster, C., "Technique Fundamentals of the Tri-Zone Polygraph Test" Available through the Backster School of Lie Detection, 861 Sixth Avenue, San Diego, Calif. 92101.

23. "Survey of Members of the Society for Psychophysiological Research Concerning Their Opinion of Polygraph Test Interpretation," *Polygraph* 13 (1984): 153–65.

24. House Committee on Government Operations, "Use of Lie Detectors by the Federal Government," 89th Cong., 1st Sess. (1965),

25. Orlansky, J., "An Assessment of Lie Detection Capability" (declassified version), Technical Report 62-16, Contract SD-50, Task 8 (Arlington, Va.: Institute for Defense Analysis, July 1964).

26. House Committee on Government Operations, "Use of Polygraphs as Lie Detectors," note 24.

27. House Subcommittee on Government Operations, "Hearings on the Use of Polygraphs and Similar Devices by Federal Agencies," 93d Cong. 2d Sess. (1974).
28. "Scientific Validity of Polygraph Testing: A Research Review and Evaluation—A Technical Memorandum" (Washington, D.C.: Office of Technology Assessment, OTA-TM-H-15, November 1983).

CHAPTER 2

1. Trovillo, P.V., "A History of Lie Detection," *Am. J. Police Sci.*, 29 (1939): 848–81, 30 (1939: 104–19.
2. Larson, J.A., *Lying and Its Detection* (Montclair, N.J.: Patterson Smith, 1969).
3. Lifton, R.J., *Thought Reform and the Psychology of Totalism* (New York: Norton, 1963).
4. Orwell, G., *1984* (San Diego, Calif.: Harcourt, Brace, Jovanovich, 1983).
5. Orne, M., "The Potential Uses of Hypnosis in Interrogation," in A.D. Biderman and H. Zimmer, eds., *The Manipulation of Human Behavior* (New York: Wiley, 1961).
6. Kroger, W.S., *Clinical and Experimental Hypnosis* (Philadelphia: Lippincott, 1977).
7. Wolfe, D., "Truth Serums Report," prepared for the Emergency Committee in Psychology of the National Research Council, Seattle (October 8, 1941).
8. Inbau, F.E., "Methods of Detecting Deception," *J. Crim. L.* 24 (1934): 1140–47.
9. Holmes, W.D., "The Degree of Objectivity in Chart Interpretation," in V.A. Leonard, ed., *Academy Lectures on Lie Detection* (Springfield, Ill.: Thomas, 1965).
10. Abrams, S. "The Penile Plethysmograph: A New Transducer Used for Detection and Therapy with Sexual Deviation Cases," *Polygraph* 13 (1984): 198–201.
11. Dektor Counterintelligence and Security, "Use of Lie Detectors by the Federal Government: An Informational Report," presented at "Hearings on the Use of Polygraphs and Similar Devices by Federal Agencies," House Subcommittee on Government Operations, 93d Cong., 2d Sess. (June 1974).
12. "Hearings on the Use of Polygraphs and Similar Devices by Federal Agencies," House Subcommittee on Government Operations, 93d Cong. 2d Sess. (June 4 and 5, 1974).
13. "Hearings on Polygraph Control and Civil Liberties, "First and Second Sessions on S. 1845," Senate Committee on the Judiciary, 95th Cong. September and November 1978).
14. Horvath, F., "An Experimental Comparison of the Psychological Stress Evaluation and the Galvanic Skin Response in Detection of Deception," *J. Appl. Psych.* 63 (1978): 338–44.
15. Kubis, J.F., *Comparison of Voice Analysis and Polygraphy as Lie Detection Procedures*, Contract DAAD85-72-C-0217, prepared for the U.S. Army Land Warfare Laboratory Aberdeen Proving Grounds, Maryland (August 1973).
16. Suzuki, A., Watanabe, S., Takeno, Y., Kosugi, T., and Kasuya, T., "Possibility of Lie Detection by Means of Voice Analysis," *Reports of the Natl. Research Inst. Police Sci.* 26 (1973: 62–66.)

CHAPTER 3

1. Steen, E.B., and Montagu, A., *Anatomy and Physiology*, Vol. I (New York: Barnes and

Noble, 1971).

2. Lacey, J.I., *Psychophysiology of the Autonomic Nervous System, Master Lectures on Physiological Psychotherapy* (1974). Available through the American Psychological Association, 1200 17th St., N.W., Washington, D.C. 20036.
3. Wenger, M.A., Jones, F.N., and Jones, M.H., *Physiological Psychology* (New York: Holt, 1956).
4. Burton, A.C., *Physiology and Biophysics of the Circulation* (Chicago: Year Book Medical, 1975).
5. Comroe, J.H., *Physiology of Respiration* (Chicago: Year Book Medical, 1974).
6. Cannon, W.B., *Bodily Changes in Pain, Horror, Fear, and Rage* (New York: Appleton-Century Crofts, 1929).
7. Fidone, E., *Physiology of the Nervous System* (Chicago: Year Book Medical, 1974).
8. Lacey, J.I., *Psychophysiology*, note 29 above.
9. Davis, R.C., "Physiological Responses as a Means of Evaluating Information," in A.D. Biderman and H. Zimmer, eds., *The Manipulation of Human Behavior* (New York: Wiley, 1961).

CHAPTER 5

1. Abrams, S., "The Question of the Intent Question," *Polygraph* 13 (1984): 326–32.
2. Reid, J.E., "A Revised Questioning Technique in Lie Detection Tests," *J. Crim. L. & Am. J. Police Sci.* 37 (1947): 542–47.
3. Backster, C., "Methods of Strengthening Our Polygraph Technique," *Police* (May-June 1962).
4. Barland, G., "A Method for Establishing the Accuracy of Individual Control Question Tests in Anti-Terrorism; Forensic Science; Psychology in Police Investigations" (Jerusalem, Israel: Heiliger, 1985).
5. Lykken, D.T., *A Tremor in the Blood* (New York: McGraw-Hill: 1981).
6. Abrams, S., "A Survey of Attitudes of the Guilt Complex Technique," *Polygraph* 6 (1977): 123–24.
7. Reid, J.E., and Inbau, F.E., *Truth and Deception* (Baltimore, Md.: Williams & Wilkins, 1977).

CHAPTER 6

1. Abrams, S., "The Control Question: A Technique for Effective Introduction, *Polygraph* 5 (1976): 290–92.
2. "Scientific Validity of Polygraph Testing: A Research Review and Evaluation—A Technical Memorandum" (Washington, D.C.: Office of Technology Assessment, OTA-TM-H-15, November 1983).
3. Lykken, D.T., *A Tremor in the Blood* (New York: McGraw-Hill, 1981).
4. Orne, M., "Implications of Laboratory Research for the Detection of Deception," *Polygraph* 2 (1975): 169–99.
5. Reid, J.E., and Inbau, F.E., *Truth and Deception* (Baltimore, Md.: Williams and Wilkins, 1977).
6. Abrams, S., "The Heart Rate Monitor," *Polygraph Update* 4 (1987): 1–2.

7. Barland, G.H., and Raskin, D.C., "An Evaluation of Field Techniques in Detection of Deception," *Psychophysiology* 12 (1975): 321–30.

CHAPTER 7

1. Keeler, L., "Scientific Methods of Criminal Detection with the Polygraph," *J. Kansas Bar Assoc.* 2 (1933): 22–31.
2. Lykken, D.T., *A Tremor in the Blood* (New York: McGraw-Hill, 1981).
3. Abrams, S., *A Polygraph Handbook for Attorneys* (Lexington, Mass.: Heath, 1977).
4. Lykken, D.T., *A Tremor in the Blood*, note 2 above.
5. "Scientific Validity of Polygraph Testing: A Research Review and Evaluation—A Technical Memorandum" (Washington, D.C.: Office of Technology Assessment, OTA-TM-H-15, November 1983).
6. Arther, R.O., "Dangers with a Known-Solution Peak," *J. Polygraph Sci.* 12 (1982): 1–4.
7. Arther, R.O., "How to Work Peak Question," *J. Polygraph Sci.* 17 (1982): 1–4.
8. Reid, J., and Inbau, F.E., *Truth and Deception* (Baltimore, Md.: Williams and Wilkins, 1977).
9. Arther, R.O., "Peak of Tension: Examination Procedures," *J. Polygraph Stud.* 5 (1970): 1–4.
10. Lykken, D.T., *A Tremor in the Blood*, note 2 above.

CHAPTER 9

1. Slowic, S., "Global Evaluation: An Inductive Approach to Case Resolution," *Polygraph* 2 (1982): 215–24.
2. Buckley, D.M., "The Validity of Factual Analysis in Detection of Deception," *Investigator* 3 (1987):9.
3. Horvath, F.S., "Verbal and Non-Verbal Clues to Truth and Deception during Polygraph Examinations," in N. Ansley, ed., *Legal Admissibility of the Polygraph* (Springfield, Ill.: Thomas, 1975).
4. Wicklander, D.E., and Hunter, F.E., "The Influence of Auxiliary Sources of Information in Polygraph Diagnosis," *J. Police Sci. & Admin.* (1975): 405–09.
5. Mullenix, P.A., and Reid, J.E., "The Pretest Interview and It's Role in the Detection of Deception," *Polygraph* 9 (1980): 74–85.
6. Polizzi, A.A., "The Validity and Reliability of Examiner's Interpretation of Polygraph Subject's Verbal Behavior," unpublished master of arts thesis, Reid College (1988); Horvath, F.S., "Verbal and Non-Verbal Clues," note 3 above.
7. Reid, J.E., and Inbau, F.E., *Truth and Deception* (Baltimore, Md.: Williams and Wilkins, 1977).
8. Jayne, B.C., "Control Question Theory in the Polygraph Technique," *Polygraph* 15 (1986): 245–54.
9. Senese, L.E., "Accuracy of Polygraph Technique with and without Card Test Stimulation," *J. Police Sci. & Admin.* 4 (1976): 274–76.
10. Kirby, S.R., "The Comparison of Two Stimulus Tests and Their Effect on the Polygraph Technique," *Polygraph* 10 (1981): 63–76.
11. Horvath, F.S., and Reid, J.E., "The Polygraph Silent Answer Test," *J. Crim. L. & Criminol. & Police Sci.* 62 (1971): 285–93.

12. Reid, J.E., and Inbau, F.E., Truth and Deception, note 7 above.
13. Reid, J.E., *Polygraph Procedure: Reid College Training Manual.* (Chicago: 1987).
14. Jayne, B.C., "Purposeful Non-Cooperation: A Diagnostic Opinion of Deception," *Polygraph* 10 (1981): 156–74; Magiera, A.C., "Patterns of Purposeful Distortions," in N. Ansley, ed., *Legal Admissibility of the Polygraph* (Springfield, Ill.: Thomas: 1975).

CHAPTER 10

1. Weaver, R.S., and Garwood, M., "Comparison of RI and MGQT Structures in a Split Counterintelligence Suitability Phase Polygraph Examination," *Polygraph* 14 (1985): 97–107.
2. Haney, K.L., "A Comparison of Control and Non-Control Question Techniques," *Polygraph* 1 (1972): 234–37.
3. Backster, C., "Anticlimax Dampening Concept," *Polygraph* 3 (1974): 48–50.
4. Keeler Polygraph Institute, *Training Guide*, 33.

CHAPTER 11

1. *DSM-111 Diagnostic and Statistical Manual of Mental Disorders,* 3d ed. (Washington, D.C.: American Psychiatric Association, 1980).
2. Thigpen, C.H., and Cleckley, H.M., *Three Faces of Eve* (New York: McGraw-Hill, 1957).
3. Heckel, R.V., Brokaw, H.C., Salzberg, H.D. and Wiggins, S.L., "Polygraphic Variations in Reactivity between Delusional, Non-delusional and Control Groups in a Crime Situation," *J. Crim. L. & Criminol. & Police Sci.* 53 (1962): 380–83.
4. Abrams, S., "The Validity of the Polygraph with Schizophrenics," *Polygraph* 3 (1974): 328–37.
5. Bitterman, M.E., and Marcuse, F.L., "Autonomic Responses in Post Hypnotic-Amnesia," *J. Exper. Psych.* 35 (1945): 248–52.
6. Weinstein, E., Abrams, S. and Gibbons, D., "The Validity of the Polygraph with Hypnotically Induced Repression and Guilt," *Amer. J. Psych.* 126 (1970): 159–62.
7. Germann, A.C., "Hypnosis as Related to the Scientific Study Detection of Deception by Polygraph Examination: A Pilot Study," *Intl. J. Clin. Exper. Hypnosis* 9 (1961): 309–11.
8. Abrams, S., "A Case of Multiple Personality," *Polygraph* 10 (1981): 212–15.
9. Abrams, S., "The Multiple Personality: A Legal Defense," *Am. J. Clin. Hypnosis* 25 (1983): 225–31.
10. Orne, M., "Special Monograph on the Hillside Strangler," *Intl. J. Clin. Exper. Hypnosis* 32 (1984).
11. Lykken, D.T., *A Tremor in the Blood* (New York: McGraw-Hill, 1981).
12. Barland, G.H., and Raskin D.C., "Psychopathy and Detection of Deception in Criminal Suspects," presented at the Society for Psychophysiological Research, Salt Lake City, Utah (1974).
13. Raskin, D.C., and Hare, R.D., "Psychopathy and Detection of Deception in a Prison Population," *Psychophysiology* 15 (1978): 126–36.
14. Abrams, S., and Weinstein, E., "The Validity of the Polygraph with Retardates," *J.*

Police Sci. & Admin. 2 (1974): 11–14.

15. Abrams, S., "The Validity of the Polygraph with Children," *J. Police Sci. & Admin.* 3 (1975): 310–11.

CHAPTER 12

1. Finkelhor, D., *A Sourcebook on Child Sexual Abuse* (Beverly Hills, Calif.: Sage, 1986).
2. Finkelhor, D., *Child Sexual Abuse* (New York: Free Press, 1984).
3. Abrams, S., "The Serial Murderer," *Oregon Police Chief* 2 (1986): 15–17.
4. Turkington, C., "Sexual Aggression Widespread," *Monitor,* American Psychological Association Newsletter (March 1987).
5. Frank, G., *The Boston Strangler* (New York: Signet Books, 1966).
6. Orne, M., "Special Monograph on the Hillside Strangler," *Intl. J. Clin. & Exper. Hypnosis* 32 (1984).
7. Levin, J., and Fox, J.A., *Mass Murder* (New York: Plenum Press, 1986).
8. Abrams, S., "A Survey of Attitudes of the Guilt Complex Technique," *Polygraph* 7 (1978): 123–24.
9. "Scientific Validity of Polygraph Testing: A Research Review and Evaluation—A Technical Memorandum" (Washington, D.C.: Office of Technology Assessment, OTA-TM-H-15, November 1983).
10. Hazelwood, R.R., and Douglas, J.E., "The Lust Murderer," *FBI Law Enforcement Bulletin* (April 1980).
11. Abrams, S., "The Serial Murderer," note 3 above.
12. Abrams, S., "The Penile Plethysmograph: A New Transducer Used for Detection and Therapy with Sexual Deviant Cases," *Polygraph* 13 (1984): 198–201.
13. Groth, A.N., *Men Who Rape: The Psychology of the Offender* (New York: Plenum Press, 1985).
14. Freeman-Lango, R., "Understanding the Distorted Perceptions and Denial Systems of Sex Offenders," presented at Alternatives to Sexual Abuse Conference, Portland, Oregon (September 1987).
15. Abrams, S., "The Question of the Intent Question," *Polygraph* 13 (1984): 326–332.
16. U.S. Department of Justice, Examining Recidivism, (Washington, D.C.: Bureau of Justice Statistics, February 1985).
17. Abrams, S., and Ogard, E., "Polygraph Surveillance of Probationers," *Polygraphy* 15 (1986): 174–82; Teuscher, T., "The Polygraph and Probation," *Polygraph* 7 (1978): 1–4.

CHAPTER 13

1. "Scientific Validity of Polygraph Testing: A Research Review and Evaluation—A Technical Memorandum" (Washington, D.C.: Office of Technology Assessment, OTA-TM-H-15, November 1983).
2. Orne, M.T., "Implications of Laboratory Research for the Detection of Deception," *Polygraph* 2 (1973): 169–99.
3. Abrams, S., "The Polygraph: Laboratory vs. Field Research," *Polygraph* 1 (1972): 145–50.
4. Larson, J.A., *Lying and Its Detection* (Chicago: University of Chicago Press, 1932).
5. Barland, G.H., and Raskin, D.C., "The Use of Electrodermal Activity in Psychological Research," in Prokasy, W.F. and Raskin, D.C., eds., *Electrodermal Activity in Psychological Research* (New York: Academy Press, 1973); Berrien, F.K., "A Note on Lab-

oratory Studies of Deception", *J. Exper. Psych.* 24 (1939): 542–46; Kugelmass, S., and Lieblich, I., "Effects of Realistic Stress and Procedural Interference in Experimental Lie Detection," *J. Appl. Psych.* 50 (1966): 211–16.

6. Abrams, S., "Polygraph Validity and Reliability: A Review," *J. Forensic Sci.* 18 (1973): 313–26.

7. Dearman, H.B., and Smith, B.M., "Unconscious Motivation and the Polygraph Test," *Am. J. Psychiat.* 37 (1963): 1017–20.

8. Floch, M., "Limitations of the Lie Detector", *J. Crim. L. & Criminol.* 40 (1950): 651–52.

9. Highleyman, S.L., "The Deceptive Certainty of the 'Lie Detector,'" *Hastings L.J.* 10 (1958): 47–64.

10. Eliasberg, W., "Forensic Psychology," *S. Calif. L. Rev.* 19 (1946): 349–409.

11. Lykken, D.T., *A Tremor in the Blood* (New York: McGraw-Hill, 1981).

12. Waid, W.M., Orne, M.T., and Wilson, S.L., "Effects of Level of Socialization on Electrodermal Detection of Deception," *Psychophysiology* 16 (1979): 15–22.

13. Raskin, D.C., and Hare, R.D., "Psychopathy and Detection of Deception in Prison Population," *Psychophysiology* 15 (1978): 126–36.

14. Hammond, D.L., "The Responding of Normals, Alcoholics, and Psychopaths in a Laboratory Lie-Detection Experiment," unpublished doctoral dissertation, California School of Professional Psychology (1980).

15. Balloun, K.D., and Holmes, D.S., "Effects of Repeated Examinations on the Ability to Detect Guilt with a Polygraph Examination: A Laboratory Experiment with a Real Crime," *J. Appl. Psych.* 64 (1979): 316–22.

16. Barland, G.H., and Raskin, D.C., "Psychopathy and Detection of Deception in Criminal Suspects," presented at the Society for Psychophysiological Research, Salt Lake City, October 25, 1974 (available through Psychology Department, University of Utah).

17. Bitterman, M.E., and Marcuse, F.L., "Autonomic Responses in Post-Hypnotic Amnesia," *J. Exper. Psych.* 35 (1945): 248–52; Germann, A.C., "Hypnosis as Related to the Scientific Detection of Deception by Polygraph Examination: A Pilot Study," *Intl. J. Clin. Exper. Hypnosis* 9 (1961): 309–11; Weinstein, E., Abrams, S., and Gibbons, D., "The Validity of the Polygraph and Hypnotically Induced Repression and Guilt," *Am. J. Psychiat.* 126 (1970): 143–46.

18. Abrams, S., "The Validity of the Polygraph with Schizophrenics," *Polygraph* 3 (1974): 328–37.

19. Heckel, R.V., Brokaw, J.R., Salzberg, H.C., and Wiggins, S.L., "Polygraphic Variations on Reactivity between Delusional, Nondelusional, and Control Groups in a Crime Situation," *J. Crim. L. & Criminol. & Police Sci.* 53 (1962): 380–83.

20. Abrams, S., "The Validity of the Polygraph Technique with Children," *J. Police Sci. & Admin.* 3 (1975): 310–11.

21. Abrams, S., and Weinstein, E., "The Validity of the Polygraph with Retardates," *J. Police Sci. & Admin.* 2 (1974): 11–14.

22. Widacki, J., and Horvath, F., "An Experimental Investigation of the Relative Validity and Utility of the Polygraph Technique and Three Other Common Methods of Criminal Identification," *J. Forensic Sci.* 23 (1978): 596–601.

23. Gustafson, L.A., and Orne, M.T., "Effects of Heightened Motivation on the Detection of Deception," *J. Appl. Psych.* 47 (1963): 405–11.

24. Davidson, P.O., "Validity of the Guilty Knowledge Technique," *J. Appl. Psych.* 52 (1968): 52–62.

25. Marston, W.M., "Psychological Possibilities in the Deception Tests", *J. Crim. L. Criminol.* 11 (1921): 551–70; Ruckmick, C.A., "The Truth about the Lie Detector," *J. Appl. Psych.* 22 (1938): 50–58.

26. Lykken, D.T., *A Tremor in the Blood*, note 11 above.

27. Lykken, D.T., "The GSR in the Detection of Guilt," *J. Appl. Psych.* 43 (1959): 385–88.

28. Lykken, D.T., "The Validity of the Guilty Knowledge Technique: The Effects of Faking," *J. Appl. Psych.* 44 (1960): 258–62.

29. Dawson, M.E., "Physiological Detection of Deception: Measurement of Responses to Questions and Answers during Countermeasure Maneuvers," *Psychophysiology* 17 (1980): 8–17.

30. Kubis, J.F., "Studies in Lie Detection Computer Feasibility Considerations," RADC-TR, 62-205, Fordham University, New York (June 1962).

31. Moore, H.W., "Polygraph Research and the University," *Law & Order* 14 (1966): 73–78.

32. Weinstein, E., Abrams, S., and Gibbons, D., "The Validity of the Polygraph," note 17 above.

33. Germann, A.C., "Hypnosis as Related to the Scientific Detection," note 17 above.

34. Corcoron, J.F.T., Lewis, M.D., and Garver, R.B., "Biofeedback Conditioned Galvanic Skin Response and Hypnotic Suppression of Arousal: A Pilot Study of Their Reaction to Deception," *J. Forensic Sci.* 23 (1978): 155–62.

35. Rovner, L.I., Raskin, D.C., and Kircher, J.C., "Effects of Information and Practice on Detection of Deception," paper presented at Society for Psychophysiological Research (Madison, Wisconsin, 1979).

36. Honts, C.R., and Hodes, R.L., "The Effect of Simple Physical Countermeasures on the Detection of Deception," *Psychophysiology* 19 (1982): 564 (abstract).

37. Honts, C.R., and Hodes, R.L., "The Effects of Multiple Physical Countermeasures on the Detection of Deception," *Psychophysiology* 19 (1982): 564–65 (abstract).

38. Stephenson, M., and Barry, G., "Use of the Motion Chair in the Detection of Physical Countermeasures," *Canadian Police Coll.* (1986): 19–32.

39. Abrams, S., and Davidson, M., "Counter Countermeasures in Polygraphy," *Polygraph* 17 (1988): 16–20.

40. Waid, W.M., Orne, E.C., Cook, M.R., and Orne, M.T., "Meprobamate Reduces Accuracy of Physiological Detection of Deception," *Science* 212 (1981): 71–73.

41. Iacono, W.G., Boisvenu, G.A., and Fleming, J.A., "Effects of Diazepam and Methylphenidate on the Electrodermal Detection of Guilty Knowledge," *J. Appl. Psych.* 69 (1984): 289–99.

42. Iacono, W.G., Cerr, A.M., Patrick, C.J., and Fleming, J.A.E., "The Effect of Antianxiety Drugs on the Detection of Deception," *Psychophysiology* 24 (1987): 594 (abstract).

43. Gatchel, R.K., Smith, J.E., Kaplan, N.M., "The Effect of Propanolol on Polygraph Detection of Deception," unpublished manuscript, University of Texas Health Sciences Center (1983).

44. VanBuskirk, D., and Marcuse, F.L., "The Nature of Errors in Experimental Lie Detection," *J. Exp. Psych.* 47 (1954): 187–90.

45. Elson, D.G., David, R.G., Saltzman, J.A., and Burke, C.J., "A Report of Research on Detection of Deception," Contract No. N6 ONR 18011, Office of Naval Research, University of Indiana, Bloomington (1952).

46. Raskin, D.C., and Hare, R.D., "Psychopathy and Detection of Deception," note 13 above.

47. Kleinmuntz, B., and Szucko, B., "On the Fallibility of Lie Detection," *Law & Soc.*

Rev. 17 (1982): 84–104.

48. Waid, W.M., Orne, E.C., and Orne, M.T., "Selective Memory for Social Information, Alertness, and Physiological Arousal in the Detection of Deception," *J. Appl. Psych.* 66 (1981): 224–32.

49. Bradley, M.T., and Janesse, M.P., "Accuracy Demonstrations, Threat, and the Detection of Deception: Cardiovascular, Electrodermal, and Pupillary Measures," *Psychophysiology* 18 (1981): 307–14.

50. Ohnishi, K., Matsuna, K., Arasuna, M., and Suzuki, A., "The Objective Analysis of Physiological Indices in the Field of Detection of Deception," *Reports of the Natl. Inst. Police Sci.* 29 (1976): 181–88.

51. Barland, G.H., and Raskin, D.C., "An Evaluation of Field Techniques in Detection of Deception," *Psychophysiology* 12 (1975): 321–30.

52. Hammond, D.L., "The Response of Normals, Alcoholics, and Psychopaths," note 14 above.

53. Raskin, D.C., and Hare, R.D., "Psychopathy and Detection of Deception," note 13 above.

54. Podlesney, J.A., and Raskin, D.C., "Effectiveness of Techniques and Physiological Measures in the Detection of Deception," *Psychophysiology* 15 (1978): 344–58.

55. Dawson, M.E., "Physiological Detection of Deception," note 29 above.

56. Abrams, S., "The Heart Rate Monitor," *Polygraph Update* 4 (1987): 1–2.

57. Barland, G.H., and Raskin, D.C., "An Evaluation of Field Techniques," note 51 above.

58. Ginton, A., Netzer, D., and Elaand, E., "A Method for Evaluating the Use of the Polygraph in a Real-Life Situation," *J. Appl. Psych.* 67 (1982): 31–37.

59. Podlesney, J.A., and Raskin, D.C., "Effectiveness of Techniques," note 54 above.

60. Widacki, J., and Horvath, F., "An Experimental Investigation," note 22 above.

61. Kircher, J.C., and Raskin, D.C., "Computerized Decision Making on the Detection of Deception," *Psychophysiology* 18 (1981): 204–05.

62. Raskin, D.C., and Hare, R.D., "Psychopathy and the Detection of Deception," note 13 above.

63. Dawson, M.E., "Physiologic Detection of Deception," note 29 above.

64. Honts, C.R., and Hodes, R.L., "The Effect of Simple Physical Countermeasures," note 36 above.

65. Honts, C.R. and Hodes, R.L., "The Effects of Multiple Physical countermeasures," note 37 above.

66. Hammond, D.L., "The Response of Normals, Alcoholics, and Psychopaths," note 14 above.

67. Abrams, S., *A Polygraph Handbook for Attorneys* (Lexington, Mass.: Lexington Books, 1972).

68. Barland, G.H., and Raskin D.C., "An Evaluation of Field Techniques," note 51 above.

69. Podlesney, J.A., and Raskin, D.C., "Effectiveness of Techniques," note 54 above.

70. Raskin, D.C., and Hare, R.D., "Psychopathy and Detection of Deception," note 13 above.

71. Rovner, L.I., Raskin, D.C., and Kircher, J.C., "Effects of Information," note 35 above.

72. Kircher, J.C., and Raskin, D.C., "Computerized Decision Making," note 61 above.

73. Widacki, J., and Horvath, F., "An Experimental Investigation," note 22 above.

74. Honts, C.R., and Hodes, R.L., "The Effect of Simple Physical Countermeasures," note 36 above.

75. Honts, C.R., and Hodes, R.L., "The Effects of Multiple Physical Countermeasures," note 37 above.
76. Hammond, D.L., "The Response of Normals," note 14 above.
77. Barland, G.J., "A Validity and Reliability Study of Counterintelligence Screening Test," Security Support Battalion, 902nd Military Intelligence Group, Fort George G. Meade, Maryland (1981).
78. Gatchel, R.J., Smith, J.E., and Kaplan, N.M., "The Effect of Propranolol," note 43 above.
79. Abrams, S., *A Polygraph Handbook for Attorneys*, note 67 above.
80. Lykken, D.T., "The GSR in the Detection of Guilt," note 27 above.
81. Lykken, D.T., "The Validity of the Guilty Knowledge Technique," note 28 above.
82. Podlesney, J.A., and Raskin, D.C., "Effectiveness of Techniques," note 54 above.
83. Giesen, M., and Rollison, M.A., "Guilty Knowledge Versus Innocent Associations: Effects of Trait Anxiety and Stimulus Context on Skin Conductance," *J. Research in Personality* 14 (1980): 1–11.
84. Davidson, P.O., "Validity of the Guilty Knowledge Technique," note 24 above.
85. Bradley, M.T., and Janesse, M.P., "Accuracy Demonstrations," note 49 above.
86. Ginton, A., Netzer, D., and Elaand, E., "A Method for Evaluating," note 58 above.
87. Balloun, K.D., and Holmes, D.S., "Effects of Repeated Examinations," note 15 above.
88. Scientific Validity of Polygraph Testing (OTA), note 1 above.
89. Larson, J.A., "Modification of the Marston Deception Test," *J. Crim. L. & Criminol.* 12 (1921): 390–99.
90. Larson, J.A., *Lying and Its Detection* (Chicago: University of Chicago Press, 1932).
91. Winter, J.E., "A Comparison of the Cardio-Pneumo-Psychograph and Association Methods in the Detection of Lying in Cases of Theft among College Students," *J. Appl. Psych.* 20 (1936): 243–48.
92. Bitterman, M.E., and Marcuse, F.L., "Cardiovascular Responses of Innocent Persons to Criminal Interrogation," *Am. J. Psych.* 60 (1947): 407–12.
93. Marston, W.M., "Psychological Possibilities in the Deception Tests," *J. Crim. L. & Criminol.* 11 (1921): 551–70.
94. Lyon, V.W., "New Deception Tests," *J. Genetic Psych.* 48 (1936): 494–97.
95. Patrick, C.J., and Iacono, W.G., "Validity and Reliability of the Control Question Polygraph Test: A Scientific Investigation," *Psychophysiology* 24 (1987): 604–05 (abstract).
96. Elaad, E., and Schokar, E., "Polygraph Field Validity," *Crime & Social Deviance* 6 (1978): 4–5.
97. Peters, R.B., "A Survey of Polygraphy Evidence in Criminal Trials," *Am. Bar Assoc.* 68 (1982): 162–65.
98. Horvath, F.S., and Reid, J.E., "The Reliability of Polygraph Examiner Diagnosis of Truth and Deception," *J. Crim. L. & Criminol. & Police Sci.* 62 (1971): 276–81.
99. Hunter, F.L., and Ash, P., "The Accuracy and Consistency of Polygraph Examiners' Diagnoses," *J. Police Sci. & Admin.* 1 (1973): 370–75.
100. Slowic, S.M., and Buckley, J.P., "Relative Accuracy of Polygraph Examiner Diagnosis of Respiration, Blood Pressure, and GSR Recordings," *J. Police Sci. & Admin.* 3 (1975): 305–09.
101. Wicklander, D.E., and Hunter, F.L., "The Influence of Auxiliary Sources of Information in Polygraph Diagnoses," *J. Police Sci. & Admin.* 3 (1975): 405–09.
102. Davidson, W.A., "Validity and Reliability of the Cardio Activity Monitor," *Polygraph* 8 (1979): 104–11.

103. Kleinmuntz, B., and Szucko, B., "On the Fallibility of Lie Detection," note 47 above.

104. Horvath, F.S., "The Effect of Selected Variables on Interpretation of Polygraph Records," *J. Appl. Psych.* 62 (1977): 127–36.

105. Patrick, C.J., and Iacono, W.G., "Validity and Reliability," note 95 above.

106. Holmes, W.D., "The Degree of Objectivity in Chart Interpretation," V.A. Leonard, ed., *Academy Lectures on Lie Detection* (Springfield, Ill.: Thomas, 1965).

107. Wicklander, D.E., and Hunter, F.L., "The Influence of Auxiliary Sources of Information," note 101 above.

108. Bersh, P.J., "A Validation Study of Polygraph Examiner Judgments," *J. Appl. Psych.* 53 (1969): 399–403.

109. Barland, G.H., and Raskin, D.C., "Validity and Reliability of Polygraph Examination of Criminal Suspects," report No. 76-1, Contract No. N1-99-0001 (Washington, D.C.: National Institute of Law Enforcement and Criminal Justice, U.S. Department of Justice, 1976).

110. Raskin, D.C., "Reliability of Chart Interpretation and Sources of Errors in Polygraph Examinations," Report No. 76-3, Contract 75-NI-99-0001 (Washington, D.C.: National Institute of Law Enforcement and Criminal Justice, Law Enforcement Assistance Administration, U.S. Department of Justice; Department of Psychology, University of Utah, Salt Lake City, Utah, June 7, 1976).

111. Balloun, K.D., and Holmes, D.S., "Effects of Repeated Examinations," note 15 above.

112. Barland, G.H., and Raskin, D.C., "Validity and Reliability," note 109 above.

113. Hunter, F.L., and Ash, P., "The Accuracy and Consistency," note 99 above.

114. Barland, G.H., "Detection of Deception in Criminal Suspects: A Field Validation Study," Dissertation submitted to the Department of Psychology, University of Utah, Salt Lake City, Utah (June 1975).

115. Horvath, F.S., "The Effect of Selected Variables," note 104 above.

116. Davidson, W.A., "Validity and Reliability," note 102 above.

117. Edel, E.C. and Jacoby, J., "Examiner Reliability in Polygraph Chart Analysis: Identification of Physiological Response," *J. Appl. Psych.* 60 (1975): 632–634.

118. Kleinmuntz, B., and Szucko, B., "On the Fallibility," note 103 above.

119. Ansley, N., and Garwood, M., "The Accuracy and Utility of Polygraph Testing," Department of Defense, Washington, D.C., 1984), Scientific Validity of Polygraph Testing, OTA, note 88 above.

CHAPTER 14

1. Starrs, J.G., "A Still-Life Watercolor: *Frye v. United States*," *J. Forensic Sci.* 27 (1982): 684–94.

2. *Frye v. United States*, 293 F. 1013 (D.C. Cir. 1923).

3. Act of Jan. 2, 1975, Pub. L. No. 93-595, 88 Stat. 1926, 28 U.S.C. App. (1976).

4. Giannelli, P.C., "General Acceptance of Scientific Tests—*Frye* and Beyond," in E.J. Imwinkelried, ed., *Scientific and Expert Evidence*, 2d ed. (New York: Practising Law Institute, 1981).

5. *People v. Williams*, 164 Calif. App. 3d, 858, 331 P.2d 251 (1958).

6. Ansley, N., *Quick Reference Guide to Polygraph Admissibility Licensing Laws and Limiting*

Laws, 12th ed. (Severna Park, Md.: American Polygraph Association, 1987). Available through APA, P.O. Box 1061, Severna Park, Md., 21146.

7. *State v. Brown,* 297 Or. 404, 445, 687 P.2d 751 (1984).

8. *State v. Lyon,* 304 Or. 221 (1987).

9. *State v. Stanislawski,* 216 N.W.2d 8 (Wis. 1974).

10. *State v. Dean,* 307 N.W.2d 28 (1981).

11. *State v. Grier,* 307 N.C. 628, 300 S.E.2d 351 (1983).

12. *State v. Melano,* 297 N.C. 483, 256 S.E.2d 154 (1979).

13. *Wynn v. State,* 423 So. 2d 294, 299 (Ala. Crim. App. 1982); *Alexander v. State,* 449 N.E.2d 1068 (Ind. 1983); *State v. Marti,* 290 N.W. 570 (Iowa 1980); *State v. Larssley,* 218 Kan. 758, 545 P.2d 383 (1976); *Corbett v. State,* 94 Nev. 643, 646, 584 P.2d 704 (1978); *State v. Renfro,* 96 Wash. 2d 902, 639 P.2d 737 (1982).

14. *People v. Kenny,* 167 Misc. 51, 3 N.Y.S.2d 348 (Queens City Ct. 1938).

15. *People v. Forte,* 279 N.Y. 204, 18 N.E.2d 31 (1938).

16. *People v. Houser,* 85 Cal. App. 2d 686, 695, 193 P.2d 937, 942 (4th Dist. 1948).

17. *State v. McNamara,* 252 Iowa 19, 104 N.W.2d 568 (1960).

18. *People v. Valdez,* 91 Ariz. 274, 371 P.2d 894 (1962).

19. *State v. Chavez,* 80 N.M. 786, 461 P.2d 919 (1969).

20. *State v. McDavitt,* 297 A.2d 849 (N.J. Sup. Ct. 1972).

21. *People v. Valdez,* Note 18 above.

22. *Commonwealth v. A Juvenile (No. 1),* 15 Ct. Cl. 2323 (D. Mass. 1974).

23. *State v. Lecar,* 86 N.M. 686, 926 P.2d 1091 (1974).

24. Beatty, T., "Admissibility Rules Eased in *New Mexico v. Dorsey,*" *Polygraph* 4 (1975): 339.

25. Forkosch, M.D., "The Lie Detector and the Courts," *N.Y.U.L.Q. Rev.* 117 (1939):202–31.

26. Barnett, F.J., "How Does a Jury View Polygraph Examination Results?," *Polygraph* 2 (1935): 262–70.

27. Inbau, F.J., "Detection of Deception Technique Admitted as Evidence," *J. Crim. L.* 93 (1935): 262–70.

28. Koffler, J., "The Lie Detector: A Critical Appraisal of the Technique as a Potential Undermining Factor in the Judicial Process," *N.Y.L.F.* 146 (1957): 3123–39.

29. *People v. Valdez,* note 18 above.

30. McCormick, C.T., "Deception Test and the Law of Evidence," *Tenn. L. Rev.* 15 (1927):108–33.

31. Cureton, E.E., "A Consensus as to the Validity of the Polygraph Procedures," *Tenn. L. Rev.* 22 (1953):728–42.

32. Ash, P., "A Survey of Attitudes on the Polygraph," *Polygraph* 2 (1973): 200–23.

33. "Survey of Members of the Society for Psychophysiological Research Concerning Their Opinion of Polygraph Test Interpretation," *Polygraph* 2 (1984): 153–65.

34. *State v. Bohmer,* 210 Wis. 651, 246 N.W. 314 (1933).

35. Smith, B.N., "The Polygraph," *Scientific Am.* 216 (1967): 25–31.

36. Lykken, D.T., "Psychology and the Lie Detector Industry," *Am. Psych.* 29 (1974): 725–38.

37. Burkey, L.M., "The Case against the Polygraph," *Am. Bar Ass. J.* 5 (1965): 855–57; Langely, L.L., "The Polygraph Lie Detector: Its Physiological Bases, Reliability, and Admissability," *Ala. Law.* 16 (1955): 209–24.

38. Raskin, D.C., "The Implications for Industrial Relations and Employment of the Introduction of the Polygraph," Hearings before the House of Commons Employment Committee Session 1983–84 (June 20, 1984).

39. *United States v. Urquidez,* 356 F. Supp. 1363, 13 Ct. Cl. 1251 (C.D. Cal. 1973).
40. *Oregon v. Lyon,* 304 Or. 221 (1987).
41. Silving, H., "Testing of the Unconscious in Criminal Cases," *Harv. L. Rev.* 69 (1956): 683–705.
42. Folick, P., "The Lie Detector and the Right to Privacy," *N.Y.S. Bar J.* (1968): 102–10.
43. Reid, J.E., and Inbau, F.E., *Lie Detection and Criminal Interrogation,* 3d ed. (Baltimore, Md.: Williams and Wilkins, 1966).
44. Tarlow, B., "Admissibility of Polygraph Evidence in 1975: An Aid in Determining Credibility in a Perjury Plagued System," *Polygraph* 4 (1975): 207–64.
45. *Commonwealth v. Saunders,* 125 A.2d 442 (Pa. 1956).
46. *Rank v. State,* 373 P.2d 734 (Alaska 1962).
47. *Anderson v. State,* 241 So. 2d 390 (Fla. App. 1970).
48. *Ballard v. Superior Court,* 49 *Cal. Rptr.* 302, 410 P.2d 838 (1966).
49. *Tyler v. United States,* 193 F.2d 24 (D.C. Cir. 1951); *James v. Commonwealth,* 204 S.E.2d 247 (Va. 1974); *State v. De Hart,* 8 N.W.2d 360 (Wis. 1943).

GLOSSARY OF TERMS

ACETYLCHOLINE (ACH): A chemical substance present in nervous tissue. Nerve fibers from the PNS are reactive to it.

ACTIVITY MONITOR: A sensor that measures movements employed as counter-measures.

ADRENAL GLANDS: A pair of endocrine glands lying on the kidneys that secrete adrenalin.

ADRENALIN: A hormone of the adrenal medulla of the adrenal glands that enhances SNS activity.

ADRENAL MEDULLA: An endocrine gland that secretes epinephrine.

AFFECT: Emotion.

AFFERENT: The conduction of nerve impulses from the periphery toward the CNS.

ANABOLISM: The part of metabolism that is associated with the building up of protoplasm.

ANALOG STUDIES: Laboratory studies that use designs that simulate actual testing conditions, such as mock crimes.

ANATOMY: The study of the structure of the body.

ANTIDAMPENING EFFECT: Backster's concept that the subject who lies to a question that is less threatening than another question that poses a greater threat responds to a lesser degree.

AORTA: The major artery of the body into which oxygenated blood enters leaving the left ventricle of the heart.

APNEA: A stoppage of breathing.

ARTERY: An elastic muscular tube that carries oxygenated blood from the heart to the various parts of the body.

AUTONOMIC NERVOUS SYSTEM (ANS): The portion of the nervous system that enervates and mediates the viscera of the body.

AXON: The part of the nerve process that conducts impulses away from the cell body and toward other neurons.

BACKSTER, CLEVE: Developed the numerical scoring system and enhanced the use of a standardized polygraph approach throughout the country.

BETA BLOCKER: The chemical used with patients with heart disease that inhibits SNS activity.

BRACHIAL ARTERY: The artery located in the inner upper arm to which the blood pressure cuff is affixed.

BRAIN STEM: The brain with the exception of the cerebral and cerebellar hemispheres.

BRONCHIA: The passageways in the lungs.

CARDIOACTIVITY MONITOR (CAM): The sensor that measures heartrate and blood pressure through a transducer on the thumb or wrist.

CARDIOGRAPH: The sensor that measures blood pressure, blood volume, and heart rate.

CATABOLISM: The part of metabolism associated with the expenditure of energy and the breakdown of protoplasm.

CELL: The basic unit structure in organisms.

CENTRAL NERVOUS SYSTEM (CNS): The brain and spinal cord.

CONDUCTIVITY: The ability of the nerve to propagate a nerve impulse from one point to another.

CONSTRUCT VALIDITY: The degree to which a test measures what it purports to measure.

CONTRACTIBILITY: The ability of the muscles to shorten or exert pull.

CONTROL QUESTION: An assumed lie to which the set of the innocent should be directed.

CONTROL QUESTION TECHNIQUE: A polygraph procedure developed by Reid in 1947 that uses the control question approach.

CRANIOSACRAL SYSTEM: The portion of the ANS involving fibers from the sacral and brain stem of the spinal cord that makes up the PNS.

DAMPENING EFFECT: Backster's concept that physiologic responses to deception can be reduced if the lie is less threatening than another lie or an outside issue.

DENDRITE: The nerve process that conducts impulses toward the cell body.

DIASTOLE: The resting phase of the heart.

DICROTIC NOTCH: The upward swing of the cardio pen caused by the secondary forward movement of the blood in the aorta after it rebounds off the aortic valve

EFFERENT: The conduction of nerve impulses from the spinal cord to the muscles and glands.

ELECTRODERMAL RESPONSE (EDR): A measure of physiologic arousal determined by the skin's resistance to electricity (GSR).

ENDOCRINE GLAND: An organ that produces a chemical that is secreted into the blood stream.

EPINEPHRINE: Adrenalin.

EXCLUSIVE CONTROLS: Bracketed controls developed by Backster in which the question formulation separates the act in question by a time bar from similar acts in the past.

EXPLORATORY TEST: Backster's equivalent of the Reid mixed question test that positions the controls next to the relevant questions.

EXTERNAL VALIDITY: Established generalizability of research findings to specific subjects and situations.

EXTRA SYSTOLE: The large contraction of the heart that follows a much smaller contraction. A skipped beat.

FALSE NEGATIVE: Diagnosing a deceptive subject as truthful.

FALSE POSITIVE: Diagnosing a truthful subject as deceptive.

FIELD RESEARCH: Studies of actual examinations in contrast to laboratory experimentation.

FRYE V. UNITED STATES: 1923 precedent-setting U.S. Supreme Court decision to reject polygraph admissibility on the basis of lack of acceptance by the scientific community.

FUNCTIONAL PSYCHOSIS: A psychiatric state with no organic basis.

GALVANIC SKIN RESPONSE (GSR): A decrease in the skin's resistance to electricity assumed to be due to sweat gland activity (EDR).

GENERALIZABILITY: The degree to which research results can be employed to evaluate present testing situations.

GLAND: An organ specialized for secretion.

GLOBAL EVALUATION: The interpretation of polygraph charts that includes using case information and interpreting the subject's behavioral reactions.

GROUND TRUTH: A determination of guilt or innocence based on some objective fact like a confession.

GUILT COMPLEX TEST: A test procedure in which the subject is tested on an unreal crime to determine whether the subject is so anxious that he or she will appear to be deceptive in response to any accusatory question.

GUILTY KNOWLEDGE TEST: A test procedure that provides a number of stimulus words, only one of which is related to the crime situation and is known only by those with guilty knowledge.

HOMEOSTASIS: Internal equilibrium.

HORMONE: A chemical substance produced by a gland.

HYSTERIA: A neurotic disorder characterized by anxiety and apparent physical disorders.

INCONCLUSIVE: A diagnosis of polygraphic findings in which neither deception (DI) nor truthfulness (NDI) can be determined.

IRRELEVANT QUESTION: A neutral question developed to bring the subject's level of reactivity down after arousal or placed in a position such as first on a test when a reaction would occur because of its position rather than the question itself.

INTENT QUESTION: A question that does not measure a concrete act but an intent to commit that act.

KEELER, LEONARDE: Developed and manufactured a portable polygraph instrument and founded the first polygraph school.

KNOWN SOLUTION PEAK: A peak of tension test in which the guilty subject and the investigators know the key.

KYMOGRAPH: The motor that controls the flow of chart paper at six inches per minute.

LARSON, JOHN: Improved Marston's polygraphic procedure and questioning approach.

LOMBROSO, CESARE: Developed and utilized the first polygraph.

LYKKEN, DAVID: A major critic of polygraphy.

MANIC DEPRESSION: The psychotic state characterized by cycles of depression, hyperactivity, and normalcy.

MARSTON, WILLIAM: A psychologist and attorney who developed one of the early polygraph instruments and attempted to have the findings from his discontinuous measure of systolic blood pressure admitted into evidence in *Frye v. United States.*

METABOLISM: The life process of cells and organisms involved in building up and destroying protoplasm.

MINNESOTA MULTIPHASIC PERSONALITY INVENTORY (MMPI): The most objective and commonly used personality test.

MULTIPLE PERSONALITY: A dissociative disorder like the one portrayed in *Three Faces of Eve.*

NERVE IMPULSE: The electrochemical change propagated along a neuron.

NEURON: The structural unit of the nervous system.

NEUROSIS: An emotional disorder that is characterized by such symptoms of anxiety, depression, and self-doubt but is not severe enough to require hospitalization.

NONEXCLUSIVE CONTROL: A Reid control without a time bar.

NUMERICAL SCORING: The procedure developed by Backster in 1963 to evaluate polygraphic tracings through a standardized scoring system.

ORGAN: A structure of the body that serves a specific function.

OXYGEN DEBT: A consumption of additional oxygen due to exercise or stress.

PARASYMPATHETIC NERVOUS SYSTEM (PNS): The part of the ANS arising from the sacral and brain stem.

PEAK OF TENSION TEST (POT): A guilty knowledge test.

PEDOPHILE: A child molester.

PENILE PLETHYSMOGRAPH: A sensor that measures blood flow to the penis.

PHYSIOLOGICAL PSYCHOLOGY: The study of the relationship between the body and behavior.

PHYSIOLOGY: The study of the functions of the body.

PLETHYSMOGRAPH: A sensor that measures blood volume through a transducer placed on the thumb or finger.

PNEUMOGRAPH: The sensor that measures respiration

POSTTEST INTERVIEW: The portion of the polygraph examination that consists of the scoring of the charts and the interrogation of the deceptive subject.

PRETEST INTERVIEW: The part of the polygraph test that precedes testing and consists of formulating questions, history taking, and explaining the examination procedure.

PROBATION POLYGRAPH TESTING: The periodic testing of those on probation or parole to serve as a deterrent.

PROTOPLASM: The substance comprising living cells.

PSYCHIATRY: The branch of medicine that treats emotional disorders.

PSYCHOLOGICAL SET: The orientation of the individual toward those areas that hold his or her interest, need, or attention. As used by Backster, the area of the test that holds the greatest threat.

PSYCHOLOGICAL STRESS EVALUATOR (PSE): A sensor that measures voice changes in an attempt at evaluating deception.

PSYCHOLOGIST: A Ph.D. who specializes in some branch of psychology.

PSYCHOLOGY: The study of human behavior.

PSYCHOPATH: A personality disorder that because of a lack of conscience, a need for excitement, and impulsivity leads to antisocial acts.

PSYCHOSIS: A severe emotional disorder that often requires hospitalization because of the individual's inability to function.

RATIONALIZATION: A psychological defense in which good reasons are given for real ones.

REID, JOHN: Developer of the control question technique, the guilty knowledge test, and other procedures that dramatically changed polygraph methods.

RELEVANT-IRRELEVANT TECHNIQUE (R-I): A procedure in which the relevant questions are compared to neutral or irrelevant questions rather than control questions.

RELEVANT QUESTION: The key question related to the crime in question.

RELIABILITY: The degree of consistency between test and retest or different evaluations of the same test.

SCHIZOPHRENIA: A psychosis associated with severe withdrawal, thought disorder, and inappropriate affect (emotions).

SEARCHING PEAK: A peak of tension test in which only the subject and not the investigator has specific crime information, such as where money is hidden.

SERIAL MURDERER: A individual in which sexual and angry feelings are welded together and who commits a series of sexual murders. A sexual psychopath.

SILENT ANSWER TEST: A test developed by Reid to give the subject the opportunity of exposing his or her deception by using countermeasures.

SPHINCTER: A muscular ring whose relaxation or contraction opens or closes body orifices.

SPHYGMOMONOMETER: The sensor that measures blood pressure.

SPINAL CORD: That part of the CNS lying in the spinal column.

STIM TEST: A procedure used to stimulate reactivity to enhance detection when a subject responds deceptively.

SUPER DAMPENING EFFECT: Backster's concept that the subject's physiologic response to a lie will be reduced if he or she is concerned that some other and possibly more threatening crime will be discovered.

SYMPATHETIC NERVOUS SYSTEM (SNS): The part of the ANS in which the fibers arise from the thoracic and lumbar spinal cord.

SYMPTOMATIC QUESTION: A question developed by Backster to determine whether the subject is concerned about an outside issue.

SYNAPSE: The functional junction between nerves and their processes.

SYSTOLE: The contraction phase of the heart activity.

TISSUE: A structure of the body composed of cells with similar functions.

VAGUS NERVE: A cranial nerve that is the major nerve of the PNS.

Validity: Degree of accuracy.

Vein: The tube that carries deoxygenated blood back to the lungs from the various parts of the body.

Viscera: Internal organs and tissues of the body.

Zone of comparison (ZOC): That technique developed by Backster that consists of a number of zones containing control, relevant, and symptomatic questions.

INDEX

tions related to, 179–181; of control questions technique, 188–191; countermeasures, 185–186; and false positives, 187–188, 192; field experimentation, 181, 199–201; of guilty knowledge test, 185, 191–193; on incomplete verification, 194–197; laboratory research, 181–188; legal aspects, 207, 209–210; and number of tests administered, 186–187; Office of Technology Assessment (OTA) on, 7–8, 193, 201; and sensors, 187

Videotaping, 13, 97; equipment, workings of, 46

Violence cases, 61

Voice stress evaluator, 14–16

ABOUT THE CONTRIBUTORS

BRIAN C. JAYNE has been dean of Reid College and the quality control officer of Reid and Associates in Chicago since 1983. In 1987 he was named editor of *Investigator*, the journal published by John Reid and Associates. Mr. Jayne is a member of the American Polygraph Association and past president of the Wisconsin Polygraph Association. He holds a polygraph license in Illinois and is certified to teach lie detection and polygraph in that state. He received a bachelor of science degree in criminal justice from the University of Wisconsin and has a master of science degree in detection of deception from Reid College. Mr. Jayne has been innovative and active in the polygraph profession. He has published over twenty-five articles in professional journals and presented seminars throughout the country.

PAUL K. MINOR is one of the preeminent polygraph examiners in the country. He rose through the ranks of U.S. Army examiners and headed a pilot program to centralize supervision of all army examiners of the Criminal Investigation Command. This pilot program was successful, and the concept was adopted on a worldwide basis. Mr. Minor was later appointed chief examiner of the Polygraph Office, U.S. Army CID Command.

From 1978 to 1987 Mr. Minor was the chief polygraph examiner of the Federal Bureau of Investigation, where he held general supervisory responsibilities over all FBI polygraph activities including criminal, foreign counterintelligence, and internal investigations and the FBI training program. He personally conducted examinations in sensitive areas.

In 1987 Mr. Minor left government service and formed American International Security Corporation, which is involved in polygraph testing and various other personnel selection and investigation programs.

Mr. Minor holds a master of science degree in criminal justice and has taught at Columbia College and the University of Baltimore.

ABOUT THE AUTHOR

DR. STAN ABRAMS is a clinical and forensic psychologist in private practice in Portland, Oregon. He received a B.A. in psychology from Wilkes College in Pennsylvania and an M.A. in psychology and Ph.D. in clinical psychology from Temple University in Philadelphia. Dr. Abrams completed an internship at Temple University Medical School in 1960.

In 1971 he completed a training program in polygraphy at the Gormac School in Los Angeles. Since that time he has done a wide variety of research and has written extensively in this area. Dr. Abrams has lectured and presented over a hundred seminars and he has written over fifty books and papers. He has served on the board of directors of the American Polygraph Association and is past president of the Northwest Polygraph Examiners Association. He was elected an honorary member of the American Association of Police Polygraphists.

Dr. Abrams has administered several thousand polygraph examinations and has testified over four hundred times in both civil and criminal cases and for both prosecution and defense.